The 100 Greatest Disasters of All Time

The 100 Greatest Disasters of All Time

Stephen J. Spignesi

CITADEL PRESS
Kensington Publishing Corp.
www.kensingtonbooks.com

CITADEL PRESS BOOKS are published by

Kensington Publishing Corp.
850 Third Avenue
New York, NY 10022

All Kensington titles, imprints, and distributed lines are available at special quantity discounts for bulk purchases for sales promotions, premiums, fund-raising, educational, or institutional use. Special book excerpts or customized printings can also be created to fit specific needs. For details, write or phone the office of the Kensington special sales manager: Kensington Publishing Corp., 850 Third Avenue, New York, NY 10022, attn: Special Sales Department, phone 1-800-221-2647.

First printing: November 2002

10 9 8 7 6 5 4 3 2 1

Printed in the United States of America

Library of Congress Control Number: 2002104525

ISBN: 0-8065-2341-7

In memory of . . .

My beloved aunt, Marie Fasano

and

My dearest father-in-law, Tony Fantarella

Faith teaches us that our eternal soul will live on after we shed our mortal skin. We are taught that death is a door, and there is a line from a sonnet by the poet John Donne that sums this up beautifully. In his sonnet "Death be not proud," John Donne scolds death and tells death not to be proud of being able to snuff out life. Donne ends the sonnet by proclaiming, "one short sleep passes, we wake eternally, And death shall be no more; death, you shall die."
So we need not worry . . .

CONTENTS

FOREWORD
Nature's Sublime Ruthlessness

From the London *Telegraph*
February 13, 2002

Millions of butterflies killed by freak storm
By Ronald Buchanan in Mexico City

Hundreds of millions of monarch butterflies have died in a freak snowstorm in the Mexican mountains, where they spend each winter after a journey of up to 3,000 miles, scientists reported yesterday.

American and Mexican researchers estimated that as many as 270 million frozen butterfly bodies littered the ground after the storm last month in their pine forest havens west of Mexico City.

"I've never seen anything like it," said Dr. Lincoln Brower, an American biologist who has followed the migration for 25 years.

The annual flight of the monarchs from as far north as Canada is regarded as one of the great migrations of the natural world.

They descend on the forests in great orange clouds each November.

Because their arrival coincides with Mexico's Day of the Dead celebrations, many villagers believe that the butterflies represent the spirit of their ancestors.

INTRODUCTION
The Empty Boast

The source of man's unhappiness is his ignorance of Nature.
—Paul Henry Thiry d'Holbach, *The System of Nature*, 1770

When it comes down to it, no matter what man does to try to control it, things really are in the hands of nature.
—Ed Skidmore, from the United States Department of Agriculture's Wind Erosion Research Unit (WERU)[1]

"One of the emptiest of man's boasts," Hal Borland wrote in *The New York Times* in 1960, "is that he has mastered his environment, this earth on which he lives." The studying of disasters, both natural and man-made, will surely elicit a concurring nod.

The first thirty-five disasters of *The 100 Greatest Disasters of All Time* are all natural; number 36, the Chernobyl nuclear plant explosion, is the first man-made disaster to appear on our list.

More than half of the one hundred worst disasters of all time were caused by Mother Nature. And the man-made disasters that do make the list—those debacles of human endeavor that resulted in death and destruction—pale when compared to the damage and deaths caused by nature itself.

Famines and epidemics dominate the Top 20, with a flood and a storm or two also making an appearance.

The disparities are striking.

The worst rail accident of all time (number 57, in Bihar, India, in 1981) claimed 800 lives. The worst epidemic of all time (number 1, the Black Death) claimed 75 million.

The worst maritime disaster of all time (number 48, the explosion of the *Mont Blanc*) resulted in the deaths of 1,635 passengers. The worst famine (number 4, in China in 1876) killed 13 million people.

The worst airplane disaster of all time (number 62, the Tenerife runway collision) took 583 lives; the worst earthquake (number 14, the 1556 China earthquake) claimed 830,000 lives.

The study of disasters throughout history quickly makes clear the power of nature. We truly had an abundance of horrific riches to choose from when compiling the top one hundred disasters.

However, this list is subjective; how could it not be?

For every earthquake covered in this book, there are hundreds more with an equal or higher number of deaths.

For every plane crash, there are dozens more on the books.

For every famine, there are countless more; enough, in fact, to warrant their own book.

And as is always the case with nonfiction, there are more disasters occurring every day, but a book is not a constantly updated Web site; thus, the finalizing of our ranking.

We were able to include details on the horrific 2002 train crash in Egypt; but by the time this book is in your hands, something even more terrible will almost certainly have happened—something that would have warranted inclusion.

But that's why we have updated editions of books.

For now, these one hundred disasters represent the things that can go wrong on this planet of ours. We assure you that we tried, in most cases, when confronted with a number of equally catastrophic disasters, to go with the one considered the worst in its category, or those disasters that had societal, cultural, or scientific significance.

A book such as *The 100 Greatest Disasters of All Time* can make us truly appreciate life.

Stephen Spignesi
April 15, 2002
New Haven, Connecticut

[1] Quoted on www.discovery.com in a Web feature about the Dust Bowl disaster (chapter 95).

ACKNOWLEDGMENTS

I am grateful for the help and support I received from many organizations, universities, museums, scientists, historians, and, of course, family and friends while researching and writing *The 100 Greatest Disasters of All Time*. My appreciation to all of you, especially my stalwart photo researcher, Michael Pye; my blessedly patient editors, Ann LaFarge and Karen Haas; and a singular and noble man with the patience of Job, my agent and friend, John White.

My gratitude to Amherst College, Ann LaFarge, Associated Press, Boston Public Library, Bruce Bender, Cat Press, Centers for Disease Control (CDC), Colleen Payne, Corbis/Bettmann, Cornell University, Dr. George Pararas-Carayannis, Dr. George Leung, Dr. Michael Luchini, Dr. Robert McEachern, Eastland Memorial Society, Federal Emergency Management Administration (FEMA), Florence Art News, Gina Sigillito, James Cole, Jay J. Pulli, Jessica Fernino, Joan Carroll, John White, Karen Haas, Kensington Books, Lee Mandato, Library of Congress, Melissa Grosso, Michael Pye, Michaela Hamilton, Mike Lewis, Morgan Williams, NASA, National Geophysical Data Center (NGDC), National Hurricane Center, National Oceanographic and Atmospheric Administration (NOAA), National Weather Service, New York Public Library, Patrick Lynch, Professor Cynthia Damon, San Francisco Museum, Southern Connecticut State University, South Florida Water Management District, Steve Zacharius, Texas City, Texas Chamber of Commerce, *Augusta Chronicle,* United States Geological Survey (USGS), University of New Haven, University of Kansas, University of Wisconsin Disaster Management Center, and The Weather Channel.

A NOTE ON NUMBERS

It is rare to find a source, contemporary or historical, that states a single quantity with certainty when discussing the number of people killed by a specific disaster, whether it is natural or man-made.

For the purposes of this book, however, we decided to most often use a single number, and we usually decided on the highest figure when a range is given.

If, for instance, historical sources repeatedly use the figure "20 to 40 million" dead when talking about a particular epidemic, famine, or flood, the logical conclusion is that there must be *some* evidence that *up to* 40 million were killed, or this figure would not be used.

Thus it was our decision to use the high figure at all times. This made for a more organized ranking as well as eliminated ambiguity as to the severity of a disaster.

FROM THE AUTHOR

Some of the chapters in *The 100 Greatest Disasters of All Time* begin with a "scene from the scene," a narrative inspired by real events, but fictionalized for purposes of illustrating the personal impact of the disaster and to bring the reader "into the moment."

The characters referred to and described in these stories are composites of people who were involved in the disaster and are not meant to depict actual people.

Specific details about locations, buildings, and attributed dialogue are based on real events, but are the author's imagining of how the scene might have taken place.

These anecdotes are fiction, and it is our hope that they make real the horrible trials and ordeals of the people who died during these disasters.

No representation of any real persons, living or dead, or the depiction of any real person's actions or words is intended.

The 100 Greatest Disasters of All Time

1

The Black Death

EUROPE

1347–1351

75,000,000 Dead

How many valiant men, how many fair ladies had breakfast with their kinfolk and the same night supped with their ancestors in the next world! The condition of the people was pitiable to behold. They sickened by the thousands daily, and died unattended and without help. Many died in the open street, others dying in their houses, made it known by the stench of their rotting bodies. Consecrated churchyards did not suffice for the burial of the vast multitude of bodies, which were heaped by the hundreds in vast trenches, like goods in a ship's hold and covered with a little earth.

—Giovanni Boccaccio

Jonathan

Jonathan's village was a metropolis of charnel houses.

There were dozens of small dwellings lining the unpaved lanes of his small

English village and the dead inhabited them all. The plague had decimated his village so quickly that entire families were left unburied and no prayers had been said over anyone's corpse. The stench of the dead town wafted across the countryside for miles.

Jonathan ignored the unseasonably warm wind and moved slowly along the side of his small house, supporting himself with his left hand as he edged toward the pit in his yard. It was the fourth day of his disease and he had less than an hour to live.

Jonathan had a blinding, throbbing headache unlike any he had ever had before, and he was so exhausted he could barely find the strength to drag himself into the yard to urinate. Even though his small one-room house was filthy with the excrement, vomit, and blood of his dead wife and children, Jonathan would not deliberately soil his own home. The Bible spoke of the godliness of cleanliness and Jonathan was a God-fearing, pious man. Thus, he shuffled step-by-step to the small hole his family used as a toilet, praying as he staggered that he would not collapse and die here, outside, away from his family.

Jonathan reached the hole and stood at its edge for a moment, swaying with dizziness and pain. When he felt steady enough to proceed, he loosened the laces of his breeches, reached inside, and withdrew his penis. He took a deep breath and when his urine began to flow, he felt a horrible burning pain across his lower back and into his groin. Breathing harshly, Jonathan looked down and saw that he was urinating a thick, blackish red fluid that scalded like fire as it exited his dying body and quickly disappeared into the black depths of the pit.

Jonathan was actually encouraged by the sight of this vile, unnatural black fluid. "Ah, the poison is leaving me," Jonathan whispered. "Praise God in all His glory."

The last few drops trickled from Jonathan, hurting even more than the full flow had, and he carefully put his penis back into his breeches and weakly pulled the laces closed.

He headed back to his house, feeling ever so slightly better from the relief of urinating.

Jonathan made it back into his house and immediately sat down at the wooden table where he and his family had eaten all their meals for almost twelve years.

He looked at the bed in the corner of the room and tears filled his eyes as he saw the dead bodies of his wife, Sarah, and their two daughters, Mary and Anna. Sarah lay on her back with one of her girls under each arm. Their skin was black, almost purple, and huge bulbous swellings jutted from their necks. They lay in a pool of filth and flies buzzed above their rapidly decaying corpses.

The Black Death had arrived in Jonathan's small village five days earlier. Sarah and the girls had gotten sick immediately and they had all died excruciating deaths within three days. Jonathan knew his time was coming and he silently prayed for a quick death. He knew better than to pray for a peaceful one.

Jonathan closed his eyes and tried to slow his breathing. As he raggedly inhaled and exhaled, his vision began to blur and his headache got suddenly worse.

In the next instant, he completely lost his sight, began vomiting, and went into a violent seizure. He fell off the chair and ended up on his back on the floor. He continued to shake and thrash about, and still, even in his final death throes, he thought of his family. Jonathan wanted to die with his wife and daughters and he actually tried to crawl to the bed where they lay.

But it was too late. Jonathan's body began hemorrhaging and blood and bodily fluids erupted from his body. His final moments were spent in a state of mindless agony and when his heart gave its final beat, he died with his right arm outstretched toward his wife and daughters.

Jonathan's village was dead.

A year after Jonathan's death, a troupe of traveling monks came upon the village and found scores of houses occupied by silent skeletons. The head friar recited prayers for the souls of the dead at the edge of the town and then nodded to his fellow monks. With pitch torches, the monks set fire to the town and waited until all the houses were ablaze before heading on their way. That night, miles away from Jonathan's village, the monks could see its black smoke rising to the heavens.

Years of the Rat

What is the difference between an epidemic and a pandemic, and which term should be used to describe the Black Death? The answer lies in geography.

An epidemic is an outbreak of disease that affects a specific geographical region or area. For instance, a typhoid outbreak in Houston, and in other cities in Texas, would be considered an epidemic. A pandemic, on the other hand, is a much more widespread outbreak covering a much larger area. A typhoid outbreak in all the southwestern states would be a pandemic, although this is certainly a question of degree. Currently, the AIDS epidemic is really a pandemic because it exists in every country on the globe. (See chapter 3.)

The Black Death outbreak in a few countries of Europe was considered an epidemic until it spread over much of the European continent. Then it became a pandemic.

The Black Death was the worst single-event disaster ever to hit mankind.

In the four-year period from 1347 to 1350, the Black Death killed upward of 75 million people in Europe, fully one-third to one-half of the European population. (Some sources cite the more conservative figure of 25 million dead, but it is likely that the 75 million figure is closer to the truth, when all deaths—even secondary deaths—due to the invasion of the plague are factored in.)

By December 1347, the Black Death had begun its attack in Europe. Its attack weapon was the flea. And the flea's mode of transport from region to region, country to country, was the ubiquitous rat. Fleas secreted themselves in the fur of rats, and leaped to human hosts whenever they had the opportunity. Fleas carried the bacterium *Yersinia pestis*, which caused three types of plague, all of which combined created the devastation known as the Black Death.

The three forms of this plague, in order of prevalence, were bubonic, pneumonic, and septicemic. All three attacked the body's lymphatic system, causing enlargement of the glands, high fevers, headaches, vomiting, and extremely painful joints. Pneumonic plague also caused the coughing up of bloody sputum; septicemic plague caused the skin to turn purple as all the cells in the body hemorrhaged. Death came quickly in all cases, and the mortality rate ranged from 30 to 75 percent for bubonic; 90 to 95 percent for pneumonic; and 100 percent for septicemic.

The Black Death was, and still is, one of the most horrible of all deaths.

Deadly Outlander

The Black Plague's deadliest years were 1347 through the beginning of 1351.

By December 1347, it had attacked Constantinople, the Italian islands of Sicily, Sardinia, and Corsica, and Marseille, France.

Six months later, by June 1348, the Black Death had invaded all of Greece, all of Italy, most of France, the eastern third of Spain, and parts of what is now Yugoslavia, Albania, Bosnia-Herzegovina, and Croatia.

In December 1348, six months later and a full year after its initial appearance in Europe, the Black Death attacked the remainder of France and most of Austria, and crossed the English Channel on ships to invade the southern third of England.

Six months later, by June 1349, eighteen months after its onset, the Black Death had overrun all of Switzerland, the southern half of Germany, the central part of England, and all of Austria.

At the end of 1349, two years after the initial outbreak, the Black Death had infiltrated all of Ireland, most of Scotland, the remaining regions of England, the central part of Germany, all of Copenhagen, and had crossed the North Sea to invade the southern third of Norway.

In June 1350, thirty months into the pandemic, the Black Death had occupied most of Norway and the remainder of Germany.

By the end of 1351, three years after the plague's debut, the Black Death burned out after storming all of Sweden and the northern third of Poland.

The Black Death had a major impact on all facets of European society, including the economy, crime, agriculture, education, and travel. Survivors with skills such as carpentry, blacksmithing, and other manual trades became critically important to the rebirth of Europe. It would take generations, however, for population growth to restore the Continent to its pre-plague levels.

The defeat of the Black Death was due in large part to improvements in sanitation, which impeded the ability of the plague-carrying fleas to survive. Some historians suggest that the Great London Fire of 1666 (chapter 93) also contributed to the ultimate elimination of the contaminated fleas in Europe, although by this time, outbreaks of the plague were scattered and infrequent.

The plague, in all its forms, has not been completely eliminated. Outbreaks have occurred regularly all over the world, including in the United States. There was a plague outbreak as recently as 1924 in Los Angeles. It was arrested quickly, but it still caused 33 deaths.

Postscript

Tuesday, February 19, 2002, 10:37 A.M.:

NICD confirms outbreak of plague
By Debjit Chakraborty

It has been officially confirmed that the mysterious disease which infected many in the villages of Himachal Pradesh and Uttranchal was pneumonic plague, reports CNBC India. Scientists at the National Institute of Communicable Diseases, NICD, confirmed this on Monday night after patients' samples were found positive for *Yersinia Pestis*, the bacteria that causes plague. Four deaths have been reported in the area so far, but authorities said the situation is under control and the worst could be over. Nearly 5,000 people in the affected areas have been given antibiotics and the area has also been quarantined.

(from Yahoo India)

2

The Great Influenza Epidemic

WORLDWIDE

1918–1919

22,000,000–40,000,000 Dead

Conditions are much worse than the public has any idea . . . I believe there are far more cases of influenza in this city than reports of the Health Department show.

—Former New York Health Commissioner Dr. Goldwater, in 1918

I had a little bird
Its name was Enza
I opened the window
And in flew Enza.

—American children's jump rope rhyme, circa 1918

Matthew knew he was sick and he also knew that this was his last chance. His family and neighbors had all died and their bodies still lay in the front rooms of their homes. There was no one to come and take them away for burial.

Matthew had gotten sick earlier that morning and he knew he had only a short time to help his body win its battle against the terrible "grippe" that had invaded his small town just outside of Boston. Matthew knew that some people had gotten sick and recovered. No one knew why they did not die, and Matthew was determined to be one of the few survivors of this terrible epidemic.

Thus, he sat on a straight chair in his bedroom, blind drunk on two fifths of gin, his chest and neck redolent and slimy with thick, cold bacon grease, the legs of his chair surrounded by four wooden bowls filled with eucalyptus oil that he had heated to boiling and now sat steaming on the floor, wafting the fragrant vapors up around his besieged body.

Matthew had heard that any of these remedies could cure a person of the grippe, so he figured that all three were as close to a guarantee of a cure as he was going to get.

Matthew's head reeled from the combination of the gin and the eucalyptus fumes. He was nauseous from the vile odor of the bacon grease and the effects of the flu. He was cold, clad as he was in only his underclothes.

And he was dying. The influenza virus that had invaded Matthew's body was relentless and was already causing many of the vesicles of his lungs to hemorrhage. Matthew would be dead within twenty-four hours. And he would die still drunk.

The two Allied vessels were ships of the dead, moving relentlessly on the same course, heading straight toward each other, in the waters off Ireland. The Great War had united many countries in a global war against tyranny, and ships of many different nations crossed paths frequently.

The crews of these two ships, though, were all sick, and there was no one on board either vessel with enough strength to change course. The two ships collided and sank. All on board both ships were lost, more innocent victims of the Spanish Lady.

After this devastating worldwide influenza epidemic stormed the United States in the fall of 1918 and overran all forty-eight states, signs were posted in American cities that warned citizens that it was illegal to cough or sneeze, and that violators would be subject to a $500 fine. Dr. Noble P. Barnes of Washington, DC, was somewhat more emphatic: "Persons at large sneezing and coughing," the good doctor proclaimed, "should be treated as a dangerous menace to the community, properly fined, imprisoned, and compelled to wear masks until they are educated out of that 'Gesundheit!' and 'God Bless You' rot!"

Thus was the desperation among civic officials and health workers trying to combat an invisible invader that was killing hundreds of thousands of people in the streets and in their homes, and for which there was no defense.

A ubiquitous public health poster of the time warned "This disease is highly communicable. . . . There is no medicine which will prevent it." The poster also included instructions on how to make a protective face mask.

The Great Influenza Epidemic occurred in two waves. The first wave began in early 1918; the second wave, after the virus had mutated, began in the summer of 1918.

The specific influenza virus of 1918–19 that exploded into the Great Influenza Epidemic, first appeared in February 1918, in San Sebastián, Spain, a small coastal town about twenty miles from the border of France.

This chance surfacing resulted in the disease being erroneously labeled the Spanish Flu, aka the Spanish Lady. Influenza was, in fact, not limited to any single country and by the time it burned out in the spring of 1919, it had attacked most of Europe and the entire United States.

By the time the influenza pandemic arrived in the United States at Camp Funston in Fort Riley, Kansas, in March 1918, the last year of World War I, it had already decimated Europe and Asia, leaving close to 16 million dead in Asia and 2 million dead in Europe. When it departed the ravaged nations, it left them devastated by social and economic turmoil.

There were many theories floating around regarding the genesis and nature of the mysterious disease. In the June 21, 1918, edition of the *New York Times*, it was suggested that the excessive consumption of turnips by the German army had given birth to the disease, which had then spread to Spain. Two weeks later, the *Times* reported that visitors from Spain were being fumigated before they were allowed to set foot in the United States. The Spanish believed that wind from France had spread the disease to Spain. In England, chemists (pharmacists) were using quinine and cinnamon in a futile attempt to arrest the disease. Others suggested snuff as an alternative cure.

Once it crossed the Atlantic, the virus made quick work of America.

In September 1918, 387 people a day died in the United States from influenza, a total of 12,000 people.

In stark contrast to September, in the month of October, 6,300 people a day died in the United States from influenza, a staggering total of 195,000 deaths for the month. This was one of the deadliest months in U.S. history and, to put this figure in perspective, the death rate per day in the United States in the year 2000 was 6,588, in a population of close to 280 million people. The population of the United States in 1918 was just over 100 million and the October death rate of that year was slightly under the death rate of today, when the population is more than two and one-half times what it was in 1918. There is no question that the Spanish Lady raged across America like an out-of-control wildfire.

This worldwide killer was astonishing in its ability to travel enormous distances. United States Coast Guard search teams came upon Inuit villages, so far away from cities that to describe them as "inaccessible" is an understatement, in which everyone had died from influenza. How did the virus travel that far and infect all those isolated people?

We still do not know the answer to that question.

* * *

The specific "Spanish" strain of virus that was responsible for the Great Influenza Epidemic has not surfaced since it disappeared in early 1920. Influenza is still with us, however, and effective vaccination programs have kept outbreaks limited in scope and brief. We have vaccinations for many known strains of influenza, but nature is clever and resourceful and there is always the chance a new strain will surface for which we have no defense.

Getting a flu shot is routine today; in 1918, all they had was bacon grease.

3

The Worldwide AIDS Epidemic

WORLDWIDE

Late 1970s–Ongoing[1]

22,000,000+ Dead[2]

Twenty years after the first clinical evidence of acquired immuno-deficiency syndrome was reported, AIDS has become the most devastating disease humankind has ever faced. Since the epidemic began, more than 60 million people have been infected with the virus . . . Worldwide, it is the fourth biggest killer.

—The UNAIDS Joint United Nations Program on HIV/AIDS

In 1991, the World Health Organization (WHO) estimated that by the end of the century, 40 million people worldwide could be infected with the HIV virus that causes AIDS.

In December 2001, the UNAIDS Program and the WHO reported that, worldwide, 40 million people *were* infected with the HIV virus. We can be certain that the World Health Organization was not pleased to have been proven correct.

* * *

AIDS—Acquired Immune Deficiency Syndrome—is a disease caused by the Human Immunodeficiency Virus (HIV). It is spread via infected blood, sexual contact with an infected person (whether homosexual or heterosexual), and from mother to fetus. The AIDS virus was isolated in 1984 by Dr. Richard Gallo of the U.S. National Cancer Institute, and Dr. Luc Montagnier, of the Paris Pasteur Institute.

Currently, there is no cure for AIDS, although treatments have advanced to the point where many in the medical field now consider the disease chronic instead of terminal. This element of fragile control has not stopped the spread of the disease, however, and it is now estimated that by the year 2004, the death toll attributed to AIDS will have surpassed the death toll of the Black Death, and that of the Great Influenza Epidemic of 1918. Dr. Ward Cates, formerly with the Centers for Disease Control and now with Family Health International, said in 1987 in David Chilton's book, *Power in the Blood,* "Anyone who has the least ability to look into the future can already see that the potential for this disease is *worse than anything mankind has seen before.*" (Emphasis added.)

AIDS was born in Africa in the 1950s, probably in green monkeys, and is believed to have spread to humans when lab monkeys infected with the HIV virus bit human lab workers. A gay airline steward known as Patient Zero brought AIDS to North America sometime in the late 1970s. This man, who died of cancer in 1984, is believed to have infected gay men in ten cities through unprotected sex, and the disease then began to spread rapidly through the gay community. It is now widespread in women and children as well as in homosexuals.

AIDS attacks the human immune system through three disease processes: immunodeficiency, autoimmunity, and nervous system dysfunction.

Immunodeficiency caused by AIDS allows a multitude of infections and cancers to attack the body, and, because of a weakened, damaged, or improperly functioning immune system, the body cannot fight them off.

Autoimmunity caused by AIDS is marked by catastrophic drops in blood platelet counts, which subsequently cause improper functioning of organs, as well as susceptibility to opportunistic diseases.

AIDS also attacks the nervous system, although researchers have not determined the specific method by which it does so. They have identified a specific dementia caused by AIDS and believe it has something to do with nerve damage caused by the HIV virus.[3]

Common diseases of AIDS patients include pneumonia, Kaposi's sarcoma (a cancer of the blood vessels), lymphoma (cancer of the lymph nodes) as well as many other infectious diseases and cancers. Treatment today is aimed at reducing the spread of the virus in the body and improving quality of life for the patient by treating the infections and cancers caused by AIDS.

The Centers for Disease Control in Atlanta reported the following alarming statistics in its June 2001 report:[4]

- Today, 40 million people are estimated to be living with HIV/AIDS. Of these, 37.2 million are adults, 17.6 million are women, and 2.7 million are children under fifteen.
- During 2001, AIDS caused the deaths of an estimated 3 million people, including 1.1 million women and 580,000 children under fifteen.
- Women are becoming increasingly affected by HIV. Approximately 48 percent, or 17.6 million, of the 37.2 million adults living with HIV or AIDS worldwide are women.
- The overwhelming majority of people with HIV—approximately 95 percent of the global total—now live in the developing world.

AIDS is a hot-button topic in many high-income industrial nations. The sexual nature of its transmission, and the fact that it first surfaced in homosexuals, has elicited strong antigay sentiments from conservatives and those who believe that their religion tells them that homosexuality is wrong. Many believe that AIDS is a punishment from God and thus they fight encouraging the use of condoms and safe-sex education, believing that only abstinence from homosexual practices will eliminate the disease from the world. This is somewhat shortsighted, since a great many people infected today are heterosexual women, children, people who received infected blood transfusions, and intravenous drug users.

Regardless of the means of transmission of the HIV virus or the societal groups most affected, the reality is that AIDS is one of the worst pandemics ever to strike mankind. If the virus happens to mutate and become airborne contagious, AIDS could very easily wipe out life on earth.

The need for a vaccine and a cure is paramount, since we cannot be sure that AIDS will burn itself out, as did the Black Death and influenza.

[1] AIDS began to surface in the late 1970s, although U.S. medical researchers have been able to trace it as far back as a blood sample in the 1950s.

[2] The UNAIDS program reported 2.8 million AIDS deaths in 1999 and, in its latest report, 3 million AIDS deaths worldwide in 2001. The death rate in climbing and the pandemic is expected to continue claiming lives in increasingly higher number around the world for the foreseeable future, short of a vaccine or cure.

[3] Rebecca J. Frey, www.gale.com *(Gale Encyclopedia of Medicine).*

[4] *The HIV/AIDS Surveillance Report*, 2002.

4

The 1876 China Famine

NORTHERN CHINA

1876–1878

9,000,000–13,000,000 Dead

The people's faces are black with hunger; they are dying by thousands upon thousands.

—Frederick Balfour, writing from Shanghai during the famine

And the king said unto her, What aileth thee? And she answered, This woman said unto me, Give thy son, that we may eat him today, and we will eat my son tomorrow.

So we boiled my son, and did eat him: and I said unto her on the next day, Give thy son, that we may eat him: and she hath hid her son.

—2 Kings 6:28–29

Chang hoped his ancestors would forgive him, and that when he met them in paradise, they would not shun him for his deeds.

His two-year-old daughter, Min, slept in the canvas sack he carried on his back. She was barely alive and was the last survivor of his three children. A month ago, Chang had killed and eaten his two oldest children, three and four years of age respectively. His wife had died of starvation at the same time, but he had refused to eat her body after she died.

He had buried his beloved in the ground behind his hut, and then had said a prayer to the gods that she be welcomed into the next world. At the time, his three children had all been in varying states of debilitation, and none of them had eaten in days. In the past nine days, Chang himself had eaten only a handful of shriveled red berries he had found by the road. They had made him sick and he had vomited them up, which had dehydrated him even more, and made him terribly dizzy and blurred his vision.

That was when he decided that, in order to live, he must sacrifice his children. He knew they would all die soon anyway, and it was better that he put them out of their misery, while also ensuring his own survival.

Chang had killed his two oldest at the same time. He had suffocated them by holding a pillow over their faces and keeping it pressed there until they stopped kicking and struggling.

He gutted them and drank some of their blood immediately. The meat from their tiny bodies, eaten sparingly, had kept him and his only daughter alive for almost three weeks. Now all the food was gone. Chang had even sucked their marrow, but now they were nothing but a pile of tiny bones. He would burn the bones and offer their spirits to the gods when he returned.

Today, he would sell his emaciated two-year-old daughter for a bag of rice. As Chang walked along the hot dusty road, he sobbed in misery. No tears wet his face, however. His body could not afford to shed any of its precious fluids. Chang cried nonetheless, and again asked his ancestors to forgive him.

This terrible famine—the worst in China's history and, in fact, in all of world history—brought about the coining of the descriptive phrase "Ten-Thousand Man Holes." A Ten-Thousand Man Hole was a mass grave so enormous it could hold ten thousand corpses. There were countless ten-thousand man holes throughout the northern provinces of China as this famine burned its way through close to 13 million people in a three-year period. Almost 12,000 people a day died for the two worst years of this famine, and it wasn't until over a year after it began that the West began to hear about what was happening in the world controlled by the Manchu dynasty.

The cause of the famine was a drought that seared the provinces of northern China from 1876 through 1878. It is almost unimaginable that such an enormous area could go without rain for years on end, but that is what happened in China, beginning in 1876. Crops died or did not grow at all, and the farmer peasants moaned over the irony that the crops in the southern provinces were being destroyed by floods from heavy monsoons while the northern regions were parched.

As would be expected in a situation of such human deprivation, crime soared, and suicides were common and continuous. Cannibalism and selling children were dreadful responses to such terrible hardship.

The Chinese government pretended the famine was not happening. They would round up the desperate thieves who stole for food and routinely mount mass beheadings. The "sorrow box" was another form of punishment common at the time. Prisoners were simply put into boxes and forgotten about. They were not fed, and before most of them died of starvation and dehydration, they were almost invariably insane (which was, perhaps, a blessing considering the horror of a death by starvation while in your right mind).

Despite the Manchu dynasty's attempts at covering up the famine (which included forbidding foreigners to travel in the affected region for the entire duration of the famine), word did get out to the world. A British envoy sent a telegram to his office in January 1878 that made clear the extent of the human tragedy in northern China:

> Appalling famine raging throughout four provinces North China. Nine million people reported destitute. Children daily sold in markets for food. Foreign Relief Committee appeal to England and America for assistance.[1]

By the end of 1878, the monsoons returned to the north. Fields were planted and crops grew again. The crime rate dropped in the area, as did instances of cannibalism, selling children, and suicide. Foreign aid also helped stabilize the northern provinces, but the death toll still stands as the single highest for any famine in history.

It is likely that the severity of the drought and famine could have been tempered by earlier aid efforts which, unfortunately, were not permitted due to the blanket of censorship imposed by the Manchu Dynasty.

[1] *Darkest Hours,* Jay Robert Nash, 114.

5

The Fourteenth-Century China Drought, Famine, and Epidemic

CHINA

1333–1347

9,000,000+ Dead

That Omnipotence which has called the world with all its living creatures into one animated being, especially reveals Himself in the desolation of great pestilences. The powers of creation come into violent collision; the sultry dryness of the atmosphere; the subterraneous thunders; the mist of overflowing waters, are the harbingers of destruction. Nature is not satisfied with the ordinary alternations of life and death, and the destroying angel waves over man and beast his flaming sword.

• • •

The Oriental Plague is, sometimes, but by no means always occasioned by pestilence, which imparts to it a character (qualitas occulta) *hostile to human nature. It originates frequently from other causes, among which this physician was aware that contagion was to be reckoned; and it deserves to be remarked that he held epidemic small-pox and measles to be infallible forerunners of the plague, as do the physicians and people of the East at the present day.*

—J. F. C. Hecker, *The Black Death*

The Fury of the Elements

For over a decade in the fourteenth century, China was devastated by a series of cataclysmic natural disasters which, through various means, claimed the lives of more than 9 million people and gave birth to the worst epidemic known to man, the Black Death.

While not a single event, this period of China's history is looked at inclusively here, for its ceaseless, monumental loss of life, and the fact that it seemed to have a "conclusion," for lack of a better word, as Professor J. F. C. Hecker states in *The Black Death.* "Floods and famine devastated various districts," Hecker writes, "until 1347, when the fury of the elements subsided in China."

Professor Justus Friedrich Karl Hecker was one of the nineteenth century's most distinguished professors of medicine, and his specialty was the historical side of medicine and how the presence and spread of disease affected the history of mankind. His 1832 *The Black Death* is a very comprehensive and thorough study of the plague in Europe. Professor Hecker also provides valuable information on the period in China from 1333 through 1347, the years that gave birth to the Black Death in Europe, which began in the year this period in China ended. (See chapter 1.)

This period began with a scorching drought in southeastern China in the area between the Kiang and the Hoai Rivers. As is always the case with prolonged lack of rain, crops withered, livestock starved, and famine ensued. As the death toll mounted and people prayed for rain, whatever gods they beseeched did oblige, sending torrential downpours that killed over 400,000 people. As the survivors were coping with such tragedy, an earthquake caused the nearby mountain Tsincheou to collapse, followed by the earth opening up and claiming many more lives.

The early months of the following year, 1334, were almost apocalyptic in their death toll. First, the southern city of Canton (now Guangzhou), which was the capital of the Chinese empire at the time, was besieged by enormous floods. At the same time, the city of Tche was experiencing a severe drought, which spawned a plague (probably bubonic) that killed upward of five million people.

A few months later, the same region was struck with a powerful earthquake that caused mountains to collapse and giant craters to flood. One such newly formed "lake" was, according to Hecker, over one hundred miles wide. Thousands of people were drowned in this earthquake-formed death hole.

The following year, 1335, in the Honan (now Hunan) region, a drought persisted for five months, bringing a plague of a different sort, a more biblical type of plague: clouds of locusts descended upon the land and devoured anything and everything that grew. Of course, when crops are gone and lack of rain prevents anything from growing, the result is famine, followed by outbreaks of plague. Tens of thousands died.

The year 1336 in southern China was a horrible seesaw of droughts followed by floods, the combined effect of which was to cause one of the worst famines in history. In 1337, it killed 4 million people. Of course, this much death and starvation was accompanied by more locusts, as well as intermittent floods and, for bad measure, an earthquake that lasted six whole days.

In 1338, the ancient city of Kingsai and the area surrounding it was struck by an earthquake that reportedly lasted for ten days. This is probably an exaggeration, yet the damage and death again spawned swarms of hungry locusts, which added to the misery.

The year 1339 continued China's streak of disasters. From Hecker's *Black Death:*

> The mountain Hong-tchang fell in, and caused a destructive deluge; and in Pien-tcheon and Leang-tcheou, after three months' rain, there followed unheard-of inundations, which destroyed seven cities . . .

The years 1340 through 1343 brought China frequent, catastrophic earthquakes; 1344 brought an enormous tsunami that destroyed the city of Ventcheou; 1345 saw more floods and famines, this time in Ki-tcheou; and this period came to a violent conclusion in 1346 with floods in Canton, more famine, and what Hecker describes as "subterraneous thunder," which can only mean the rumblings of earthquakes.

The plague that began in 1333 and so devastated China made its way to Europe over fifteen years, until it first appeared in Constantinople in December 1347. The plague made the journey to Europe in the bloodstream of fleas that rode in the fur of rats who hitched a ride on trade ships headed for the European countries.

No matter the distance, no matter the time, anyone can be a victim of a disease from another corner of the world.

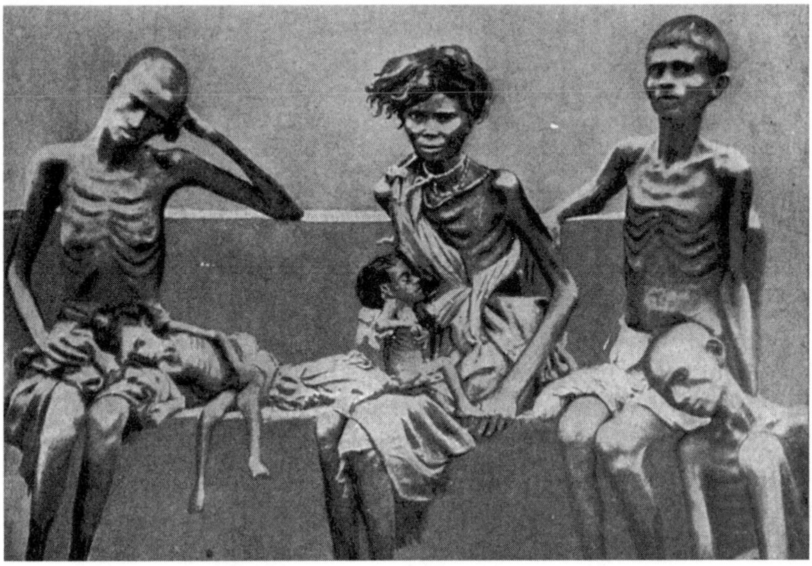

6

The 1896 India Drought, Famine, and Disease Disaster

Southern and Western India; the Punjab Region of Northwestern India

1896–1901

8,250,000 Dead

Poor emaciated women, clothed only in thin rags, came and fell down at our feet and said, "Oh, sir, we cannot live, we cannot keep from starving on two and a half cents a day, with grain so high priced, and breaking stones [for money] is such hard work."

—A missionary in southern India in 1898, one of the worst years of the drought and famine[1]

Yesterday I saw sixteen corpses; today, within the same distance, ten. Must people really see ribs and skeletons to make them give?

—Reverend J. Sinclair Stevenson, a missionary in Parantij, Gujarat[2]

The Poorhouse

The young girl was always terrified, but she never let herself cry. She had been found a few days earlier on the side of the road, squatting next to the body of her dead mother, and she had been picked up and brought to this place, a combined orphanage and poorhouse. The place was a madhouse of noise and filth, a macabre asylum inhabited by people with parts of their faces and hands missing, and by men who would not leave her alone. Lepers were here, stretched out on rotted mats, as well as people coughing with tuberculosis, and women with cholera and typhoid lying in their own waste. The man in charge of the poorhouse scowled all the time. He also threatened not to feed her if she did not do what he demanded. So, she obeyed. She worked, and she did other things, and she kept quiet. She may have been young, but she was wise enough to realize one critically important fact: at least she was being fed. And that was much more than could be said of the countless people who had died of starvation and whose bodies seemed to be everywhere.

During the five-year period from 1896 through 1901, India was plagued by continuing, pernicious droughts that caused relentless, lethal famines, which subsequently caused epidemic levels of disease and death. This five-year human tragedy claimed a staggering 8,250,000 lives, or over 4,700 deaths per day, *every* day, from 1896 through 1901.

Beginning in 1896, southern and western India suffered a seemingly endless drought that stretched over a three hundred thousand-square-mile area, and culminated in the terrible famine of 1896–98, in which 6 million Indians died. The drought and famine affected more than 61 million Indians, and was soon followed by another two-year drought and famine nightmare that claimed 2,250,000 Indians.

Corpses, such as the one of the young girl's mother, littered the streets, and children were left homeless. The poorhouses of India overflowed with the destitute and the helpless. Millions were left with no choice but to go to poorhouses, and these government-supported havens soon turned into dens of crime, as well as freely operating brothels and last-stop hospices (minus medical care) for the terminally ill.

Young girls were used as prostitutes, and also forced to work endless hours for almost no money. One English woman who had visited an Indian poorhouse wrote in a letter home, "Bad men, immoral women, pure young girls and innocent children were freely mixing . . . Many were suffering from leprosy and other unmentionable diseases. God help the young girls who are obliged to go to the relief camps and poorhouses."[3]

At first, the starving people of India's hardest hit areas resorted to scavenging the land for anything that could even remotely be considered edible. Russia had gone through this several years before when its starving citizens resorted to eating "hunger bread" made from weeds, straw, tree bark, and even sand. (See chapter 16.) In India, the hungry ate cactus plants, roots, whatever berries could be found, and even grass. The average man in India earned 75¢ a month, if he was fortunate enough to be working. But with the price of wheat at $3.60 a bushel, it is obvious that native Indians could not afford to buy the food their own country produced, a paradigm we have seen repeatedly throughout history. (See chapter 12 for a particularly vivid illustration of this type of governmental iniquity.) Some men, desperate to provide for their families, would travel on foot for days to towns where they had heard there was work. Frequently there were jobs, but the overseers, exploiting the men's distress about and fears for their families, often hired workers for 2¢ or 3¢ a day, and this paltry amount was paid for brutally long hours of physical labor that would be taxing for men in good health and strong physical shape, and was unbearable for half-starved men who had just walked days with little or no food.

Ultimately, the number of deaths and the breadth of hunger and starvation led to the inevitable: cannibalism. As it has often been seen throughout history, humans will resort to eating human flesh when hunger becomes apocalyptic. Corpses are everywhere during a wide-ranging famine, and such a source of meat and protein does not go overlooked for long.

The Indian government could do little but add the starving people to the welfare rolls. A drought cannot be prevented, but famines can be minimized or alleviated and diseases can be treated. Unfortunately, India was a poor country, and thus the death toll during this five-year period was a stunning loss of human life, and an epic of untold instances of human suffering.

[1] Jay Robert Nash, *Darkest Hours,* 262.
[2] Lee Davis, *Natural Disasters,* 118.
[3] Jay Robert Nash, *Darkest Hours,* 262.

7

The 1932 Ukraine Famine

THE UKRAINE, THE SOVIET UNION

1932–1933

7,000,000 Dead[1]

I saw the ravages of the famine of 1932–1933 in the Ukraine: hordes of families in rags begging at the railway stations, the women lifting up to the compartment window their starving brats, which, with drumstick limbs, big cadaverous heads and puffed bellies, looked like embryos out of alcohol bottles . . .

—Arthur Koestler, *The God That Failed*

No one was keeping count. —Nikita Khrushchev

Andrew Gregorovich, in his 1997 "Black Famine in Ukraine 1932–33: A Struggle for Existence," which appeared in the *Forum Ukrainian Review,* called this tragic famine "the most immense of Stalin's crimes."

Today, the collectivization of farms is almost unanimously considered to be the single most inefficient method of crop and livestock production. To Stalin and the Bolsheviks, collectivization was a glorious implementation of the Communist doctrine. Many Russian farmers, already indoctrinated to the confiscatory abuses of the Communist system, did not protest collectivization. In the Ukraine, however, where private ownership of farms and land was a centuries old, ingrained practice, peasant farmers did not so willingly accede to the mandate.

As reported in James Cornell's *The Great International Disaster Book,* the Soviet Union exported 1.7 million tons of grain in 1932 and 1.8 million tons in 1933, food that could have provided 17.5 million people with one thousand calories a day for two whole years.

A July 18, 1932, article in the Russian newspaper *Svoboda* (later cited in *The Ukrainian Weekly),* titled "Famine in Soviet Ukraine and its Main Reason," noted, "The harvest of 1931 was plentiful, but the government took such harsh measures with the peasants that they were forced to give up 70 percent of everything harvested."

Some of the Ukrainian kulaks (well-off farmer peasants) did fight back against collectivization. Many of them killed their livestock rather than allow them to become part of the collective. Many tried to flee the Ukraine to Romania or Poland, but were shot to death by Soviet troops as they tried to cross the borders. (Sometimes the corpses were left to rot in the wild, hoping to discourage other Ukrainians from attempting to leave Mother Russia.) There are also accounts of the Bolsheviks setting fire to Ukrainian villages to prevent peasants from fleeing to another country.

The farmers who stayed in the Ukraine were treated almost as badly. Peasant farmers—even as they were starving to death—were sent to jail, to exile in Siberia, or shot to death if they could not meet the extreme Soviet grain production quotas.

Some peasants tried to survive by selling everything they owned, including some of their clothes, in order to buy some black market rye bread, loaves that were often contaminated with fungus which would cause gangrene and, in worst cases, disease and death.

Some tried to hide food that they had grown from the government collectors. This, too, was treated harshly. In August 1932, the Soviet government issued a directive that any peasant caught hiding food would be shot.

As in other catastrophic famines throughout history, cannibalism was a last resort for starving people. Human flesh sausages and jellied meats were often sold secretly. Sometimes, a finger or toe (or worse) would show up in a crock of potted meats.

The Soviet government under Stalin kept word of this terrible famine from the outside world and strictly controlled what foreign journalists were allowed to see. (Reportedly, foreign journalists were the only ones outside of the government who had access to as much food as they wanted, whenever they wanted it.)

The Ukrainian Weekly reported that the headlines in the Russian newspaper *Svoboda* on September 30, 1932, read "Crisis in the Soviet Union Deepens." According to the article, it was determined that the Russian government had three major problems to tend to immediately. It had to somehow find food for the USSR's population; it had to dramatically develop the country's foreign trade; and it had to immediately produce all necessities for everyday life for Soviet citizens.

According to *Svoboda*, *"The government was searching for a socialist solution to the situation."* (Emphasis added.)

Stalin could have put an immediate end to the famine by releasing confiscated grain to those who were starving. That he did not, combined with the unachievable grain quotas imposed upon the Ukrainians, is evidence that Stalin's policies were genocidal, and that he intended the double assault of "dekulakization" and collectivization to help him with the "Ukrainian problem."

Seven million people died horrible deaths from this government-orchestrated disaster. To this day, there are still pro-Stalinists who insist that there was no man-made famine and that the "few" deaths that did occur were due to a long drought in the Ukraine, even though there are many reports that rainfall for the area during the period of the famine was normal.

[1] This figure is from Robert Conquest's *Harvest of Sorrow: Soviet Collectivization and the Terror-Famine.* Conquest acknowledges that it is difficult to separate the number of deaths caused by the "dekulakization" of the Ukraine and the number from famine, but ultimately concludes that 7 million dead is probably accurate, if conservative, with the possibility that the total deaths from famine alone in the 1932–33 period could have been as high as 10 million. (*The Ukrainian Weekly* also uses the 7-million-dead figure when writing about the famine. Stalin himself, during an August 1942 conversation with Winston Churchill, said that 10 million died from collectivization.) This is Conquest's final summation:

Peasant dead: 1930–37		11 million
Arrested in this period; dying in camps later		3.5 million
TOTAL		14.5 million
Of these:		
Dead as a result of dekulakization		6.5 million
Dead in the Kazakh catastrophe [famine]		1 million
Dead in the 1932–33 famine		
in the Ukraine	5 million	7 million
in the N. Caucasus	1 million	
elsewhere	1 million	

8

The 1921 Ukraine Famine

The Volga Region, the Ukraine, the Soviet Union

1921–1923

5,000,000 Dead[1]

The villages were as quiet as death. No one stirred from the little wooden houses, though now and again we saw faces at the windows—pallid faces with dark eyes staring at us. In one village I remember we had as our guide a tall, middle-aged peasant who had blue eyes and a straw-colored beard. When he spoke of the famine in all those villages hereabouts he struck his breast and tears came into his eyes. He led us into timbered houses where Russian families were hibernating and waiting for death. In some of them they had no food of any kind.

—Philip Gibbs, *The Pageant of the Years*

In *Harvest of Sorrow,* Robert Conquest's 1986 seminal book about the policy of collectivization in the Soviet Union and its result, what he calls the "terror-famine," he has this to say about the 1921 Ukraine famine:

> The great famine of 1921 was not the result of any conscious decision that the peasant should starve. Nevertheless, to attribute it simply to drought is quite untrue. The weather, though bad, was not at the disaster level. The factor which turned the scale was, in fact, the Soviet Government's methods of crop requisition—partly because it took more of the peasant's product than would leave him with subsistence; partly because, over the past three years, it had efficiently removed much of the incentive to produce.
>
> The starvation which now possessed the land followed inevitably from the ruling that (as with Lenin's frank admission), the peasant's needs were not to be taken into account.[2]

As in the 1932 Ukraine famine (chapter 7) that claimed 7 million lives, the 1921 famine was starvation in a land of plenty. The government took away the peasants' food to sell it, and, as Conquest notes, Vladimir Lenin (and, of course, later Joseph Stalin) not only knew about it, but encouraged it and didn't care about the consequences.

True, there was a drought in the Ukraine in the spring and summer of 1921, which resulted in crop failures of up to 75 percent in the region, and it was especially bad in seven provinces on the Volga River. However, the crops that survived in the Ukraine as a whole, and that were eventually harvested, were enough to feed the inhabitants of the region who were starving, particularly those in the southern Ukraine. The new Bolshevik government needed to do two things to prevent the famine from taking hold: stop exports of grain, and put in place a food distribution program that would have shifted harvested grain to the southern Ukraine.

This was not done, and the famine became a devastating tempest that roared through the region and resulted in 1.2 million people starving by September 1921.

The government, in a lame attempt at assistance, set up orphanages and shelters for the children, facilities that consisted of nothing but buildings where the children orphaned by the starvation deaths of their parents waited to die.

The American Quakers were active in relief efforts during the famine and one worker wrote about a home that was built for 50 children but actually housing 645, its total increasing at a rate of approximately 80 children each day. He described the stench in the house as "indescribable" and wrote about the constant cacophony of crying and screaming that went on twenty-four hours a day. In the morning, the dead bodies were removed from the piles of children on and under the beds and placed in a shack for later disposal.

As with all prolonged famines, disease became the secondary killer. Starving people are prone to fatal diseases that can spread rapidly, and this is what happened in the Ukraine. Typhus and cholera resulted in hundreds of thousands of deaths. Medicine was not available and, even if it was, curing someone who is starving to death of a disease would not have done much good.

As with all prolonged famines, cannibalism became commonplace. Children were eaten by their parents; corpses were cut up and consumed by starving peasants. The Quakers, working in the region trying to alleviate suffering and feed those that they could, would often buy inexpensive home-cured sausages to supplement their own food stores. In 1922, the Quaker relief workers met and unanimously decided to stop buying the local meats. They had learned that they almost all contained human flesh, and the Americans decided to stick with food brought in from areas outside the Soviet Union.

In July 1921, Russian novelist and playwright Maxim Gorky wrote (with Lenin's permission) to Herbert Hoover (who would become the U.S. president eight years later), then head of the American Relief Administration. The ARA had been doing relief work in Europe for some time, and Gorky requested American aid for the Ukraine famine victims. Hoover went to Congress and was able to persuade it to appropriate $20 million for immediate Russian aid, which, when combined with contributions from individual Americans and future appropriations, would result in a total of $45 million in American funds going to the starving in Russia.

The 1921–23 Ukraine famine ended in the fall of 1923 when the region enjoyed an enormous harvest. The damage done by the famine, however, did not go away, and for several years following, relief efforts concentrated on housing orphaned and abandoned children, replacing broken (or eaten) equipment (starving peasants actually boiled and ate saddles and other leather gear), and replacing the horses and livestock that had either died from starvation or had been killed and eaten.

By the end of the 1920s, conditions were far better in the Ukraine, and yet this relative prosperity would be short-lived. The famine of 1932 was only months away.

[1] Robert Conquest, *Harvest of Sorrow,* 53.
[2] Robert Conquest, *Harvest of Sorrow,* 55.

9

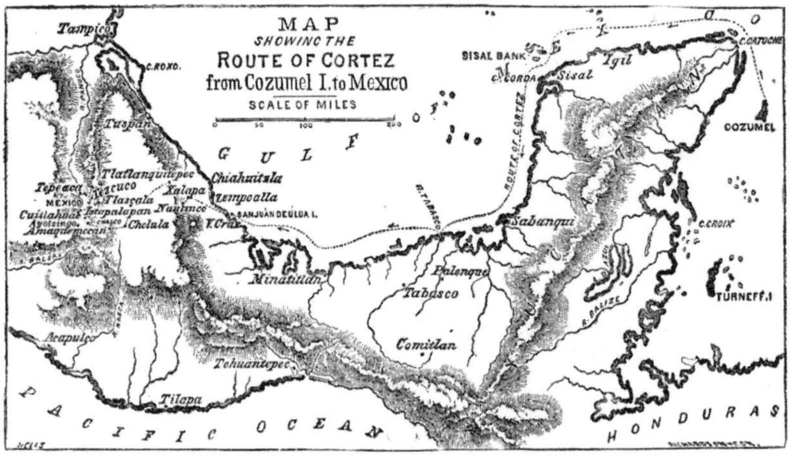

The 1520 Mexico Smallpox Epidemic

MesoAmerica: Mexico, Guatemala, Belize, Honduras, Nicaragua

1520–1521

4,000,000 Dead

A sorer disease cannot befall [them], they fear it more than the plague . . . [F]or want of bedding and linen and other helps they fall into a lamentable condition as they lie on their hard mats, the pox breaking and mattering and running one into another, their skin cleaving by reason thereof to the mats they lie on. When they turn them, a whole side will flay off at once as it were, and they will be all of a gore blood, most fearful to behold. And then being very sore, what with cold and other distempers, they die like rotten sheep.

—William Bradford, on post-Cortés smallpox in the Native American population[1]

Hernando Cortés felt vindicated. After what he and some of his men had just seen take place, he had no qualms whatsoever about mercilessly conquering the Aztec people, their leader Montezuma, and their capital Tenochtitlán (now Mexico City).

From a distance, the Spaniards had watched as the Aztec priests, all of whom were dressed in elaborate robes, ornaments, and headgear, placed a naked young man on a large stone altar. After many chants and prayers, the head priest raised a large dagger, plunged it deep into the sacrificial victim's chest just below his throat, and dragged it down to his waist, opening a deep slit in his torso. The priest withdrew the knife and waved it around, allowing the precious blood to splatter on his acolytes.

The young man was conscious, but moaning and clearly in shock. The priest then handed the knife to the priest on his right, reached into the gaping hole in the victim's chest, felt around, found the heart, and then violently ripped the fist-sized muscle from the young man's chest.

He held it up, the blood dripping down his arm, and all attending the ceremony bowed their heads. The priest placed the heart in a golden bowl and nodded to four of his priests. They picked up the body of the now-dead young man, walked to the top of the long flight of stone stairs, and hurled the body down the steps. It bounced, spun, and twisted in bizarre positions until it reached the bottom of the pyramid. The broken body was then taken away. Its limbs were removed, cooked, and served to the king and his guests that evening. It is said that Montezuma preferred thigh meat cooked with tomatoes and chile peppers.

The story of Spanish explorer Hernando Cortés's smallpox-assisted defeat of the Aztecs is a vivid illustration of how a disease can change the world.

In 1519, Cortés brought smallpox from Puerto Rico to the North American continent, specifically Mexico, which resulted in the deaths of between 3 and 4 million biologically defenseless Aztec natives, one of the most devastating epidemics in human history.

Smallpox had been brought to Puerto Rico from Santo Domingo, having been brought there by Christopher Columbus. The Spaniard explorers were mostly immune to the deadly disease, as were their slaves. In fact, it was not Hernando Cortés himself who exposed the Aztecs to smallpox. It was one of his black slaves who was infected yet immune (slaves also served as soldiers in Cortés's invading army) and his contact with the Aztecs started the epidemic.

Pánfilo de Narváez was an unwitting agent of contamination whose 1519 visit to Mexico with Cortés resulted in the deaths of 4 million native Aztecs. A similarly infected person wandering through New York could conceivably wreak similar havoc and devastation.

The story of Narváez cannot help but remind us of one of today's most widespread fears: that a terrorist organization will inject a "suicide contaminator" with stolen smallpox virus and set that person loose in a heavily populated city—such as New York—and let him walk among the unprotected, passing the smallpox virus to all he meets. As was the case with the Aztecs in 1520, today, no one is immune. Smallpox was believed to have been completely eradicated in 1980, with the last case appearing in Somalia in 1977. Samples of the smallpox virus have been stored in labs in Russia and the United States, and that it can come into the hands of terrorists cannot be discounted.

When Cortés first invaded Tenochtitlán, he was met with quite a bit of resistance. This is no surprise, considering that the Aztecs were healthy, well-fed, and weeks away from feeling the effects of the smallpox virus with which they were being infected. Cortés chose to retreat and fully expected the Aztecs to follow him and engage his troops in battle.

After several weeks of peace and no sign of being pursued, Cortés sent spies back to Tenochtitlán. They returned with tales of a weakened city, where thousands were sick and dying.

Shortly thereafter, Cortés returned, completed his conquest in three short months with only five hundred men, and appointed himself king. He then ordered the surviving Aztecs, many of whom were sick and dying, to leave their city. Once they were gone, he and his men plundered the city of its gold and jewels, and then leveled it. When Cortés finally left, the Aztec empire was no more.

What made Cortés's job even easier, and led to mass surrenders and the city's eventual downfall, was the Aztecs' superstitious belief that Cortés's gods were more powerful than their own. What else would explain why Cortés's men did not get sick?

Smallpox was now in the land, and in less than one hundred years, the disease would appear in Boston, and would attack the nonimmune Native Americans as it did the Aztecs, leading to mass deaths that, coupled with the European colonists' genocidal annihilation of the indigenous population of what would shortly thereafter be America, led to the near extinction of the Native American people.

[1] Howard Simpson, *Invisible Armies,* 680.

10

The English Sweating Sickness

England

1485–1551

3,000,000 Dead

A newe Kynde of sickness came through the whole region, which was so sore, so peynfull, and sharp, that the lyke was never harde of to any mannes rememberance before that tyme.

—R. Grafton, *A Chronicle at Large, and Meere History of the Affayres of Englande* (1569)

No One Was Safe

In 1533, fourteen-year-old Catherine Willoughby married fifty-year-old Charles Brandon, the duke of Suffolk, and they quickly had two sons, Henry and Charles.

Twelve years later, in 1545, the duke died, making Catherine a twenty-six-year-old widow with two boys, Henry, ten and Charles, nine.

Six years later, Catherine sat on a wooden stool between the two beds on which her sons lay dying, and cursed the God that had led her to marry Charles and suffer through the loss of first a husband, and now two sons.

Her two young boys had gotten sick the day before and she knew they would not see the next day's morning light. Their sickness started at the same time, as if the two brothers had to share even the cause of their deaths. Catherine found them both in bed, holding their heads in their hands, crying from blinding headaches. Their sickness quickly progressed to head-to-toe body pain, followed by a fever that brought on terrible sweating. Within hours, they were both gasping for breath as the fever raged and the pain imprisoned them in their beds.

The two boys lapsed in and out of consciousness. Catherine tried to soothe them by soaking a thick cloth in cold water and holding it to their hot, sweaty brows. She also sang softly to them, believing fervently that they could hear her voice and hoping that it calmed them.

As the sun set, and the servants moved through the castle lighting wall torches, Catherine sat silent, tending to her two boys, waiting for their suffering to be over.

Henry and Charles Brandon died that night, with their mother beside them. A high mass was held for their souls and they were buried in a sacred ceremony befitting their royal station. Their mother ordered their clothes burned. She was so grief-stricken she did not want to come upon a painful reminder of them even by chance.

The two heirs to England's throne were victims of the fifth wave of English Sweating Sickness, a deadly disease also known as *Sudor Anglicus*, that swept through England five times and the European mainland once, and which was responsible for, in its five incarnations, upward of 3 million deaths in a sixty-six-year period.

The disease first appeared in 1485 and the first written mention of it was by an Italian, Polydore Vergilio:

> [In 1485] a new disease pervaded the whole kingdom . . . a pestilence horrible indeed . . . suddenly a fatal sweat attacked the body wracking it with pains in the head and stomach, moreover there was a terrible sensation of heat. Therefore the patients cast off the bed coverings from the beginning; if they were dressed they stripped off their clothes, the thirsty ones drank cold water, others suffering from this fetid heat, provoked a sweat which had a foul odor . . . all of them dying immediately or not long after the sweat had begun; so that not one in a hundred evaded it.[1]

The epidemics always began in the summers. Sweating Sickness lay dormant for twenty-three years after its first appearance before surfacing again in 1508, followed by summer waves of disease in 1517, 1528, and 1551. It is believed that the 1528 epidemic was the worst. Sweating Sickness killed within one day and, in some cases, as quickly as three hours. Treatment was futile, and yet, as is always the case among people desperate to save their loved ones, bizarre remedies were attempted. For some reason, many believed that the way to cure Sweating Sickness was to *make the patient sweat more.* As soon as someone manifested any of its symptoms, he or she would be wrapped up in clothes and blankets and put to bed covered with spreads and quilts. Between the fevers, the sweating, and the thick coverings, most sufferers died quickly. Their families believed that they had simply begun the treatment too late.

After 1551, Sweating Sickness was never seen again in England or Europe.

Grief in the Liver

In 1552, the English doctor John Caius wrote a treatise in which he chronicled this mysterious invader, and described how it made itself known in the patient:

> First by peine in the backe, or shoulder, peine in the extreme parts, as arme, or legge, with a flusshing, or wind as it semeth to certaine of the patientes, feling the same. Secondly by the grief in the liver and nigh stomach. Thirdly, by peine in the head, and madness of the same. Fourthly by a passion of the hart . . . the patientes breathed rapidly and heavily of necessity . . . with a whining, sighing voice . . . it lasteth but one natural day.[2]

What was this deadly epidemic, how was it transmitted, and why did it die out?

The United Kingdom's Drs. Guy Thwaites, Mark Taviner, and Vanya Gant, writing in the February 20, 1997, issue of the *New England Journal of Medicine,* came to some logical conclusions in an attempt to answer those questions, although they admit that only DNA testing will confirm their hypotheses.

They believe that English Sweating Sickness was some form of Hantavirus contracted by inhaling rat feces.

Once again, this ubiquitous rodent and its ubiquitous fleas brought a plague to mankind and caused enormous numbers of deaths.

It is not known if some species of rat crawling the earth today still carries the Sweating Sickness virus. An outbreak will be the only way to know and, by then, it will probably be too late for countless people. It is hoped, however, that modern medicine will be able to vanquish it quickly this time around.

[1] Geoffrey Marks, *Epidemics,* 100–01.

2 J. Caius, "A boke, or counseill against the disease commonly called the sweate, or sweatyng sicknesse." London: Richard Grafton, 1552:8.

11

The Yellow River and Yangtze River Floods

CHINA

2297 B.C.—the Twentieth Century

Countless Millions Dead

The tops of poplars which lined the roads now float like weeds on the water, but here and there an old tree with thick strong branches has strong men clinging to it crying for help. In one place a dead child floated to shore on top of a chest where it had been placed for safety by its parents, with food and name attached. In another place a family, all dead, were found with the child placed on the highest spot . . . well covered with cloths.

—News report in the *North China Herald*[1]

A hydrolic engineer once described the Yellow River as "the greatest outdoor laboratory in the world for flood control."[2]

The Yellow and Yangtze Rivers in China have been flooding for millennia, and these deluges have consistently taken an enormous number of lives on a regular basis while also causing massive multibillion-dollar losses and destruction.

We are looking at many of these floods in this chapter inclusively, in much the same way we look at a global epidemic spanning decades (chapter 3) as an all-inclusive event, considering them as an ecological pandemic for the country of China in general, and particularly the Yellow and Yangtze River floodplains. We believe that the enormous number of deaths within a specific geographic region—the Yellow and Yangtze Rivers' valleys—is a valid criterion for including these floods in a single ranking.

The Yellow River in northern China is known as "China's Sorrow" because of the misery it inflicts upon the people who live within reach of its life-giving and life-taking waters. The Yellow River, 2,903 miles long, is the sixth longest river in the world. It drains and irrigates over 400,000 square miles and is a mile wide at some points along its length. China's Sorrow rises in the Kunlun Mountains in northern China and flows eastward to the Gulf of Bo Hai. The river's high content of yellow loess gives it its name. The Yellow River has reportedly flooded over one thousand five hundred times since 2297 B.C.

The Yangtze River is 3,434 miles long, flowing from Tibet to the East China Sea. The Yangtze has been a trade and transportation route since ancient times.

The triangle of land formed by the three cities of Beijing, Shanghai, and Hankow comprises the worst areas for flooding in China. In this triangle, it is estimated that between 1851 and 1866, 40 to 50 million people died in floods.

Here is a review of some of the major floods of the Yangtze and Yellow Rivers over the past eleven or twelve decades (with a nod to the first recorded Yellow River flood, which occurred four thousand years ago).

- **2297 B.C., the Yellow River:** According to ancient records, this flood lasted for thirteen years. As might be expected, not much else is known with certainty about this catastrophe.
- **September–October 1887, the Yellow River:** The river broke through seventy-foot levees at Cheng-chou in Honan province, completely flooding 11 cities and 600 villages (some estimates say upward of 1,500 villages were swallowed). At least 900,000 died from drowning, followed by many more dying from disease and starvation; 2 million were left homeless; and 50,000 square miles were submerged. Journalist A. H. Godbey wrote of this flood, "The actual loss of life could not computed accurately, but the lowest intelligent estimate placed it at 1.5 million, and one authority placed it at 7 million." By 1889, the floods had receded, but the water left behind cholera, and famine, adding to the death toll.
- **September 1911, the Yangtze River:** The Yangtze overflowed into Nganhwei, Ichang, Hupei, and Hunan provinces, as well as the city of Shanghai, flooding a total of 700 square miles of land. At least 200,000 people died from drowning and another 100,000 from starvation in the

weeks that followed. During the aftermath of this flood, roving mobs of starving men robbed and murdered flood survivors. Missionaries traveling to Hankow on steamboats on September 6 of that year saw the Yangtze River dotted with floating coffins. The floods had washed away a cemetery and sent the coffins drifting. Over 500,000 refugees fled to Manchuria and Mongolia.

- **August 1931, the Yellow River:** This flood, preceded by a two-year drought, drowned 140,000 people and left 10 million people homeless. During this flood, aviator Charles Lindbergh flew food and medicine into the devastated areas. The flood affected over 51 million people, and the grand total of deaths from drowning, disease, and famine is reported to be 3.7 million.
- **1933, the Yellow River:** Historian Dr. George Cheung told us "The flood of 1933 affected the lives of 2.7 million people and killed 12,700 people. The river flooded again in 1935 and 1938 (which was man-made to stop the invading Japanese army)." A total of 4,500 square miles were submerged.
- **July 1935, the Yellow River:** When the river flooded Hankow province, 30,000 people drowned and 5 million were left homeless.
- **April 1938, the Yellow River:** Chiang Kai-shek ordered a levee dynamited to stop the invading Japanese. This created a flood of cataclysmic proportions, in which probably 500,000 (some sources say 800,000) people died, and millions more were left homeless.
- **1939, the Yellow River:** At least 500,000 people drowned and several million more died from famine following the flood. All the rice crops were wiped out, all of the houses in northern China were washed away, and 25 million people were left homeless.
- **August 1950, the Yangtze River:** A total of only 489 people drowned, but 10 million people were left homeless, 890,000 houses were destroyed, and 5 million acres of croplands were completely flooded.
- **August 1954, the Yangtze River:** This flood claimed 40,000 lives and left 1 million people homeless. (The Communist government ordered 600,000 workers to use their bodies to form a levee to hold back the waters. It didn't work.) An area twice the size of Texas was completely under water. Interestingly, before the Communists took over, the United States was planning to build the world's largest dam on the Yangtze. The new Communist government threw the plan out and went with what became known as the Bhukov Plan, a program that used clay soil to build levees, instead of constructing dams out of wood. The clay levees collapsed in the floods of 1954.
- **April 23, 1969, the Yellow River:** Several hundred thousand people died, and 1,000 square miles of Shantung province were completely flooded. (The Japanese troops who were occupying much of the flooded area intercepted Red Cross shipments of food for the flood victims.) A

staggering 10 million people were homeless and 90 out of 130 districts in Hopei province were under water for months.

- **July 1981, the Yangtze River:** In Szechwan province, 753 people drowned, 28,140 were reported missing, and 1.5 million were left homeless from the floods.
- **July–August 1996, the Yellow and Yangtze Rivers:** Some 2,775 people drowned, 234,000 were injured, 8 million were evacuated, 4.4 million were left homeless, and 8 million acres of cropland were ruined. The flood did $20.5 billion in damages and affected in some way a total of 200 million people.
- **July–August 1998, the Yangtze and Shoshun Rivers:** This was the worst northern China flood in forty-four years. A total of 4,150 people drowned, and 180 million people were affected in some form. A staggering 18.3 million acres were evacuated, 13.3 million houses were damaged or destroyed, and the floods did $26 billion in damages.

China's sorrow, indeed.

[1] Joyce Robins, *The World's Greatest Disasters,* 75.
[2] Roger Smith, *Catastrophes and Disasters,* 106.

12

BEGGAR-WOMAN AND CHILDREN.

The Irish Potato Famine

IRELAND

1845–1850

1,029,552 Dead

1,180,409 Emigrated

$725 Million in Economic Losses[1]

Six famished and ghastly skeletons, to all appearances dead, were huddled in a corner on some filthy straw, their sole covering what seems a ragged horsecloth, their wretched legs hanging about, naked above the knees. I approached in horror, and found by a low moaning they were alive—they were in fever, four children, a woman, and what had once been a man. In a few minutes I was surrounded by two hundred such spectres as no words can describe.

—Nicholas Cummins, *The Times of London*, 1847

Tha shein ukrosh. ("Indeed, it is the hunger" in Celtic.)

—A starving Irish farmer during the potato famine

The Irish Potato Famine and Stalin's collectivization policies share some grim similarities.

Stalin allowed millions of his own people to starve as he exported tons of grain to fatten the state's coffers. When Ireland's potato crops failed in 1845 due to a blight, Great Britain continued to export the country's cash crops and livestock to England as the Irish people starved to death or died from disease brought on by malnutrition. The English did allow the Irish to buy grain, but none of the working farmers in Ireland could afford to pay for it. Catharina Japikse of the U.S. Environmental Protection Agency, writing in the fall 1994 issue of the *EPA Journal,* makes the telling point that "in fact, the Irish starved not for lack of food, but for lack of food they could afford."

The potato had been introduced in Ireland in the mid-1600s and it soon became the country's most important and ubiquitous crop. Potatoes mixed with a little buttermilk, and sometimes eaten with a small portion of cabbage, was the main diet of the native Irish peasant. The typical Irish potato farmer ate close to eight pounds of potatoes a day, and less than a single acre of potatoes could feed an Irish family of four for an entire year and still leave acreage for other cash crops. Many Irish tenant farmers also grew one or more grain crops and raised livestock, all of which had to be sold to pay their high rents.

In 1845, a parasitic fungus, *Phytophthora infestans,* was brought to Ireland on ships from North America, especially Mexico. This alien fungus was deadly to Ireland's potatoes and it attacked and wiped out Ireland's entire potato crop. This resulted in the working Irish farmers and their families having nothing to eat except a few ounces of cornmeal, which they would receive through limited British government assistance. They would mix the cornmeal with milk or water into a stirabout, a hot corn mush with no flavor, little substance, and almost zero nutrients.

As the population grew weaker and crossed over into starvation, disease, including typhus, cholera, dysentery, fever, pneumonia, and many other ailments brought on by poor nutrition, weakness, and starvation, began to run rampant.

People began dying in droves and the grave diggers were too weak to dig more than a foot below the surface. Coffins were too expensive and there were no carpenters to build them anyway, so the skeletal remains of the dead were often buried in the rags in which they had lived and died.

Animosity, hostility, and religious prejudice between Protestant Britain and Catholic Ireland were rampant in the 1800s. Some Irish still believe that the half-hearted efforts on the part of the British government to help the starving Irish were due in large part to a pervasive desire on the part of the English to be rid of the Catholic Irish completely. Nonetheless, the British government did implement a public works program, putting the potato farmers to work building bridges, roads, canals, docks, and other elements of Ireland's infrastructure. Some of these projects were often unnecessary "make work" projects, similar to FDR's work programs during the Great Depression, and today there exist in Ireland structures built during the Potato Famine that are still in use.

The downside of the British work projects was that it required emaciated, feeble men to do hard physical labor, with no subsequent increase in their food intake. The workers were paid meager amounts by the British government, and they were not fed during the workday. Men often collapsed from hunger and exhaustion and many died. They left behind widows with children who were then deprived of even the pittance their husbands had been earning on the work crews.

Many Irish farmers and their families, no matter how much they loved their homeland, refused to lie down and die. They crowded onto ships headed for America and Canada, resulting in a massive immigration movement.

In the early 1840s, the population of Ireland was approximately 8 million people, more than 5 million of whom were dependent on agriculture for their livelihood. By the end of the decade and after the famine, a quarter of the population—over 2 million people—was gone from Ireland: over a million had died during the famine, and over a million more had left the country for the hopefully brighter shores of America and Canada. By 1900, following continuing post-famine emigration, the population of Ireland was down to around 4 million people. The current population is approximately 3.5 million people.

Unfortunately, the conditions on the ships headed away from the Emerald Isle were often atrocious, and many died from disease on their way to a better life. Tellingly, these ships of immigrants were cynically nicknamed "coffin ships." It is estimated that at least 20,000 Irish émigrés died on their way across the sea.

The Irish Potato Famine changed the face of Ireland and left deep wounds that still hurt today. It is one of history's saddest tragedies. The blight and crop destruction could not have been prevented, but the suffering, starvation, deaths, and massive emigration could have been, with a more effective, and more compassionate government response to the crisis.

[1] £16 million in 1848 equals approximately $725 million in 2002 dollars.

13

The 1970 Bangladesh Cyclone

The Ganges Delta, East Pakistan

November 13, 1970

1,000,000 Dead

As we hovered for a landing, the sickening smell of rotting corpses—human and cattle—came wafting up from the ground . . . We touched down, and men, boys, and girls below the age of puberty ran toward us across the ruined fields . . . There was a mad scramble for the packages . . . A little girl came running up to me, pointing at her swollen belly and asking for food, but I had none to give. Nearby a small boy collapsed on top of his relief bundle and broke into tears.

—Maynard Packer, *Newsweek*

Dead bodies carpeted the land and it was difficult to walk without stepping on corpses. Cadavers were lodged in trees like macabre, rotting fruit that had faces and limbs. A million dead cows floated in the Ganges River and Delta and their waters quickly turned red. Scores of ships were strewn inland, far from the waters where they had been anchored. Vultures ate very well for many days after the storm waters receded. The gigantic fifty-foot tsunami that accompanied this cyclone rose high above the many small offshore islands in the Bay of Bengal, slammed down upon them with fury, leaving the tiny islets looking as though they had never been inhabited.

(A tsunami is an enormous ocean wave caused by an underwater earthquake or an underwater volcanic eruption. A tsunami can do more damage and claim more lives than the earthquake or volcano that created it. This water monster rises up out of the sea with little or no warning and slams down on coastal areas with great fury and destructive force. When it retreats, it takes with it houses, cars, animals, and people.)

The initial death toll from this tropical storm was reported in the November 15, 1970, *New York Times* as 11,000 confirmed, with the caution that "the final toll might be at least twice that number." The final toll was considerably more than that; at least 500,000 people were dead from this devastating cyclone and tidal wave, and many sources reporting up to a million dead. If we factor in the great number of deaths from injuries, starvation, and the cholera and typhoid epidemics that followed this storm, then the 1-million-dead figure seems not only likely, but perhaps even too low.

Three days before this calamitous cyclone struck, it was tracked approximately eight hundred miles south of the Ganges Delta of East Pakistan, which is now Bangladesh. A report from the coastal city of Cox's Bazar in Burma (now Myanmar) warned the coastal islands and areas of the Ganges Delta that the storm was located in the Andaman Islands and was moving straight for them at around ten miles per hour.

These reports were either dismissed, ignored, or not heard for two reasons. First was the fact that a month or so earlier, a similar report had been issued and the predicted storm had turned out to be minimal with little loss of life, and minor injuries and damage. Many believed that this would be the case with this latest storm.

The second reason the alert was not taken seriously was that many of the most vulnerable people did not hear it. The offshore islands of East Pakistan were dotted with small, agricultural villages and many did not have electricity or even battery-powered radios. Thus, many who were right in the killer's path were in complete ignorance of the oncoming storm.

The tidal wave arrived first, at around midnight on November 12. This was followed by winds of up to 150 miles per hour that, combined with the force of the water, wreaked enormous havoc, and left the islands and coastal area of the Ganges Delta utterly devastated. Some people survived by climbing trees and holding on for hours until the storm passed. Others climbed onto the roofs of their flooded houses and prayed that the roofs would not be ripped off by the incredible wind. Their prayers were not always answered, however, and survivors told stories of watching their neighbors go flying by, either hanging off a detached roof, or being carried off by the water.

After the storm subsided, damage assessments began. Once the world learned of the horrible devastation the storm had left behind, relief efforts started, with the United States and Great Britain leading the way. British cargo planes brought in enormous amounts of food and supplies; American helicopters likewise dropped massive amounts of food; worldwide relief organizations sent contingents of medical people and engineers to help fight the cholera and typhoid, and to begin the daunting task of rebuilding roads and bridges and other elements of the area's infrastructure.

Sadly, the Pakistani government seemed to be the least concerned about helping the people in the Ganges Delta area. Foreign governments were quicker, more generous, and more eager to help than were the nation's own leaders. This apathetic and totally inadequate response from Pakistan's capital, Karachi, ultimately resulted in a revolution. The Pakistanis who had survived the cyclone mounted a bloody civil war to free themselves from Pakistani rule and the country of Bangladesh was born.

Bangladesh today has its problems, including poverty, illiteracy, slow economic development (its per capita gross domestic product is extremely low), and a high birth mortality rate. Foreign aid and domestic programs targeting specific problems have resulted in some overall progress, but the country still has high levels of poverty, and a troubled banking system. Bangladesh has created jobs, though, in the garment industry, and its exports have steadily risen, with the United States one of its biggest customers.

Adding to Bangladesh's internal economic woes are recurrent problems with devastating storms. The country experiences one to two major cyclones every year, plus floods, typhoons, and other calamities that impede agricultural stability.

The 1970 cyclone, while considered the worst tropical storm of the century, did result in the birth of a nation, albeit a nation with troubles that a change in name did not erase.

14

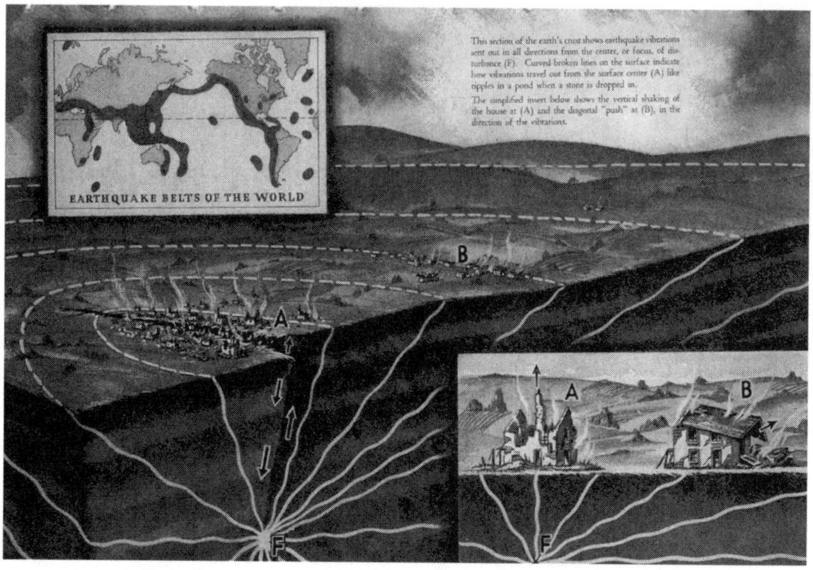

EARTHQUAKE BELTS OF THE WORLD
This section of the earth's crust shows earthquake vibrations sent out in all directions from the center, or focus, of disturbance (F). Curved broken lines on the surface indicate how vibrations travel out from the surface center (A) like ripples in a pond when a stone is dropped in.
The simplified insert below shows the vertical shaking of the house at (A) and the diagonal "push" at (B), in the direction of the vibrations.
A
B
F

The 1556 Great China Earthquake

Shensi, Honan, Shansi Provinces, China

January 23, 1556

830,000+ Dead

Does the earth breathe before earthquakes?
—William R. Corliss, *Handbook of Unusual Natural Phenomena*

Li Ming lay on her stomach on her reed bed mat, staring out through the hole that was the entrance to the cave where she lived with Mama and Papa. In the early hours of the morning, she would stare out the opening and watch as the sun rose slowly over the plains surrounding the hills where she and her family, and many other Chinese families, all lived.

Li Ming remembered when her father and many other men and their sons had dug the caves, using wooden tools, and sometimes their hands, to pull away the soft gray soil, moving deeper and deeper into the mountains. First they had hacked out steps up the side of the mountain so they could climb up and down easily, and then the men had put their backs into digging the caves.

Li Ming's cave was one of the bigger ones and she knew her father was proud of the shelter he had been able to make for his family. The cave was warm in the winter and cool in the summer, and Papa had even dug out a small flat alcove next to their cave where Mama could put clothes to dry or breads to cool. The cave was bright enough during the day for Li Ming to practice her letters, and at night, after darkness fell, Papa would light one of their precious suet candles until they all went to bed.

This morning, Li Ming had wakened early, roused by some inner disquiet that, if asked to, she probably would not have been able to describe. She looked over at Mama and Papa asleep on their mat, and shifted her little body so she could see outside more clearly. The sky was a flat gray color that bore no trace of the rising sun. It was bright enough for Li Ming to see quite a distance, but the light was strange and unsettling. Li Ming began to get a little frightened, but was comforted by the presence of her parents a few feet away.

The little girl decided she would feel better if she had Lui, her doll, with her, so she reached beneath her covers and felt around for the cloth doll filled with grass that Mama had made for her. Just as her hand landed on the soft doll, Li Ming heard a tremendous roaring sound, as though some giant bear-god had awakened furiously angry and was venting his wrath. Li Ming started to crawl off her mat when everything began to shake.

The sides and ceiling of her cave began to tremble, and fine sand poured down like dry rain as the soft walls began to break apart from the shaking.

"Mama! Papa!" Li Ming screamed as she began to crawl across the floor to her parents. They had been awakened by the sound but the whole mountain was now shaking so violently that they could not even get to their feet.

As Li Ming continued to crawl to her parents, and as Mama and Papa held on to each other with all their strength, suddenly the entire mountain collapsed on top of the hundreds of caves and the thousands of people inside its cavernous depths.

The earth shook and heaved like a raging ocean and Li Ming's mountain was soon nothing but an enormous field of rocks and silt. Some of the Chinese peasants trapped inside the mountain were still alive when the earth stopped shaking. But they were the living dead, for there was no way of getting out and there was no one who would come and rescue them.

Blessedly, Li Ming and her parents died instantly and did not have to wait for the agonizing death of suffocation or blood loss. Their bones lie still beneath the mountain that once was their home in Shensi, China.

The Shensi, China, earthquake in 1556 holds the sad title of being (so far) the deadliest earthquake known in history. A staggering 830,000 lives were lost and the earthquake was felt in 212 provinces in China. Experts believe that, using today's 1 to 10 Richter scale, the Shensi earthquake was at least a level 8, and possibly as high as an 8.3. (See "Measuring an Earthquake's Intensity," page 320.)

Many thousands of the deaths from this earthquake were from people being buried alive. Thousands of Chinese peasants (including Li Ming's father) had dug caves in the sides of the soft cliffs in the region and they lived in these hollow places. The Shensi cliffs were made of loess, which is a gray silt that is easy to tunnel into and, unfortunately, not very strong or solid.

When the powerful January 23 earthquake struck, the mountains literally came down on top of thousands of unsuspecting Chinese, all of whom died beneath the tons of rubble. Included in the death toll as well were the people living in weak, poorly contructed houses that could not withstand the earthquake.

The destruction covered five hundred square miles but few other details are known of this most tragic of all earthquakes.

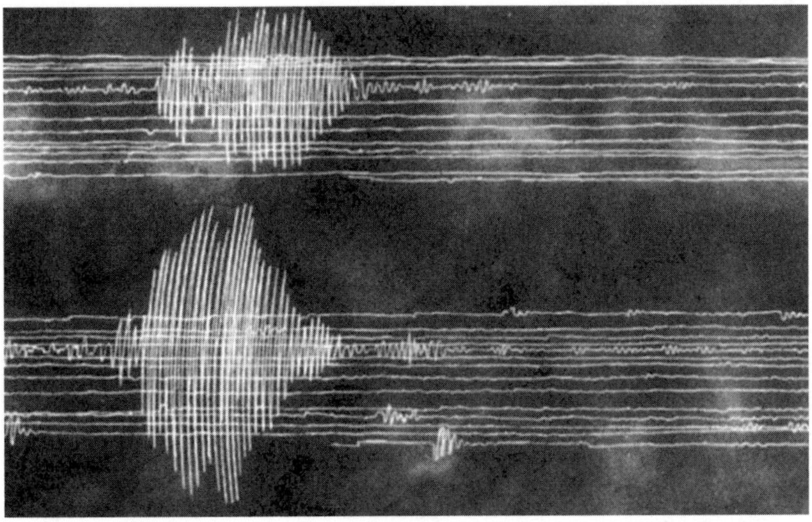

15

The 1976 Tangshan, China, Earthquake

TANGSHAN, CHINA

July 27, 1976

655,000 Dead

The transformation from rural near-normality to scenes of urban destruction is swift and shocking. One minute the train is speeding by waving fields of wheat, the next it is crawling through a desert of rubble as far as the eye can see.

—Journalist Peter Griffith, in the *Times* (London)

The 1976 Tangshan, China, earthquake is believed to be the deadliest quake of the twentieth century, and yet the Chinese government has never released an accurate death toll for the disaster. China initially told the world that the number of dead was 655,000 but has since stated it believes the number was between 240,000 and 255,000, a figure many experts consider to be much too low. A 1988 book written by members of the Chinese Seismological Service states with certainty that no more than 242,419 people died in the quake.

Dr. George Pararas-Carayannis, world-renowned earthquake and volcano authority, and author of *The Big One: The Next Great California Earthquake*, related the following regarding the number of deaths in Tangshan in 1976:

> A couple of days following this Tangshan earthquake of 28 July 1976 in China, United Press International (UPI) contacted me by telephone at my office in Honolulu . . . to provide them with an estimate of the death toll, since the Chinese would not reveal that information (and did not do so for over a year).
>
> I told UPI that approximately 700,000 to 750,000 people must have lost their lives from this quake. I based my estimate on the death toll caused by the earthquake in 1556—which devastated 98 counties and 8 provinces of Central China. The historic record documents that destruction from the 1556 quake—centered primarily in Hausien in the Shensi province—affected a total area of 500 square miles, and that in some counties the average death toll was 60 percent of the total population. In the 1556 event, 830,000 people lost their lives, so the estimate I gave to UPI for the 1976 quake was reasonable since the magnitude of this event was similar to that estimated for the 1556 quake—and since construction standards for this rural area had not changed significantly. As it turned out—a little over a year later—the Chinese gave the death toll at 655,000—so I was not very far off in my earlier estimate.[1]

A year before the Tangshan earthquake, Chinese scientists, using a new network of earthquake monitoring stations and equipment, successfully predicted an earthquake in Haicheng in time to evacuate the population and save countless lives. The system failed in 1976, however, and the only signs of the enormous, pending 8.3 magnitude[2] earthquake were natural: strange lights appeared in the sky, goldfish leaped out of their tanks, chickens refused to eat and ran around as if in a panic, droves of mice scurried about looking for a place to hide, and the water levels in wells began going up and down randomly. (The failure of the government to adequately warn of such a catastrophe may be why the Chinese government has consistently insisted that the death toll from the quake was significantly lower than what most experts believe.)

The physical activity of the ground in Tangshan during the 1978 quake was awe-inspiring evidence of the incredible power trapped beneath the surface of the earth.

According to reports, at 3:42 A.M. local time, a fault seven miles beneath the surface of Tangshan began to move. The energy from the shifting traveled through the earth, and when it reached the surface, the ground turned clockwise for a few seconds, then counterclockwise, then thrust upward.

This kind of violent ground movement took down 96 out of 100 houses (650,000 total), and 90 out of 100 factories.

Hundreds of thousands of citizens asleep in their beds were killed immediately; hundreds of thousands were injured; and thousands of deaths would ultimately follow from injury and disease, particularly typhoid, dysentery, influenza, and encephalitis. All 4 of Tangshan's hospitals were leveled, killing everyone inside. The enormous number of unburied corpses added to the disease outbreaks.

Also adding to the toll of death and destruction was a 7.1 magnitude aftershock the following afternoon that finished the job. As survivors were digging through the rubble looking for the injured or trying to salvage any possessions or valuables they could, the 7.1 quake struck and took down almost everything remaining standing, significantly adding to the death toll.

A major hydroelectric electricity generating plant was destroyed, bridges collapsed, reservoirs were ruined. Every road in the area was destroyed, and over 250 miles of railroad track in the region were ripped up and rendered useless by the quake, all of which severely hampered the attempts of rescue teams to get to Tangshan. Telephone and radio lines were devastated and it took hours for anyone in China's capital, Beijing, to hear of the disaster.

The Tangshan earthquake did not intimidate its survivors and the decision was made to rebuild the city in the same location. The massive construction effort took almost ten years and cost close to $8 million.

[1] See Dr. George Pararas-Carayannis's in-depth Web sites for more information:

- Dr. George's Tsunami Page
  www.geocities.com/DrGeorgePC
- Dr. George's Earthquake Page
  www.geocities.com/DrGeorgePC_1

[2] As registered at the United States Geological Survey station in California on the day of the initial quake.

16

The 1891 Russia Famine

16 Provinces in Southwestern Russia[1]

Winter of 1891–1892

407,000 Dead[2]

When hungry, one is not choosy about what one eats.

—Chinese proverb

Starvation is a slow, insidious way to die.

The deprivation of nutrients from the human body leads to much more than just hunger. Every human organ and body system is affected and the resultant symptoms are terrible. The journey to death begins with dreadful hunger *pains*—not just pangs—accompanied by weakness, swelling of the legs, chronic diarrhea, low body temperature, and a drastically reduced resistance to infection and disease. The majority of the 407,000 Russians who died during the country's 1891–92 famine died from opportunistic diseases that their debilitated bodies and starvation-weakened immune systems were unable to fight off.

* * *

People will eat literally anything when they are starving, just to put something in their screaming, empty stomachs. Starving people have been known to swallow stones, sand, and even their own feces when the hunger becomes apocalyptic.

In Russia in 1891–92, this level of desperation was widespread.

People called it "hunger bread," or "famine bread." It was a disgusting lump of mainly weeds, combined with chopped straw, tree bark, and sand. People would mix these substances together with some water and maybe a tiny amount of rye (if they had it) and bake it all into a hard yellow-black lump of detritus that provided no nutrients and served only as something solid inside an empty stomach. In "Russia's Conflict with Hunger," in an 1892 issue of the *American Review of Reviews,* W. Edgar describes a loaf of famine bread as "so disgusting in smell, taste and appearance that it is difficult to imagine that mankind could be reduced to such an extremity as to be forced to eat it."

Weakened digestive systems could not, of course, digest such a "food," and diarrhea, vomiting, and stomach pain often followed the ingestion of a piece of famine bread. Since the components of famine bread were found in the wild, fleas, lice, and mites were often mixed into the "recipe," which resulted in widespread typhus among many of those who ate off an infested loaf.

In Shakespeare's *As You Like It,* Amiens sings that there is "no enemy but winter and rough weather," and one of the most vivid illustrations of this is the contribution the winter and the weather made to this devastating Russian famine.

The Russian harvest of 1891 was very bad because of the five-month period with little or no rain before the harvest. The total harvest was approximately half of the harvest of the region's best year, which had been 1888. There were areas that did better than others, but the harvest in general was much lower than in previous, wetter years.

There were grain reserves in the country that hungry peasants could have tapped—if the Russian government had allowed this. As we have seen throughout the history of famines, it has been quite common for governments to continue to export grain while their own citizens starve. During the 1891–92 season, as crop production dropped precipitously, Russia's grain exports *remained the same.* The government tapped the reserves so as not to lose export dollars.

The farmers without a crop? They ate famine bread.

Russian Minister of Finance I. A. Vyshnegradskii often stated his policy regarding the country's grain business. *"Nedoedim no vyvezem,"* he would proclaim. "We may not eat enough, but we will export."

In *Famine in Russia, 1891–1892*, Richard G. Robbins Jr. describes what a traveler passing through a Russian village crippled by the famine might find:

> In the company of the village *starosta* [elder] and the local *zemski nacahl'nik* [land captain], the traveler might be invited to visit some of the houses. The *zemski nacahl'nik* is checking, no doubt for the third or

> fourth time, to see if the peasants have hidden away stores of grain in the stable or under the floorboard. The stable, when examined, proves devoid of both grain and animals. Nor is this exceptional; in many villages, from one-half to two-thirds of the livestock has been sold. As for the contents of the *izba* [hut], even men hardened to the realities of Russian country life are shocked by what they encounter. The appalling stench of burning dung, human perspiration, and sickness is the first impression. When eyes adjust to the gloom of the hut, an old *baba* [woman] and an ancient *muzhik* [peasant man] come into view. Two children are curled on top of the stove. All are listless, with the dirty yellow skin, bloated features, and dropping eyes that are symptomatic of advanced hunger. The mother of the children lies on a bed in the corner of the room, stricken with typhus. Her husband and the oldest boy have left the village to seek work in a nearby town.

And what else does the traveler see in this sad place of suffering? Sitting on the table is a loaf of *golodnyi khleb*—hunger bread.

Although the famine mainly struck an area of Russia five hundred miles long by nine hundred miles wide (the Volga River bisecting the area north to south), the disaster impacted the entire country and spurred the government to take steps. The government's pathetic efforts included a misguided and poorly organized public works program, as well as the purchase of grain from other areas. The purchased relief grain was useless, however, since it could not get to the famine area because of the inadequacies of the country's railway and shipping lines.

Improved harvests ultimately pulled the provinces out of famine, and it is now known that the botched handling of the crisis by the Russian government contributed to its severity and duration.

Lessons were not learned, however, and Russia suffered several more famines in its recent history. (See chapters 7 and 8.)

[1] Kazan, Kursk, Nizhni, Orel, Orenburg, Penza, Perm, Riazan, Samara, Sartov, Simbirsk, Tambov, Tula, Ufa, Viatka, Voronoezh.

[2] Some estimates of the number of people who died during the famine go as high as 655,000, but this is the number of deaths in the whole country for the period. If the deaths are limited to the sixteen famine provinces, and unrelated cholera deaths (there was an epidemic in 1892) are deducted, then the number comes down to around 407,000, which is widely accepted by most experts as the more accurate total.

17

The Plague of Justinian

CONSTANTINOPLE

542

300,000 Dead

During these times there was a pestilence, by which the whole human race came near to being annihilated . . . For it did not come in a part of the world nor upon certain men, nor did it confine itself to any season of the year, so that from such circumstances it might be possible to find subtle explanations of a cause, but it embraced the entire world, and blighted the lives of all men . . . respecting neither sex nor age . . .

—Procopius, *The Secret History*

In Constantinople (now Istanbul) during the mid–sixth century, the life expectancy for males was between twenty-five and thirty years.

It was less for women, and the age at which females married was around fourteen. In order for the population to continue to grow, the birth rate had to maintain an extremely high level. The mid–sixth century birthrate of eighty births per one thousand is almost triple today's birthrate of around thirty per one thousand.

Life was short and difficult for the average citizen during the final years of the Roman Empire, and into this trying maelstrom was thrown the first ever pandemic of bubonic plague.

Now known as the Plague of Justinian, the plague that struck Constantinople in 542 is believed to have been the bubonic form of plague, because historical records, especially the writings of Procopius, prove that it was not contagious, as are the pneumonic and septicemic forms. Procopius writes of family members caring for loved ones infected with the plague and not getting sick. If it had been either of the other two airborne contagious types, anyone caring for a plague victim would also have died in short order.

Procopius wrote that "neither physicians nor other persons were found to contract this malady through contact with the sick or with the dead, for many who were constantly engaged in either burying or in attending those in no way connected with then held out in the performance of this service beyond all expectation . . ."

It is believed that the plague began in Egypt and Ethiopia in 540, made its way down the Nile, and traveled on ships to Constantinople along trade routes and in fleas on the bodies of rats, arriving in Constantinople the spring of 542. Once the merchant ships landed and the rats invaded the city, the disease began to spread rapidly.

It is estimated that the plague killed 300,000 people in Constantinople that one year. At one point, 10,000 people a week were dying. Houses were filled with rotting corpses and mass burials were common. Soon the death toll grew so high, and so fast, that the grave diggers could not dig pits, the enormous makeshift tombs, fast enough to keep up with the thousands dying daily. Myriad bodies were brought to the shore and piled on the beaches to rot; bodies were also stacked up on the streets, causing a pervasive stench of rotting flesh that hung over the town like a pall. After a while, no one bothered to continue to count corpses or keep track of the identities of the dead.

The estimated population of that area during Justinian's reign was approximately 500,000 and it is believed that the Plague of Justinian decimated 60 percent of it in a single year. The plague then moved on to Italy, France, Spain, Sweden, and Germany, and there is even evidence that it may have attacked Great Britain and Ireland in 544.

The plague manifested itself in glandular swellings in the groin, in the armpits, and the throat. It also caused the vomiting of blood, delirium, diarrhea, sore throat, black blisters, and terrible pain. Some victims tried to kill themselves; some lapsed into comas from which they would never awaken. In what had to have been a bizarre scene, Procopius writes that "those who were under the spell of the coma forgot all those who were familiar to them and seemed to be sleeping constantly. And if anyone cared for them, they would eat without waking . . ."

This sudden, massive tempest of death devastated commerce, crippled the food chain, and left the military without the necessary manpower it needed to defend the empire. Even the emperor Justinian was not immune to the plague. He contracted the disease but miraculously survived.

The plague left Constantinople ravaged and Justinian a weakened emperor who would not be able to rebuild the empire he had ruled. In a single year, disease transmitted by the almost invisible flea did what armies and conquerors could not: brought about the end of the Roman Empire and the start of the Dark Ages.

18

The 526 Antioch, Syria, Earthquake

ANTIOCH, SYRIA

May 20, 526

250,000+ Dead

Except for the soils of the field, the fire surrounded everything in the city, as if it had received a command from God that every living thing should be burned.

—A survivor of the Antioch earthquake[1]

It must be the will of God that my baby and I shall live, the young pregnant girl named Diana thought as she brushed the white dust from her face and tried to breathe slowly.

Diana had been in the kitchen when the earthquake hit. The house had collapsed around her and she was somehow saved when she dropped into a small cave created when a wall fell on top of some rubble. She would learn later that her entire family had died, but she had survived under mountains of stone and rubble.

Diana was nine months' pregnant and the midwives had told her that the baby was due at any time. Now she was buried alive, and she could feel her heart pounding in her temples and the baby kicking inside her. The cavern she was in was long enough for her to lie down, but too low for her to stand up, or even kneel. Diana didn't mind, though. She felt better lying down.

As she started to pray to God for her and her baby's lives, she suddenly felt a soaking rush of wetness on her legs and her bottom. Her water had broken as she lay in the darkness, all alone.

Her immediate response was to panic, but then she calmed herself and tried to breathe normally. The pains the older women had told her about were beginning. They were gripping, agonizing spasms that felt as though her entire womb was repeatedly clenching like a fist, with each squeeze sending bright blades of razor pain through her entire groin and abdomen.

Over the next nine hours, Diana suffered the agony of labor pains without even a sip of water to wet her parched throat. She lay flat on her back with her knees up and her legs spread, gripping a small rock in each hand and pounding them on the hard floor of her cave during the worst of the pains. When the baby's head came out, it was so excruciating, she thought she was going to die, but then she kept pushing and breathing, and banging the rocks, and eventually the newborn—a girl—slithered out from her womb, landing in the dust at her feet.

She picked Mary up—the earthquake had occurred during the Feast of the Ascension and Diana had already named her daughter for the Blessed Mother—and wiped her off as best she could. She used her teeth to gnaw through the umbilical cord, and then brought Mary to her breast. First, she squeezed her nipple and used a little of the fluid to wash Mary's dusty face. She then fed Mary and tried to relax away the lingering spasms.

This story of life amid so much death has a happy ending: Several days after Mary was born, mother and child were found by rescuers, and both lived to tell the tale.

The Antioch earthquake that buried Diana killed 250,000 people—fully one-half of the city's population.

Antioch was a thriving religious and cultural metropolis of the ancient world, being the third arm of the triumvirate with Alexandria in Egypt and Rome in Italy. The city had churches, markets, theaters, public baths, glorious monuments, and beautiful esplanades. Christianity had been brought to Syria by the apostle Paul around 38, and religion thrived in Antioch. Constantine the Great had built the Great Church at Antioch in 327, dedicating it to "Harmony, the Divine Power which unites the Universe, the Church, and the Empire."

The earthquake, which had to have been a magnitude 7 or greater, struck in the early evening, at around six o'clock. The damage was immediate and apocalyptic. Almost every building in Antioch collapsed during the quake, crushing to death close to 250,000 people. After this initial shock, there was silence and calm, which was followed shortly by an aftershock that completed the devastation. Fires started almost immediately, burning alive those who had been trapped in the rubble.

Miraculously, the Great Church did not fall during the earthquake. Many survivors looked to this as a sign that God had triumphed over whatever power had done this terrible thing to Antioch. This sense of peace and relief, however, was short-lived. Two days after the quake the Great Church burst into flames and burned to the ground.

The survivors were terrified and homeless and many decided to flee the city. They gathered up what few belongings they could rout from the rubble and headed out of town.

Throughout history, there has been a common thread running through many of the world's worst natural disasters, and that has been the sudden appearance of predatory looters following a mass tragedy.

Antioch was no exception; bands of thieves waylaid the refugees, robbing them and killing them at will. Looters also tore through the ruins of Antioch, digging out of the stone anything of value, likely ignoring the dying and the wounded.

When the dust settled, there were still thousands of Antiochans who had survived and stayed behind. They set about rebuilding their city, determined not to allow the earthquake to make then lose hope, give up, and forsake their beloved city. For two years, they worked. Houses were built, rubble and debris was removed, churches were planned and begun.

Fate (and the geological faults below the surface of Syria) had other plans for the people of Antioch, however. Two years after the devastating 526 quake, another earthquake struck Antioch. This one was not as severe as the earlier one, but it took down all the new buildings and killed 5,000 people.

Thus, history bid farewell to Antioch.

[1] Stuart Flexner, *A Pessimist's Guide to History*, 33.

19

The 1920 Gansu, China, Earthquake

Gansu Province, China

December 16, 1920

200,000 Dead

It is a bitter and humiliating thing to see works, which have cost men so much time and labour, overthrown in one minute; yet compassion for the inhabitants is almost instantly forgotten, from the interest excited in finding that state of things produced in a moment of time, which one is accustomed to attribute to a succession of ages.

—Charles Darwin, March 1835

Natural disasters can spontaneously elicit unexpected awe from observers and victims, an emotion that is not a common reaction to man-made disasters except in the most large-scale of tragedies.

A massive explosion that levels a town, such as the Texas City harbor explosion in 1947, can do this; but usually there is a psychic numbness that results from a plane crash or a train wreck or an urban fire.

The really colossal natural disasters, on the other hand, can stun mortal man with their impossible doings. The enormity of what actually happens during catastrophes such as earthquakes, or tsunamis, or tornadoes is almost too much for witnesses to bear.

The earth is not supposed to open up and swallow people and buildings as though they were toys. The water in a harbor is not supposed to retreat a half mile from land, exposing the seabed to the shocked eyes of the people on the shore. A house is not supposed to be picked up, carried for a mile or so, and then dropped onto a car. These things are so antithetical to the natural order of things that they become surreal, and they often stun observers into a bewildered catatonia.

The 1920 earthquake that roared through Gansu province in China was one of those natural catastrophes that was replete with "impossible doings." During this 8.6 magnitude earthquake, an area 300 miles wide and 100 miles long was transformed into something akin to a "solid ocean." The land moved up and down in waves as though it were water, and mountains were violently shaken and wrenched apart, leading many survivors to state with conviction that the land had walked, that ruthless stone giants had stomped through the Gansu province with impunity. December 16, 1920, is still, to this day, known in China as *shan tso-liao* ("when the mountains walked").

The first harbinger of the earthquake was an earsplitting roar from the bowels of the earth on the evening of December 16. The rumbling from underground was as though those stone giants were shouting out to the people above, "Beware!" This alarming noise was followed by violent winds that tore through the region like a sudden, landlocked hurricane. However, it was not a hurricane; it was much, much worse.

The wind created huge, blinding dust storms that reduced visibility to zero and pelted the people with sand and rocks. Adding to the peril was the fact that December 16 was a bitterly cold night in Gansu province.

Then the earthquake ripped open the earth, shook the mountains, and caused horrifying landslides of boulders and huge slabs of rock that came crashing down, wiping out entire villages in seconds. The landslides formed dams of boulders and trees, and, after the earth stopped shaking, the stunned survivors had to work desperately to remove the dangerous dams, or risk flooding that would likely kill the few who had miraculously lived.

National Geographic magazine covered one unusual result of the earthquake in Gansu:

> At the junction of the valley stands Swen Family Gap, a town of several thousand souls, in which one-tenth was killed by the collapse of buildings and cave dwellings; and the other nine-tenths were saved by the miraculous stoppage of two bodies of earth shaken loose from the mother hill and left hanging above the village, lacking only another half-second's tremor to send them down. A third avalanche, having

> flowed from the hills on the opposite side of the valley across the valley floor and the stream bed, is piled up in a young mountain, near enough to the village to overshadow the wall. In each case the earth which came down bore the appearance of having shaken loose, clod from clod, and grain from grain, and then cascaded like water, forming vortices, swirls, and all the convolutions into which a torrent might shape itself.[1]

In 1556, an enormous earthquake struck Shensi province in China. At that time, many of the Chinese peasants lived in hollowed-out caves in the mountains formed by loess, a soft siltlike soil. These fragile honeycombs of "homes" collapsed quite easily during the quake. (See chapter 14.) In 1920, there were still Chinese peasants making their homes in the mountains of loess, and, as in 1556, these hills also collapsed, burying alive hundreds of thousands.

After the 1920 earthquake, the death toll was calculated at approximately 180,000. An additional 20,000 souls perished from the cold during the winter. It was reported that many of these people did not have to die, and that they perished because they refused to build themselves new shelter. Why? Because of the awe and shock caused by such a mind-boggling catastrophe. Many of the survivors were so terrified of new tremors and quakes that they spent the winter out of doors, thereby finishing the job the earthquake started.

There was some validity to the survivors' fears, for earthquakes struck Gansu province again, but not during the 1920 winter following the 8.6 magnitude earthquake. The area was hit by a major quake in 1927, in which 100,000 died; and yet again in December 1932, during which 70,000 died. In a twelve-year period, 370,000 people died in one geographical region in China.

[1] Jay Robert Nash, *Darkest Hours,* 303.

20

The 1908 Messina, Sicily, Earthquake

Messina, Sicily

December 28, 1908

160,000 Dead[1]

We were all sleeping in my house when we were awakened by an awful trembling which threw us out of our beds. I cried out that it was an earthquake, and called to the others to save themselves . . . Finally, with my brother and sister, I succeeded in gaining the street, but soon lost them in the mad race of terror-stricken people who surged onward, uttering cries of pain and distress. During this terrible flight chimneys and tiles showered down upon us continuously. Death ambushed us at every step.

—A woman survivor of the Messina earthquake[2]

Surreal Sights from Sicily

Drunken transvestite prisoners roamed the streets, cutting off the fingers of the dead. Vultures dive-bombed for corpses' eyes. Naked survivors looking for food broke into the few buildings that were still standing. Men disemboweled other men as they fought for a handful of found beans. Streets opened and belched fire, and then slammed shut after swallowing hundreds of screaming people. The sea opened and sailors could see the ocean floor before their ships fell into the vast chasm. Buildings collapsed as though they were made of cards. A manic father ran back into his destroyed house and raced to the third floor looking for his infant son, but his son was gone and the boy's bed was full of fish. A naked woman rushed up to an Italian marquis who had just arrived in Messina and demanded from him a pair of shoes. Trapped victims chewed their own hands to the bone before they died. Those fortunate enough to have escaped their buildings ran through the ravaged streets as bodies, living, dead, and suicidal, rained down on them from above. Rats, dogs, and pigs fed on the dead and attacked the living. A naked family sat beneath an umbrella in the rubble that was their home. King Victor Emmanuel spent hours digging through the ruins for survivors. Russian sailors lined up looters in groups of twelve and executed them. An old man held the body of a dead child in his arms and danced at the edge of the water. Wriggling arms and legs thrust out of the rubble, waving blindly and pleadingly for help. Mountains of dead bodies burned long into the night. Entire villages were reduced to nothing but the bricks with which they had been built.

And through it all, Jesus Christ remained standing. The mosaic figure of Christ in the dome of Messina's Duomo cathedral did not fall, or shatter, as the building collapsed around it.

The first tremors hit at 5:25 A.M. They arose from beneath the waters of the Strait of Messina, the thin ribbon of water separating the peninsula of Italy from the island of Sicily. Immediately following this first "wake-up" shock, a series of enormous tremors struck, one after another, each one lasting approximately a half minute. The cumulative effect of these wrenching earth movements collapsed building after building, as though each were rigged to explode and crumble, and someone was pushing the switch every minute or so. A five-hundred-mile-per-hour, fifty-foot tsunami followed the earthquakes. Gas pipes ruptured, water mains exploded, fires raged, and the dead were everywhere.

On the Italy side of the Strait of Messina, the earthquake reached as far north as Cosenza, leveling Terranova and Reggio di Calabria, as well as countless small villages in between on the coast of the Tyrrhenian Sea.

On the Sicily side of the strait, the quake demolished the city of Messina and its neighbor Patti and did enormous damage as far south as Noto and Vittoria. Catania was severely damaged, as was inland Paterno. (The city of Corleone, the inspiration for the central character in Mario Puzo's *Godfather,* was safely ensconced in the northwest corner of the island of Sicily and was untouched by the quake and subsequent flooding and fires.)

The first help arrived the morning after the earthquake when three Russian Navy battleships rushed to the strait and dropped anchor off Messina. Six hundred armed Russian sailors immediately moved into the city, evaluated the situation, and set about establishing order and rescuing survivors. The Russian navy commanders took it upon themselves to take full charge of the city, and within an hour they had treated over one thousand survivors in a rapidly built open-air hospital. The Russians also mounted search and rescue missions, as well as rounding up and executing looters. Two hours after the Russians arrived, five British ships reached Messina and the British soldiers were equally expeditious in setting up kitchens and hospitals as well as assisting the Russians in looking for survivors.

U.S. ships did not join the Russian and British fleets. America was still angry that the anti-American governor of Kingston, Jamaica, had refused its help the previous year following an earthquake there. The United States' policy after that was to go only where asked. The official policy following the Messina disaster was that U.S. warships and relief vessels would go to Sicily, only if personally requested to by King Victor Emmanuel. America did, however, immediately send millions of dollars of relief supplies, but U.S. ships remained at sea.

[1] There is still disagreement today as to the actual number of people who died in this terrible earthquake, and from related tsunamis and fires. A check of eight sources (books, but Web sources were equally inconsistent) turned up nine different figures: 70,000, 83,000, 85,000, 100,000, 120,000, 150,000, 160,000, 250,000, and 300,000. Three separate sources each cited 160,000 dead, so we went with this figure, confident that it is as close to accurate as possible (although still an educated guess) and, if anything, perhaps too low. Regarding this disaster, historian Charles Morris, in his 1909 book, *Morris' Story of the Great Earthquake of 1908,* may have been correct when he wrote, "The actual loss of life will never be known."

[2] *New York Times,* December 30, 1908.

21

The Great Kanto Earthquake

Tokyo and Yokohama, Japan

September 1–3, 1923

156,000 Dead[1]

At the moment when the news of the great disaster which has befallen the people of Japan is being received, I am moved to offer you in my own name and that of the American people the most heartfelt sympathy, and to express to your Majesty my sincere desire to be of any possible assistance in alleviating the terrible suffering to your people.

—President Calvin Coolidge, telegram to Japan's Emperor Yoshihito after hearing of the Kanto earthquake

If personality is an unbroken series of successful gestures, then there was something gorgeous about him, some heightened sensitivity to the promises of life, as if he were related to one of those intricate machines that register earthquakes ten thousand miles away.

—F. Scott Fitzgerald, *The Great Gatsby*[2]

Thousands of terrified Japanese huddled in the waters of Yokohama Bay, keeping everything but their heads submerged. Their beloved city was burning, and tens of thousands of their fellow citizens had already died, either from being crushed to death in the cataclysmic earthquake and buried in the rubble that was everywhere, or burned to death in the enormous fires that quickly followed the earth's somersaults. (And "somersault" is what the earth did in some places. There are reports of enormous tracts of land literally turning upside down from the power of the quake.)

Most of these earthquake refugees felt relatively safe in the water. After all, they knew that fire cannot live in water. So they thought.

The Standard Oil building and its huge oil storage tanks stood on the Yokohama waterfront. Tankers arrived daily from around the world and filled the enormous tanks with oil for Yokohoma and Tokyo, cities in a country that relied almost solely on imported oil for its energy needs.

The raging fires that covered Yokohama with a blanket of flame edged nearer and nearer to the Standard Oil building and its full oil tanks until the inevitable happened. The building and the tanks violently exploded and one hundred thousand tons of burning fuel oil gushed into Yokohama Bay, drenching the thousands of people floundering helplessly in what had earlier been a fireproof sanctuary.

The oil stuck to their bodies and burned them to death, or it burned them to the point where they chose to drown rather than continue to endure the agony of being covered in flaming oil that no amount of water could put out.

The Great Kanto Earthquake, named for Japan's Kanto plain spanning Tokyo and Yokohama, struck at precisely one minute before noon on Saturday, September 1, 1923. It is estimated that the quake measured between 7.9 and 8.3 on the Richter scale, packing a force greater than a one-megaton nuclear explosion.

Over the next three days, more than 1,700 earthquakes struck the area, and Tokyo Imperial University recorded 237 that could be felt by the inhabitants of Tokyo and Yokohama, and the people in the area between the two cities.

The initial earthquake destroyed a staggering 75 percent of Tokyo's buildings. About 20 percent of Yokohama's buildings were likewise demolished. Following the quake came the fires—huge firestorms and rare fire tornadoes that had to have made the Japanese feel as though the very gates of Hades had been opened. Some people tried to flee the fire, which also brought winds that could lift people bodily off the ground and incinerate them as it tossed them about like stray leaves or random pieces of paper. Over thirty-five thousand people gathered in a park by the side of the Sumida River because they believed that fire would not be able to attack them in an open area where there were no buildings to burn and where a river stood nearby.

Unfortunately, they misjudged the fire demon's powers and the conflagration attacked them in toto, killing every one of them in one awesome and lightning-fast firestorm. After the fire departed, there remained a giant, smoldering, burned-to-death throng of people who had been packed together so tightly, they had all died standing up.

The fires raged through Tokyo and Yokohama for over two days, destroying communications, water supplies, electrical facilities, and food stockpiles.

By the time the fires were put out and the tremors ceased, almost 200,000 people were injured, 500,000 were homeless, and 80,000 homes had been destroyed. And perhaps upward of 200,000 people had died.

Part of the reason for such an enormous physical property loss was the fact that the buildings in Tokyo and Yokohama were constructed with flimsy, lightweight woods. Few had brick or cement foundations, and the walls were often draped with flammable wall hangings. In addition, Japanese families liked to cook using small charcoal, tabletop braziers. When the earth started to shake to the great degree it did (the quake occurred during lunchtime), thousands of these lit braziers were flung off tables, hurling flaming coals against flammable furnishings and hangings, and, in effect, giving the fire to come a helping hand.

The permanent geological changes resulting from the Great Kanto Earthquake were breathtaking in their enormity. In the middle of Sagami Bay (the earthquake's epicenter), the sea bottom dropped between 300 and 600 feet from the quake. In the northern end of the bay, however, the sea floor rose an astonishing 750 feet.

Japan would be struck again by a major, devastating earthquake in 1995, when Kobe was truck by a 7.2 magnitude quake that would do over $131 billion in damages. (See chapter 41.)

[1] As is often the case with mass disasters, this figure is arguable. Some sources report 140,000 deaths; some say 143,000; some say upward of 200,000.

[2] It is believed that Fitzgerald is referring to the Kanto earthquake in this passage.

22

The 1815 Eruption of Tambora and the Year Without a Summer

SUMBAWA, INDONESIA; THEN THE WORLD

April 5, 1815–Spring 1817

150,000+ Dead

Billions in Lost Crops and Other Damages

Three distinct columns of flame rose to an immense height, and the whole surface of the mountain soon appeared covered with incandescent lava, which extended to enormous distances; stones, some as large as the head, fell in a circle of several miles diameter, and the fragments dispersed in the air caused total darkness . . . the abundance of the ashes expelled was such that at Java, a distance of 310 miles, they caused complete darkness in midday, and covered the ground and roofs with stratum several inches thick.

—Sir Stamford Raffles, Governor of Java[1]

About 8 A.M. began to snow—continued more or less till past 2 P.M. The heads of all the mountains on every side were crowned with snow. The most gloomy and extraordinary weather ever seen.

—Bennington, Vermont, farmer Benjamin Harwood, in an early June 1816 diary entry[2]

Nuclear Winter

If the missiles fly, and the unimaginable happens, mankind will have to deal not only with the death and destruction meted out by the nukes, we will also (according to many renowned scientists, including the late Carl Sagan) have to contend with a nuclear winter.

Nuclear explosions can produce temperatures ranging from five thousand four hundred to seven thousand two hundred degrees Fahrenheit. Almost anything will burn at these temperatures, and, if the burned material is organic (trees, people), then the resulting smoke, while thick and unhealthy to breathe, will probably not be toxic. If the burned material, however, is plastic, or glass, or chemical, or synthetic, then the gases produced and present in the ensuing smoke might quite possibly be fatal.

A nuclear winter—a worldwide darkening and cooling of the atmosphere—would occur when the smoke from one or more nuclear explosions blocks the sun from hitting the ground, causing drastically lower temperatures, widespread crop death, as well as freak weather that could include summer snowstorms and thick polluted fogs. (See chapter 39.)

A nuclear winter would also destroy countless life forms, and, since it is estimated that a full-scale nuclear war between the United States and either Russia or China would instantly kill at least one billion people, it is believed that the nuclear winter that followed would kill another billion.

In 1816, the northeastern United States was given a preview—on an infinitesimally smaller scale—of something akin to a nuclear winter when the New England and Atlantic seaboard states suffered through a year without a summer.

Why did it snow in June in Connecticut?

Why was there frost in July in New Hampshire?

The answer is because the Mount Tambora volcano on the Indonesian island of Sumbawa erupted the year before, spewing the largest quantity of volcanic ash into the air in all of recorded history. It would take 104 years for scientists to figure out the connection; in 1920 they finally did, and from then on, there was an explanation for the year without a summer—and a new understanding of the effect volcanic eruptions can have on the earth's weather.

Tambora

Everyone thought Tambora was extinct. It wasn't. On April 5, 1815, the thirteen thousand-foot sleeping Goliath awakened and let out a series of rumblings that announced its presence and could be heard a thousand miles away. For five days, the volcano spewed ash in such quantity that houses on Sumbawa collapsed under the weight. The ash was so impenetrable to sunlight that island residents could literally not see their hands in front of their faces. On April 10, the eruption peaked with enormous columns of fire that snaked around each other and intertwined above the glowing mountain.

This was followed by a violent wind, which was probably similar to the meteorological phenomena of the firestorm—fire tornadoes formed during enormous forest fires. (See chapter 92.) Like a vacuum cleaner, this maelstrom swept people and animals and houses up into the air. The living things were dismembered and burned up; the inanimate objects were smashed and torn apart into countless pieces.

The power of Tambora's eruption was more than the mountain and the island on which it stood could handle, however. As it discharged tons of rock and lava and ash, the volcano began to shrink, from thirteen thousand feet to nine thousand, and, ironically, the surface of the island began to rise as foot upon foot of ash piled up. This ash—which would ultimately be over three feet deep and would also choke the water around Sumbawa—would finish Tambora's job of executing the people within its sphere. The ash killed all the vegetation, and the subsequent famine, combined with a cholera epidemic, added 80,000 deaths to the 12,000 killed immediately during the eruption.

The Year Without a Summer

One observer of the Tambora eruption mused that the ash ejected by the volcano, if spread out evenly, would probably cover all of Germany. The majority of the ash did not land on the ground, though; instead, it remained in the atmosphere and began traveling around the world via the jet stream.

This immense cloud of effluvia caused a drop in the world's temperature and in Europe and New England devastation to the summer crops that had already begun to mature.

June temperatures were well below normal, which contributed to the damage already being done by an ongoing drought. Farmers resorted to feeding whatever corn they could harvest to their cattle so as not to loose livestock. In Switzerland, starving people ate stray cats and dogs. New York farmers were forced to dig up newly planted potatoes to feed their families. Bizarre summer frosts killed crops as soon as they were planted. People started hunting raccoons and pigeons for food. It is estimated that starvation and disease added another almost 50,000 deaths to Tambora's total, although at the time, no one knew of the connection between the year with no summer and the eruption of a volcano thousands of miles away and hundreds of days in the past.

Even if they did, it is likely that the stoic and taciturn nineteenth-century New England farmers wouldn't have believed it anyway.

[1] Karen Farrington, *Natural Disasters*, 44.

[2] Keith Heidom, "Eighteen Hundred and Froze to Death," *The Weather Doctor* at www.islandnet.com/~see/weather/history/1816.htm.

23

The 1864 Calcutta Cyclone

CALCUTTA, INDIA

October 5, 1864

80,000 Dead[1]

The glories of our blood and state
Are shadows, not substantial things;
There is no armor against fate;
Death lays his icy hand on kings . . .
And in the dust be equal made . . .
—James Shirley, *The Contention of Ajax and Ulysses* (1659)

The largest city in India and the capital of the West Bengal state, Calcutta, was founded in 1690 as a British East India Company trading post, and over several centuries, it has borne a notorious reputation as a stifling place of poverty, disease, massive overcrowding, and vile, unsanitary conditions. Calcutta is also known for being the home of both the humanitarian Mother Teresa and the infamous Black Hole,[2] as well as being the site of some of the worst natural catastrophes in history.

Calcutta is a teeming metropolis of contradictions. Internet sites that offer tips for tourists often start off by telling potential visitors to Calcutta that it is dirty. To many Westerners, that is enough to discourage a visit; yet, the experts go on to then extol some of the wonders of Calcutta, which is also known as the "City of Joy" and is described by native Calcuttans with words such as *enchanting* and *fascinating.*

Today, Calcutta is a tourist destination, boasting many world-renowned sites, including the Nakhoda Mosque (which can accommodate ten thousand worshippers at a time), St. Paul's Cathedral Church, the Mother Teresa Mission of Charity, the Japanese Buddhist Temple, the Birla Planetarium, the Academy of Fine Arts, the National Library, the Indian Museum, the Nehru Children's Museum, the Floating Museum, the Botanical Garden, the Zoological Garden, the Ranji Stadium as well as a race course, golf course, and polo grounds.

Calcutta in 1864 was a quite different place. Although British-controlled, the city was desperate with poverty, and catastrophes such as the October 5, 1864, cyclone compounded Calcutta's miseries and problems. Many of the native Indians lived in rickety huts, while the British colonials and their families enjoyed more well-built, spacious houses, often staffed by natives. The cyclone that struck Calcutta on October 5 did not play favorites, though. The storm was so powerful that, in addition to thousands of huts being blown away like wood chips, the roofs of the more solid houses of the British were torn off and the buildings themselves severely damaged by the high waves and typhoon-strength winds of the storm.

The cyclone came up from the Bay of Bengal, into the Hooghly River, and headed straight for Calcutta and its busy port. Close to three hundred ships were moored in the Calcutta harbor and every vessel was destroyed and sunk, all with their crews and cargo on board.

The cyclone's winds created a forty-foot high wave of water, which was what the Calcuttans saw coming toward their city. This wave essentially put Calcutta under water, drowning more than 50,000 people immediately. There was nowhere to run and there was nothing anybody could do to save either life or property. The cyclone was a force that was able to exploit the geographical configuration of the Bay of Bengal to strengthen itself, while using the bay's water as a deadly weapon of destruction. The cyclone had moved through the bay for an entire day before arriving at Calcutta at 10:00 A.M. on the morning of October 5, probably the worst possible time. It was high tide and this made the sea wave that much higher and gave it a longer "reach."

The kind of destruction that the storm wreaked on Calcutta was not over when the winds subsided and the water retreated. In addition to the public health catastrophe of having to contend with 50,000 corpses, the city's entire water supply was destroyed. Reservoirs were contaminated with all manner of effluvia, including human waste and human remains, and the vermin that are always attracted by the stench of death arrived and began spreading disease and death.

Within a few weeks, an additional 30,000 Calcuttans died from all manner of water-borne bacterial diseases, including typhus and cholera, and opportunistic diseases such as pneumonia, enteritis, influenza, malaria, and dengue fever.

A cholera epidemic had started in 1863 in the lower basin of India's Ganges

River and quickly raged throughout all of India, as well as China, Japan, and Indonesia. This pandemic was most likely exacerbated in eastern India by the death and unsanitary conditions from the 1864 cyclone, and the aftermath of the storm may have hastened its transmission along the Mediterranean coasts, into north Africa, and eventually the Caribbean Islands and the east coast of the United States. The disease outbreak in Calcutta and environs certainly did not help *stem* the cholera pandemic.

Aside from the spread of disease throughout India and beyond, the 1864 cyclone was surgically precise in its attack on Calcutta. Records reveal that as the storm was drowning Calcutta and tearing the city into pieces at 10:00 on the morning of October 5, at the same time, the city of Contai, a short distance from ground zero, was completely untouched. Calcutta was the target and the devastation was complete. An 1864 drawing published in the *Illustrated London News* after the storm painted a grim picture of the city's harbor: ship's masts were strewn about the water like matches in a puddle; buildings were flattened; and debris covered the coastline for miles.

The Bay of Bengal would be visited again many times by catastrophic storms.

Sometimes geography can be a death sentence.

[1] Fifty thousand were killed during the storm; another 30,000 died shortly thereafter from injuries from the cyclone and disease brought on by contaminated water supplies.

[2] The Black Hole was a cell in the jail of a British fort in Calcutta in 1756. That year, a battle took place at the fort between British and Indian soldiers. The Indian troops imprisoned 146 British soldiers in the Black Hole, which measured fifteen feet by eighteen feet. Most of the British soldiers—123 men—were dead from suffocation by the following morning. J. Z. Howell, one of the men who survived, told of his ordeal in the 1758 *Annual Register:*

> Many to the right and left sunk with the violent pressure, and were soon suffocated; for now a steam arose from the living and the dead, which affected us in all its circumstances, as if we were forcibly held by our heads over a bowl of strong volatile spirit of hartshorn, until suffocated; nor could the effluvia of the one be distinguished from the other; and frequently, when I was forced by the load upon my head and shoulders, to hold my face down, I was obliged, near as I was to the window, instantly to raise it again, to escape suffocation . . .
>
> About a quarter of six in the morning, the poor remains of 146 souls, being no more than three and twenty, came out of the black hole alive, but in a condition which made it very doubtful whether they would see the morning of the next day . . . The bodies were dragged out of the hole by the soldiers, and thrown promiscuously into the ditch of an unfinished ravelin, which was afterwards filled with earth.

24

The 1970 Peru Earthquake and Landslide

CHIMBOTE, YUNGAY, HUARAS

May 31, 1970

66,794 Dead

$250 Million in Damages

We had been terrified by the quake, and most of us were praying in the streets amid the wreckage of the city when we heard the infernal thunder of the huayco coming down from Huascaran. For God's sake, send us help. We have no medicine, no food . . . All night the women have cried and prayed; some men were cursing, raising their fists to heaven.

—A radio message from a survivor of the May 31, 1970, Peru earthquake, sent after the *huayco* [landslide][1]

Some of the survivors lived by running to the city of the dead.

The ninety-two residents of Yungay, Peru, who fled to Cemetery Hill to escape a ferocious landslide all survived. The entire city of Yungay and everyone else in it—almost three thousand souls—were wiped out in the landslide, and yet these ninety-two people survived. After the massive surge of rocks and mud was over, the ninety-two dazed survivors looked around to see everything gone, except for a statue of Jesus Christ with his arms outstretched, standing tall above the rubble. (Coincidentally, in 1908, in Messina, Sicily, after a huge earthquake had totally devastated the town, including the majestic Duomo cathedral, and the dust had settled, the giant mosaic figure of Jesus Christ in the Duomo was still standing.)

The May 1970 Peru earthquake struck at 3:23 P.M. on the last day of the month and measured 7.75 on the Richter scale.[2] The United States Geological Survey declared the quake "possibly the most destructive historic earthquake on the western hemisphere." The earthquake emanated from a crack in the ocean floor in the harbor of Chimbote, Peru, a little over thirty miles from the coast.

The quake itself did horrific damage to the coastal cities, especially Chimbote, which was almost completely destroyed. Casma and Huramey also suffered enormous devastation and a large loss of life. The shock waves from the quake spread in concentric circles over northern Peru in an area six hundred miles wide.

Huaras, a popular resort town, was erased from the earth. There was no food or water for survivors (few as they were) and great billowing clouds of dust choked the stunned handful that had lived. The dust also made rescue efforts very difficult. Helicopter pilots could not see the ground as they flew over the devastated areas, thereby delaying medical and emergency personnel from moving in.

As is always the case with a disaster of this scale, an immediate and pressing problem was the vast number of dead bodies. The fear of disease from the unburied bodies prompted action that living loved ones found intolerable, and yet completely necessary. Giant mass graves were dug and corpses—usually unidentified and unclaimed—were simply piled in until no more could fit. They were then covered over, thus solving both the problem of sanitation as well as the overwhelming shortage of coffins and single graves.

A total of 66,794 people died; more than 100,000 were injured, many seriously; and a staggering 800,000 people were left homeless. Five thousand of the homeless were children who had been orphaned by the earthquake.

The Infernal Thunder of the *Huayco*

The earthquake was not finished after tearing through cities, burying people, and causing an estimated 95 percent of the buildings in its reach to collapse. It triggered an enormous landslide from Mount Huascaran, which brought 3.5 billion cubic feet of mud, rock, and water crashing down on the city of Yungay, including a one hundred-foot-thick glacier.

This immense amount of weight broke dams throughout northern Peru, adding even more devastation to the area. Cities were flooded, and one source described the effect of the landslide as "finishing the damage" that the earthquake "overlooked."

Some of the rocks that flew down from Mount Huascaran were the size of small houses, and many of them weighed seven hundred tons or more. A United States Geological Survey photo from the disaster showed one such rock with a man standing next to it. The man was dwarfed by the gigantic boulder, and, when we consider that a rock this size and weight came hurling through the air at speeds upward of two hundred miles an hour, it is not surprising that many reports from the scene describe houses exploding into tiny fragments when these missiles struck them. There is a law of physics that states that force is a factor of weight and speed. The seven hundred-ton rocks hitting the houses in Peru were a compelling demonstration of that law. The rocks that did not hit houses left gigantic craters in the earth where they landed.

Peruvians are used to earthquakes. They get them every twelve or fifteen years on average, and some have been severe; many have been ignorable.

The May 31, 1970, Peru earthquake with its ensuing landslide was the kind of earthquake Peruvians fear, and the kind they hope is a once in a millennium event.

[1] Stuart Flexner, *The Pessimist's Guide to History*, 307.

[2] Some sources say 7.5; others, 7.7 or 7.8. Regardless of the fractional component of the magnitude, the fact that it was very close to a magnitude 8.0 is what is most telling about the destructive power of this quake. A magnitude 7.0 earthquake releases the amount of energy equivalent to 199,000 tons of TNT. The Richter rankings increase logarithmically by a factor of 10; thus, a magnitude 8.0 is equal to the energy equivalent of 6.3 *million* tons of TNT. (A magnitude 9.0 is equivalent to an unimaginable 99 *million* tons of TNT.) The 1970 Peru earthquake was closer to a magnitude 8.0 than a magnitude 7.0, and the destruction left in its wake was powerful evidence of the difference one ranking can make.

25

The 1988 Armenia Earthquake

ARMENIA, THE SOVIET UNION

December 7, 1988

55,000 Dead[1]

$14.2 Billion in Damages

I have Chernobyl behind me, but I have never seen anything like this. The scope is just catastrophic.

—Yevgen I. Chazov, Soviet Minister of Health[2]

The effects of a natural disaster such as this 1988 earthquake in Armenia magnify exponentially when the areas hit are staggeringly poor without any "help" from a catastrophe.

Countries such as Armenia have had difficulty providing basic services such as education, clean water, and abundant electricity. The cataclysmic destruction wrought by a major earthquake can set the country back not months, or even years, but decades. For instance, ten years after the 1988 quake, in the city of

Spitak, Armenia, tens of thousands of families still lived in temporary slumlike housing, and elsewhere the mayor of a small Armenian town boasted that a new building had central heating. Consider: The area is so poor that central heating is something of which to be extraordinarily proud. In Yerevan in 1992, four years after the quake, people were still being forced to live with only one to two hours of electricity a day.

The epicenter of this earthquake, which measured 6.9 on the Richter scale, was twenty-five miles northeast of the Armenian city of Leninake. It struck at the unfortunate hour of 11:41 A.M., a time when all the factories and schools were filled. The earthquake lasted less than one minute, and, four minutes later, there was an aftershock that measured 5.8. This quake was the worst earthquake catastrophe since the 1976 earthquake in Tangshan, China, which measured 7.8 and killed 655,000 people. (See chapter 15.)

Within the thirty-mile circumference around the epicenter of the earthquake, *every* building with more than two stories came down, crushing to death or burying alive everyone inside at the time. Most of the people who were buried beneath the tons of concrete, wood, and glass, died there.

More than 15,000 people were injured in the quake, and in a terribly sad development, the hospitals that tended to the injured did not have enough antibiotics for the number of people hurt, and thousands died from infections that could have been treated. This also dramatically illustrates the life and death difference between the resources of the poorer countries and the developed nations.

In the United States, when a major disaster hits, the full resources of the U.S. government—from FEMA to individual state governments and agencies—are marshaled to help in any way possible. Rebuilding begins immediately, as much medication as is needed is flown in from all over the country, and individual charitable donations begin pouring in for the affected people. There is no way that an area of our country would still exhibit earthquake damage ten years after a catastrophe, and yet this is commonplace in poor countries with an aging infrastructure and the inability to begin the recovery process without an enormous amount of outside aid.

The National Oceanic and Atmospheric Administration (NOAA) described the reasons the 1988 Armenian catastrophe did so much damage:

> Many factors contributed to the magnitude of the disaster, including freezing temperatures, time of day, soil conditions, and inadequate building construction. A large number of medical facilities were destroyed, killing eighty percent of the medical professionals. In this earthquake both design deficiencies and flawed construction practices were blamed for the large number of building collapses and resulting deaths. Many of the modern multi-storied buildings did not survive. Soil conditions also contributed to building failures. The high death rate may in part be attributed to the way the buildings fell apart. When concrete floor panels about three feet wide collapsed into compact rubble piles, little open space was left where trapped people might sur-

> vive. The proportion of survivors among people trapped in the rubble of multi-storied buildings was approximately 3.5 times higher for the ground floor than for higher floors. The collapse of a large number of apartments which had many occupants on upper floors added to the number of fatalities.[3]

Soviet Premier Mikhail Gorbachev was in the United States when the quake struck. He cut his visit short and immediately flew back to the Soviet Union.

The Armenia earthquake occurred during the time of perestroika—which literally translates to "again build order." Perestroika was evident in the Soviet Union's new policy of openness and a willingness to accept help from countries around the world. Gorbachev was nurturing and promoting this new course of action, one that involved a bureaucratic and economic restructuring of the Soviet Union. In the past, the Soviet government would have denied that the quake had done any damage at all, and whatever damage *had* been done, the glorious Soviet government would take care of and the people were happy to have such an efficient regime handling the situation.

In the new era, the Soviets broadcast nonstop coverage of the effects of the quake, and welcomed any and all relief organizations and workers—no matter what country they were from—to come to Armenia and help—first rescue and recover, then rebuild. This was an enlightened policy, but it did not negate, or hide, the devastating poverty of the region and the Soviet government's inability to do what was necessary.

The help flowed in, the tent cities rose, the medical aid began, and yet over 500,000 people were homeless and entire cities were nothing but piles of rubble.

Many years after this historic quake, Armenia is still struggling to recover.

[1] The official death toll for this earthquake was 28,854; yet unofficial reports, which often account for many deaths overlooked by authorities, claim 55,000 deaths. Considering the magnitude of destruction, the inadequacy of many local census records, and the number of people missing and never found, the higher number seems not only possible, but likely. In a December 1988 British Civil Defence briefing for the Soviet authorities by Patrick Stanton on the earthquake, Stanton writes, "The true figures however, will probably never be known and those questions have carefully been avoided."

[2] In the Russian newspaper *Izvestia,* shortly after the earthquake. Also, see chapter 36, on the 1986 Chernobyl nuclear disaster, referred to by the minister of health.

[3] www.ngdc.noaa.gov/cgi-bin/seg/m2h?seg/haz_volume2.men+Earthquake+Damage,+ Armenian+ SSR,12/1988_help.

26

The 1755 Lisbon, Portugal, Earthquake

LISBON, PORTUGAL

All Saints' Day, November 1, 1755

50,000–100,000 Dead[1]

Scarcely had they ceased to lament the loss of their benefactor and set foot in the city, when they perceived that the earth trembled under their feet, and the sea, swelling and foaming in the harbor, was dashing in pieces the vessels that were riding at anchor. Large sheets of flames and cinders covered the streets and public places; the houses tottered, and were tumbled topsy-turvy even to their foundations, which were themselves destroyed, and thirty thousand inhabitants of both sexes, young and old, were buried beneath the ruins . . . After the earthquake, which had destroyed three-fourths of the city of Lisbon, the sages of that country could think of no means more effectual to preserve the kingdom from utter ruin than to entertain the people with an auto-da-fé, it having been decided by the University of Coimbra, that the burning of a few people alive by a slow fire, and with great ceremony, is an infallible preventive of earthquakes.

—Voltaire, *Candide*

Allhallows, 1755. November 1 is the day Roman Catholics pay honor to all the saints in heaven, thank them for their intercession, and promise them their best efforts in living a holy life, following the example of Jesus Christ Almighty.

All Saints' Day, 1755, the churches in the Roman Catholic city of Lisbon, Portugal, are filled with worshippers at morning mass.

Here is one possible scenario, in one doomed cathedral.

The priest is resplendent in his robes; the acolytes and altar boys are solemn and worshipful.

At approximately 9:30 in the morning, the priest begins reciting the *Commemoration of the Living:*

> Memento, Domine, famulorum famularumque tuarum . . . vel qui tibi offerunt hoc sacrificium laudis, pro redemptione animarum suarum, pro spe salutis et incolumitatis . . .
>
> (Remember, Lord, your male servants and female servants . . . who to You offer this sacrifice of praise, for [their] soul's redemption, for hope of salvation and safety . . .)

As the word *incolumitatis*—safety—echoes in the glorious cathedral, a rumbling sound is heard, followed immediately by a violent earth tremor that shakes the interior of the cathedral from side to side. Statues fall from pedestals. The enormous crucifix hanging above the altar comes crashing down on top of the priest, killing him instantly. The glorious stained-glass windows shatter as the marble surrounding them cracks and collapses.

In seconds, the cathedral's high, vaulted ceiling comes crashing down, taking colossal marble pillars with it, crushing to death hundreds of worshippers under tons of stone.

This All Saints' Day earthquake was one of the largest to hit Europe and is estimated to have been at least 8.6 on the Richter scale.

Its reach was astonishing. Buildings collapsed in Spain; earth tremors were felt in Scotland and Sweden; fifty-foot waves slammed into Helsinki from the Gulf of Finland; 10,000 people were killed in Fez and Meknes in inland Morocco; the ground opened up in Devonshire, England. It is not farfetched to report that fully a third of the European continent and parts of Africa felt this earthquake.

However, Lisbon would have much more to deal with than just a catastrophic 8.6 magnitude earthquake. Following the three massive waves of tremors in the city, the water in the Lisbon harbor receded a half mile, allowing stunned survivors to gaze in shock at the exposed seabed. This was followed within minutes by a massive tsunami upward of sixty feet that destroyed almost all of the remaining structures in the city and drowned thousands who had managed to escape death from the earthquake.

Still the All Saints' Day holocaust was not over. Following the earthquake and the waves came the fires. Burning candles in the razed churches, along with cooking fires in the destroyed homes, started a conflagration that raged through Lisbon for three days, completing the annihilation of the city.

The destruction was estimated at approximately 90 percent of all structures: 18,000 out of 20,000 buildings were heaps of rubble by the end of the three-day period of devastation.

But a recitation of numbers does not express the losses *not* represented by a death toll or the number of destroyed buildings.

Lisbon was a cultural center of Europe. The city boasted many libraries, museums, art galleries, and other repositories of priceless art, documents, and incunabula—books printed before 1501, often one of a kind.

It is believed that more than 200 paintings by masters such as Titian, Rubens, and Correggio, were incinerated in the fires that raged throughout the city. The number of rare books lost was close to 100,000,[2] if not more. A history handwritten sometime in the sixteenth century by Holy Roman emperor Charles V was lost; as were hand-drawn maps of Portuguese explorers. Two Dominican convents housing illuminated manuscripts (books adorned with beautiful ornaments and elaborate hand lettering) were burned to the ground.

The triple assault of earthquake, water, and fire was so enormous—so "Old Testament"—that it wasn't long before the priests concluded that the wrath of God had been unleashed on Lisbon because the city was filled with sinners. To prevent further disasters of this scale, it was decided by church leaders and the ruling monarchy to get rid of the sinners. Public hangings and beheadings of suspected transgressors began immediately after the cessation of natural assaults. (This was, after all, still the Inquisition.) There had to have been a reason for the infliction of such dolor, and, the common wisdom went, it was the sinners' fault.

Cooler heads did prevail, however, and that year scientists such as English physicist John Mitchell undertook a study of earthquakes as natural phenomena.

Lisbon was rebuilt. It took ten years and the new Lisbon had wider streets and no slums.

Lisbon has been rocked by hundreds of quakes over the centuries, but the 1755 catastrophe was the worst disaster in all of the ancient city's history.

[1] As with many disasters of old, calculating the death toll is an inexact science. Sources use figures in the 50,000 to 100,000 range (in a city of 275,000), some stating with certainty 50,000; some, 60,000; some, preferring to use the range. Modern students of this massive earthquake would probably not be amiss erring on the high side.

[2] At least 70,000 books were lost when the king's palace was destroyed; another 18,000 when the Marques de Lourical's palace fell (Jay Robert Nash, *Darkest Hours*, 336, 338).

27

The 1939 Erzincan, Turkey, Earthquake

ERZINCAN, SIVAS, SAMSUN PROVINCES, TURKEY

December 27, 1939

50,000 Dead

The famous Erzincan earthquake (M~8.0) on 26 December 1939 generated many effects—surface ruptures, landslides, microseismic intensities up to 11 degree, tsunami in the Black Sea, as well as big destruction and many human deaths (more than 30–40,000). There are very clear descriptions from this time (mainly by the newspapers) about the anomalous behaviour of the meteorological weather in the epicentral area—extremely low temperatures, very large snowfalls, freeze winds, big storms. All these events make very difficult all rescue operations. During the following days, very large rains occurred to the south and southeast and generated very big flooding and mudflows to the southern, eastern and south eastern parts of Turkey. These negative meteorological events add more than several thousands deaths and many injured accompanied by destruction of the buildings and expected summer harvest.

—Boyko Ranguelov and Arnd Bernaerts of the Geophysical Institute of Bulgaria, in a report for the Second Balkan Geophysical Congress and Exhibition

Erzincan is no longer a city, but a great cemetery.
—One of the survivors of the Erzincan earthquake

On December 29, 1939, İsmet İnönü, president of Turkey, arrived in Erzincan to survey the damage done by the earthquake two days earlier.

Arriving shortly thereafter was the Red Crescent organization (the Turkish Red Cross) and a huge contingent of the Turkish army. The president surveyed the damage and his heart ached for the loss of life and at the sight of the devastation. İnönü had served in the military as war minister and had seen action at the front, but this wholesale obliteration was unlike anything he had seen in combat. Nature could easily do far more damage than man's mortars and bombs, he likely thought as he gazed at the remains of what had once been a bustling village.

Suddenly, an elderly woman wearing a black dress that was covered in dust came running toward İnönü. His soldiers moved to stop her, but the president beckoned her to approach him. The woman was crying and gasping for breath. She grabbed his hand and held it to her cheek. *"Bafikan! Bafikan!"* the woman cried. *"Benim aile ol git! Nicin? Nicin?"* "President! President! My family is gone! Why? Why?"

President İnönü shook his head and embraced the woman, trying to offer her some bit of small comfort in her overwhelming grief. As he stood among the rubble, holding the weeping woman in his arms, dust still rose from the horrific ruins of the Turkish town of Erzincan. The woman's family had all died when the roof of their house collapsed from the weight of the rocks and sand her husband and sons had placed there as makeshift insulation against the brutal Turkish winters. As her bed was closest to the door, she had managed to flee, but the rest of her family had not been so lucky.

For three hours in the early morning of December 27, 1939, two days after Christmas, a total of seven earthquakes wiped out entire towns and killed tens of thousands in northern and eastern Turkey, including cities on the edge of the Black Sea.

The first quake hit at 2:00 A.M., and six more followed until finally ceasing at 5:00 A.M. A blizzard then followed the earthquakes, adding further misery to the wretched survivors.

Erzincan was obliterated, along with its 25,000 occupants, except for one building and one group of citizens. The prison remained standing and the convicted murderers inside its stone walls survived. The prisoners subsequently escaped, but, in a stunning tribute to the essential goodness of man, none of them fled the scene. Instead, they all worked to dig over a thousand people out of the rubble, as well as build shelters and fires against the snow, and defend the wounded from packs of roving dogs.

The epicenter of the Erzincan earthquake was estimated to be sixteen miles below the surface of Turkey. A staggering 80 villages were completely destroyed by the quake, which measured an 8 on the Richter scale. It was, and still is, the worst earthquake in Turkish history.

Interestingly, within twenty-four hours of the Erzincan earthquake, a sequence of earthquakes was felt all over the world, including Nicaragua, El Salvador, Honduras, South Africa, Rome, Italy, and even the west coast of the United States. High-rise buildings in Los Angeles swayed, but the shocks were relatively minor. Nonetheless, some experts believed that the enormity of the Turkish earthquake started a chain reaction of quakes. This theory was discounted by most seismologists, most notably William Lynch of Fordham University.

The 1939 earthquake in Turkey was not the end of Turkey's seismic problems. A major quake would strike Izmit in 1999, killing at least 18,000 and doing over $40 billion in damages. (See chapter 31.)

28

The 1990 Iran Earthquake and Landslide

Zanjan and Gilan Provinces, Northwest Iran

June 21, 1990

50,000 Dead[1]

A rock as big as a building crushed my home.
—An earthquake survivor in the town of Rudbar

Sometimes, terrible events occur that tear down walls, eradicate political and cultural differences (if only temporarily), and summon forth humanitarian efforts, offered freely, for those once considered an enemy.

This devastating 7.3–7.7 magnitude[2] earthquake in northwestern Iran in 1990 was one of those transforming events, and there is no more compelling evidence of this than the fact that then–U.S. President George Bush, who had recently cut off all diplomatic and trade ties with Iran, offered whatever help

America could provide, and also sent a message of condolence to Iran's president Hashemí Rafsanjani.

This earthquake was the worst ever to strike this area of the Caspian Sea region, and the damage and death figures were enormous. It struck at 12:30 A.M. local time and it registered aftershocks as large as 6.5 magnitude for four days after the initial quake. The epicenter of the quake was in the Caspian Sea.

The cities of Rudbar, Manjil, and Lushan, along with 700 small villages, were completely destroyed, and at least 300 more villages were damaged. There was $7 million in damages in the Gilan and Zanjan provinces alone, and 100,000 dried clay houses either were severely damaged or completely collapsed. In addition to the 50,000 people killed, there were more than 60,000 injuries, and a half million people were left homeless.

The United States National Geophysical Data Center assessed the massive damage and concluded that most of the destruction was due to the following causes:

- *Construction materials*: the use of brittle construction materials, brick, block, adobe, wooden timbers, and modern materials inappropriate for use in traditional structures.
- *Construction techniques and workmanship*: the use of unreinforced masonry, and unreinforced sheer walls, poor welding of connections in steel frames, failure to tie steel support beams together, and the use of heavy masonry without adequate support in flooring, ceilings, and roofs.
- *Inadequate design and detailing*: Some modern structures lacked the symmetry of earlier traditional structures. Earthquake resistant designs were not used. Building codes were inconsistent or unenforced.
- *Liquefaction and failure of the soils:* This was especially prominent on the shores of the Caspian Sea. Pressure from the earthquake forced ground water droplets between the grains of sand. The soil temporarily lost strength and behaved as a viscous liquid. With no firm support, structures sank or were spread apart by the liquefied soil. The unconsolidated soils may also have amplified the seismic vibrations.
- The single most important factor in building failures was the use of unreinforced masonry walls.[3]

There were stories of heroism and poignant loss during this earthquake. Patrick Stanton of the British Civil Defence told of coming upon a grief-stricken old man in the front yard of what had once been his house. The old man told the UK defense workers that his wife had gone back into their house three times to rescue people, and when she went in a fourth time, the house collapsed on top of her, killing her. The man's heartache was overwhelming and the British team consoled him, telling him that she had died a hero, and that her death had not been in vain.[4]

One woman in Hir, who had managed to survive in her house beneath mountains of rubble for three days, was ultimately rescued, only to die the moment she was placed on the ground outside her ruined home.

Rescue teams from France, the United Kingdom, Spain, and Japan arrived at the affected area within hours and immediately began assessing needs and working with the Red Crescent relief organization. Sometimes things did not go as smoothly as they should have. Stanton reported the following, which he hoped would serve to prevent similar disorganization at future disasters:

> In the international camp many of the same past mistakes were evident (with the exception of the medical units); too much equipment, too many personnel, too much flag flying, too much media, too many people standing around doing nothing. The French and the Spanish were the only ones to show any kind of organisational initiative.[5]

Northwest Iran sits on a fault line that receives the energy from the collision of two tectonic plates—the Arabian and the Eurasian—resulting in frequent, often very destructive earthquakes.

There is nothing that can be done to prevent these catastrophes. What can be done, however, is to build better (the USGS report cited above is stunningly damning), and better prepare for the inevitable. This may not be possible, considering the isolation Iran incurs for a number of political and military reasons.

As is often the case, the innocent suffer when governments clash.

[1] This figure may not be completely accurate. In a field report, Patrick Stanton of the British Civil Defence states, "Facilities for documentation of missing, injured, dead and survivors appeared non-existent." Also, he says, "At no time, from any source, could we be sure of reliable information as to: how many people had died; or were injured; or were missing; nor how many survivors there were. Survivors we spoke to were confused about how many people had died in their own street." Stanton adds, "Survivors living in the area seemed confused when questioned about how many people had died or had been injured," further suggesting that death tolls may be inaccurate (*Assessment of the Iranian Earthquake*). In addition, many of the dead were immediately buried in mass graves to prevent the spread of disease, further muddying the accuracy of the number of deaths.

[2] The Teheran University measured the quake as a 7.3 magnitude; the United States Geological Survey measured it as a 7.7 magnitude.

[3] www.ngdc.noaa.gov.

[4] Patrick Stanton, *Assessment of the Iranian Earthquake.*

[5] Ibid.

29

The Eruption of Mount Pelée

Martinique

May 8, 1902

40,000 Dead

The first relief parties have ventured into the streets of St. Pierre. It was not expected that survivors would be found, and so there has been no disappointment at the mournful reports that have been returned.

All of the earlier stories of the disaster worked by Mount Pelée have been verified. THE DESTRUCTION OF THE CITY IS COMPLETE. Not a building remains standing. The desolation is appalling.

Piles of dead in the vicinity of the site of the Cathedral tell a story of the attempt to find sanctuary and refuge in the great structure of worship. Men and women, panic-stricken at the cataclysm, turned in the moment of despair to the Cathedral and were apparently overcome before they could reach its doors.

—*New York Herald,* Monday, May 12, 1902

Little Isabella knew her mommy was worried about something. Isabella could always tell.

The five-year-old girl crouched barefoot in the front yard, drawing circles in the sand with a stick. For the past several days, she had heard the big people talking about the Dragon. Daddy had said that the Dragon was not sleeping anymore. Mommy wanted to leave and go away. Isabella did not want to go away. She liked her house and her room and her friends and her school. But she was afraid of the Dragon. Would the Dragon come and eat them all up? As Isabella drew a big circle around her feet, leaving her standing in the middle, she suddenly heard a noise louder than she had ever heard before. She looked up toward the mountain and it was as though the sky had caught fire. Mommy ran out of the house toward her. "Come, Isabella!" she screamed. "The Dragon is awake!" Just as Mommy reached out her hand to grab Isabella's little arm, a giant blanket of fire slammed down on their hometown of St. Pierre. Isabella, standing like a bull's-eye in the center of her hand-drawn target in the sand, and her frantic mommy, were instantly incinerated. Fortunately, they were dead before they had time to realize that they were being burned alive. The wave of flames then swallowed their house, leaving nothing but the gaping cement foundation. Isabella's last thought had been, "Are we going away now?"

On Thursday, May 8, 1902, it took Mount Pelée three minutes to completely eradicate the town of St. Pierre on the French island Martinique in the West Indies.

After suffocating the townsfolk for weeks with the most horrible sulfur fumes imaginable, the long-dormant Mount Pelée erupted at 7:49 A.M. By 7:52 A.M., St. Pierre and its 28,000 inhabitants, save two, were no more. A clock found in a military hospital was frozen at eight minutes to eight. The area that once was the town continued to burn ferociously for another five hours. In addition to the total devastation of the town, 18 ships anchored in the harbor, and all their crew and cargo, were caught in the hurricane of fire and lost.

One of the two survivors of the eruption of Mount Pelée was twenty-five-year-old Auguste Ciparis, a prisoner on death row whose execution was scheduled for the following day. Ciparis was incarcerated in a stone cell that had thick walls, a tiny window, and a heavy door. The cell was so small and had such a low ceiling it could be entered only on hands and knees. Being in this cell saved Ciparis's life. He was severely burned and remained buried in his cell beneath the hot rubble for three days before rescuers found him. Ciparis was taken to a hospital on Martinique, and upon his recovery, his death sentence was repealed. He later toured with Ringling Bros. and Barnum & Bailey Circus in a replica of his jail cell as the "Survivor of Pelée."

The enormous number of deaths from Mount Pelée was due, in large part, to bureaucratic self-interest, to the deluded editorial stance of the local paper, and to the refusal of the citizens of St. Pierre and environs to take the volcano's many warning signs seriously.

The local governor, who was worried about his reelection bid, ordered outgoing roads blocked, preventing worried citizens from leaving before the election on May 10. The local newspaper took a mocking tone in its editorial approach to the widespread worries about the volcano. (The editor of the paper was killed in the eruption.) Local citizens went about their daily lives in complete denial, even as they held wet handkerchiefs to their faces to prevent breathing in the sulfur fumes, and as they saw horses drop dead in the streets from inhaling the toxic gases from Pelée.

On Monday, May 5, 1902, three days before the major eruption of Mount Pelée, the volcano poured a river of boiling mud down the side of the mountain. This flood of death swallowed a sugar mill, killing all of its 100 workers, and it continued to cascade down the slopes of the mountain. This initial onslaught of destruction caused *some* of the residents of St. Pierre to try to flee the city; there was not, however, a mass exodus from the town.

Then on Thursday, the entire side of the mountain exploded, sending a massive, one thousand eight-hundred-degree Fahrenheit firestorm traveling a mile a minute toward nearby St. Pierre. Within three minutes, everything in the town was ablaze. There literally was no time to escape.

The assistant purser on the U.S. steamer *Roraina* anchored in the harbor described the eruption vividly as a "hurricane of fire." Hot gases killed most of the victims, but some died when all their body fluids boiled and they literally exploded.

Martinique rebuilt St. Pierre, and Mount Pelée still stands looking down on it, a chilling reminder of 1902, and a terrifying reminder of what could happen again.

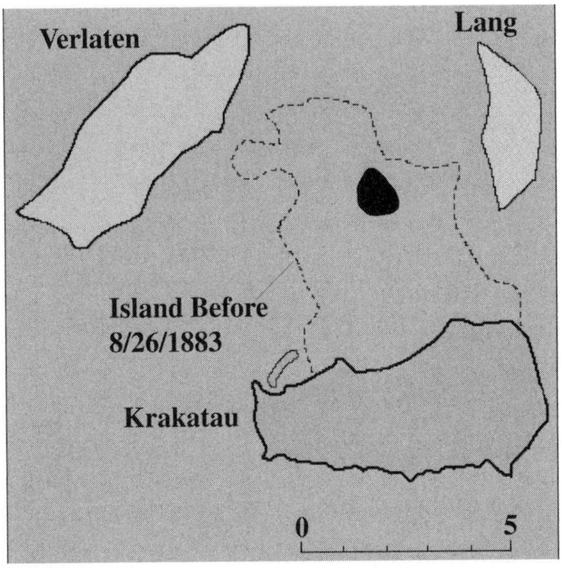

30

The Eruption of Mount Krakatoa

Krakatoa Island, Sunda Strait, Indonesia

August 26–27, 1883

36,417 Dead

Suddenly, we saw a gigantic wave of prodigious height advancing from the seashore with considerable speed. Immediately, the crew set to under great pressure and managed after a fashion to set sail in face of the imminent danger; the ship had just enough time to meet with the wave from the front. After a moment, full of anguish, we were lifted up with a dizzy rapidity. The ship made a formidable leap, and immediately afterwards we felt as though we had plunged into the abyss.

—N. van Sandick, engineer of the ship *Loudon*, which survived Krakatoa's tsunami

How loud was the Krakatoa volcanic eruption, reportedly the loudest sound ever heard in all of human history? If an explosion occurred in Los Angeles,

California, equivalent in magnitude to that of the Krakatoa explosion, it would be heard in New Haven, Connecticut.

Other natural disasters have had a higher death toll than Krakatoa had, but the eruption of this Indonesian volcanic island in late August 1883 is a panoply of incredible geophysical superlatives. In fact, the awesome power of the Krakatoan eruption dramatically illustrates the colossal forces of nature and the minuscule-in-comparison powers of man. Granted, we can theoretically destroy the planet with the combined nuclear weapons of the countries that have them, but we have never created a weapon that even comes close to having the power of the eruption of the Krakatoan volcano.

Krakatoa sits in the Sunda Strait between the Indonesian islands of Java and Sumatra. Throughout its history, it was uninhabited, although there were frequent visitors to the island volcano.

The first recorded eruption of Krakatoa occurred in 1680. It then remained silent for over two hundred years until a cycle of eruptions began in May 1883. Nearby residents of Java and Sumatra did not consider the eruptions alarming. Some people even visited the island and climbed to the peak of the volcano to peer down inside the cavernous opening. No one evacuated and people went about their lives.

The summer passed.

Then, at midday on Sunday, August 26, 1883, a series of enormous explosions issued forth from Krakatoa. People nearby could hear the eruptions, and ash and pumice began to rain down on houses and ships in the Sunda Strait.

This went on for twenty-four hours until the following day, when four enormous explosions, the largest occurring around ten in the morning, literally shook the world. This explosion woke people up in southern Australia, over two thousand five hundred miles away.

The shock wave from Krakatoa circled the earth an estimated seven times at close to seven hundred miles an hour—three times in one direction, four times in the opposite direction.

The ash cloud from Krakatoa rose as high as fifty miles into the air and the dust of the volcano circled the earth many times, depositing dust almost everywhere on the planet. The dust was so thick that the Sunda Strait experienced two full days of complete darkness.

Krakatoa also caused seventeen other smaller volcanoes to erupt on the island, and the combined heat of all these explosions raised the temperature of the surrounding ocean an astounding sixty degrees. In addition, a *ten-foot-thick* blanket of pumice covered the waters for miles around Java and Sumatra. The eruption also caused a tsunami—a tidal wave—that wreaked the most destruction and was experienced all the way as far as Cape Horn in South America.

Krakatoa's 100- to 120-foot tidal waves swallowed close to 300 nearby coastal villages and ports and killed over 36,000 people, either from drowning or from being crushed to death as their houses collapsed on top of them. Very few deaths were actually from being incinerated by lava or from shock waves. The Krakatoa's tsunami was the primary killer—it was so big it was reportedly felt on the west coast of the United States.

The explosions sank a fifty-square-mile section of coastal land as well as several smaller islands in the Sunda Strait.

The *Berow,* a Dutch gunboat in the Sumatran port of Telok Betong, was picked up by Krakatoa's tsunami, transported in the air, and dropped more than a mile inland into a forest on Sumatra. Countless ships in the waters around Indonesia were not so fortunate; most of them sank and were never recovered.

Krakatoa sent five cubic miles of debris into the atmosphere and this detritus stayed there for two whole years. This material made the midday sun look blue in South America, and the setting sun look green in Hawaii for months after the eruption.

The dust also created spectacular sunsets all over the world for many months after the eruption. Some were so dramatic that they looked like enormous fires some distance away.

Two months later, in October 1883, many people in New Haven, Connecticut, called the fire department because they thought the red flaming sunsets they were seeing were huge fires burning out of control. These sunsets were also seen elsewhere in many areas along the eastern coast of the United States.

Krakatoa ultimately sank into the sea, its pent-up energy spent, its power exhausted. In its place is now Anak Krakatoa ("child of Krakatoa"), a smaller volcanic island that manifested a minor eruption in 1928, and continues to erupt periodically. It is highly unlikely, though, that Anak will ever achieve the cataclysmic power of Krakatoa. An eruption of equal or greater magnitude is definitely possible elsewhere on earth, but so far, Krakatoa holds the record as the most powerful volcanic eruption of all time.

31

The 1999 Izmit, Turkey, Earthquake

IZMIT, TURKEY

August 17, 1999

30,000–40,000 Dead[1]

$40 Billion in Damages[2]

It was as if something had grabbed hold of us from underneath, turned us upside down and was shaking us. Then the house was moving from one side to another without stopping. While this was going on there were terrible deep noises coming from the ground. Just as it was finishing, there was a loud noise of buildings collapsing. Screams, the noise of breaking glass. Our house was buried in a deep silence . . . In the inky black darkness I couldn't feel my own feet . . . For two days we slept in the street.

—Izmit earthquake survivor Pinar Onuk[3]

In Golcuk, Turkey, the new buildings came crashing down, killing those inside and leaving the area piled high with rubble and bodies. The city's enormous mosque, however, built centuries ago, remained standing and suffered little damage.

At 3:01 in the morning local time, a 7.4 magnitude earthquake struck Izmit, Turkey, along the North Anatolian Fault (a fault geologically very similar to the San Andreas Fault in California), causing massive destruction and enormous loss of life.

One year after this quake, tens of thousands of people were still living in tent cities. The streets looked like war zones, with many destroyed or damaged buildings still untouched and left standing as they were in August 1999. Many of the survivors were still fearful of living in solid houses after seeing three-quarters of the homes in the area come crashing down, killing everyone inside.

The earthquake was felt more than two hundred miles away, and the damage estimates and deaths were horrific. Because the epicenter was in Izmit, it affected one of Turkey's most populated and industrialized areas.

At least 20,000 people were killed instantly during the quake, most of them crushed to death in their beds as their homes collapsed on top of them. Close to 50,000 people were seriously injured, and the death toll would rise to somewhere between 30,000 and 40,000. The *entire country* of Turkey lost electricity in the quake; a refinery that supplied one-third of Turkey's oil caught fire and had to be shut down for weeks; and people within a three-mile range had to be evacuated. Approximately 600,000 people were made homeless by the quake, and half of them ended up living on the streets. It is believed that the affected population was close to 15 million people, and that 10 percent of Turkey's economy was damaged by the quake.

At least 20,000 buildings collapsed during the quake and what was most alarming about the destruction was that the majority of the razed structures had been built within a few years before the earthquake.

How could brand-new buildings—presumably built to much stricter building codes than older structures were—come down so easily? Turkey's building code was an adaptation of California's Uniform Building Code, which mandated earthquake-resistant design specifications. If Turkey was using California's building standards, why weren't the buildings as resistant to earthquake damage as they were supposed to be?

An investigation by the engineering group EQE International following the Izmit quake uncovered alarming answers to those questions. Most of the buildings constructed in the years before the quake, and supposedly designed according to the California code were *not* built to the code's standards. From the EQE report:

> Most of the buildings did not meet the design requirements of the code and included details that are not earthquake resistant. Those include inadequate vertical and horizontal reinforcing steel and the widespread use of smooth (as opposed to deformed) reinforcing steel.[4]

EQE also learned that design engineers never inspected ongoing construction to make sure that the contractor was building according to the plan specifications. The design engineer worked directly for the contractor so there was zero independent oversight on most building constructions. The materials used were often of low quality, and the workmanship on most building sites was substandard and, in many cases, just plain shoddy. Peter Yanev, an engineering consultant quoted on CNN.com, described the construction in the area as "absolutely inadequate."[5]

The Turkish government's response to the earthquake was also completely inadequate, and wildly disorganized. Turkish Prime Minister Bulent Ecevit, in defense of his government's seeming incapability in coping with a crisis of such magnitude, told CNN's Jerrold Kessel, "[Responding to such a crisis] would be a difficult task for any country in the world. It was not confined to one city, to one province, but to a large area. Telecommunications were completely cut off for at least two days in the three provinces which are badly hit. And transportation in Turkey was handicapped because bridges were destroyed, roads and highways were destroyed."[6]

Regarding the allegations that buildings had been constructed with inferior materials and with a disregard for the building code, Ecevit admitted that "mistakes" had been made but that the Turkish government "would remedy them."[7]

As in all major disasters in urban areas, the threat of disease became very real, very quickly. Relief workers and medical personnel were worried about outbreaks of the usual postdisaster visitors: cholera, typhus, pneumonia, as well as the range of problems caused by dehydration and lack of food. Rotting bodies were everywhere and workers sprayed lime and chemical disinfectants on the streets, sidewalks, and the rubble. Unfortunately, rain followed the earthquake, and washed away the chemicals; officials became concerned that rainwater running off corpses would contaminate groundwater.

Izmit is continuing to rebound, although the damage from the earthquake is still evident and was compounded by another quake in the same area in November of the same year.

Turkey's North Anatolian Fault is not finished either. It remains to be seen if Golcuk's mosque will still be standing after the next big earthquake.

[1] The original death toll for this earthquake was approximately 20,000, but unofficial estimates place the number of deaths at between 30,000 and 40,000.

[2] This figure includes close to $7 billion in property damage, and the rest in economic damage and impact caused by the earthquake.

[3] Lee Davis, *Natural Disasters,* 89.

[4] "Izmit, Turkey Earthquake of August 17, 1999." An EQE Briefing, 1999.

[5] "Rescues bring flash of hope amid grim toll of Turkey quake." www.cnn.com, August 20, 1999.

[6] "Turkish leader admits mistakes in quake response. www.cnn.com, August 24, 1999.

[7] Ibid.

32

The Great Hurricane of 1780

The Windward and Leeward Islands of the Caribbean; Jamaica and Puerto Rico

October 10–12, 1780

28,000–30,000 Dead

Had I not been an eyewitness, nothing could have induced me to have believed it. More than six thousand persons perished, and all the habitations are entirely ruined . . . The whole face of the country appears an entire ruin, and the most beautiful island in the world has the appearance of a country laid waste by fire, and sword, and appears to the imagination more dreadful than it is possible for me to find words to express.

—Admiral George Rodney, from his diary entries about the hurricane's toll on Barbados

There has never been a deadlier hurricane than the Great Caribbean Hurricane of 1780.

On the Windward and Leeward Islands, a staggering 22,000 people lost their lives; in addition to this terrible death toll on land, thousands of sailors were also lost at sea as defenseless ships anchored offshore were hit with the full brunt of this great storm.

It was during the American Revolution, a year before the Battle of Yorktown, when the Caribbean was hit with the worst hurricane in world history. It formed around Cape Verde off the coast of Senegal in Africa, and spent ten days moving slowly westward, gathering moisture, building strength, increasing in size, until it struck Barbados on Tuesday, October 10, 1780.

The hurricane inflicted massive death and destruction on that small, sun-drenched island, leveling almost every building and killing 6,000 people. It next moved on to St. Lucia, but not before sinking the British fleet anchored off its coast and drowning 6,000 sailors. Then it devastated the island itself. From there it went to Martinique, where it killed an estimated 9,000 people and destroyed another naval fleet, this one consisting of 40 French ships. More than 4,000 French sailors died in the hurricane.

Then the storm continued on its relentless drive through the Windwards, into the Leeward Islands, striking and decimating Dominica, Guadeloupe, and St. Eustatius, killing upward of 9,000 people.

Veering slightly southwest, the hurricane next headed straight for Jamaica, where it leveled buildings and wiped out crops, resulting in the deaths of countless slaves for whom no food could be imported, because of the shipping restrictions caused by the Revolutionary War.

Interestingly, one week before the Great Hurricane hit Jamaica, that island was brutalized by an enormous tidal wave that did enormous damage to the west coast port town Savanna-la-Mar, killing approximately 300 people.

The governor of Jamaica, Colonel John Dalling, described the damage to Savanna-la-Mar in his official reporting of events to London:

> The sky on a sudden became very much overcast, and an uncommon elevation of the sea immediately followed. Whilst the unhappy settlers at Savanna-la-Mar were observing this extraordinary Phenomenon, the sea broke suddenly in upon the town, and on its retreat swept everything away with it, so as not to leave the smallest vestige of Man, Beast, or House behind.[1]

Nature was not finished with Jamaica, however, and a week later, it was hit by the Great Hurricane.

The Great Hurricane then turned northward and hit Puerto Rico, where it sank another fleet, this time a Spanish armada, killing at least 2,000 sailors.

"A General Convulsion of Nature"

The following is an excerpt from a letter from Major General Vaughn, commander of British naval forces anchored off the Leeward Islands, to King George III.

> October 30, 1780
> I am much concerned to inform your Lordship, that this island was almost entirely destroyed by a most violent hurricane, which began on Tuesday the 10th instant. And continued almost without intermission for nearly forty-eight hours. It is impossible for me to attempt a description of the storm; suffice it to say, that few families have escaped the general ruin, and I do not believe that ten houses are saved in the whole island: scarce a house is standing in Bridgetown; whole families were buried in the ruins of their habitations; and many, in attempting to escape, were maimed and disabled: a general convulsion of nature seemed to take place, and an universal destruction ensued. The strongest colours could not paint to your Lordship the miseries of the inhabitants: on the one hand, the ground covered with mangled bodies of their friends and relations, and on the other, reputable families, wandering through the ruins, seeking for food and shelter: in short, imagination can form but a faint idea of the horrors of this dreadful scene.[2]

The Great Hurricane of 1780 has the highest death toll of any hurricane that has ever hit a populated area, and it is extremely likely that its record will stand. Today, we know not only where a hurricane will make landfall, we know when. This allows preparation (stocking up on food, candles, water; boarding up windows) and, when the hurricane looks to be extremely dangerous, evacuation. In 1780, the first warning that a storm was coming were the first gusts of a peculiar wind, or the first drops of rain. By the time people knew they were in trouble, it was far too late.

Today, the dollar value of loss from a major hurricane is enormously higher than it was in the eighteenth and nineteenth centuries, but, thankfully, the death toll is a fraction of what it was before we could tell that we were in the crosshairs for a storm like the Great Hurricane of 1780.

[1] *Jamaica Gleaner,* August 17, 2001.
[2] Patrick J. Fitzpatrick, *Natural Disasters: Hurricanes,* 154–55.

33

The 1896 Japanese Tsunami

NORTHEASTERN COAST OF HONSHŪ, JAPAN

June 15, 1896

28,000+ Dead

The wounds suffered by the survivors and shown by the bodies of the dead are of a shocking description. In some cases, the flesh is torn into shreds, exposing the bones beneath; in others the eyes are forced out of their sockets; in others the trunks seem to have been wrenched asunder by forces acting in opposite directions; in others the victim looks as though it had been plunged in boiling water and almost every body shows purple spots as if it had been fiercely pelted with fragments of stone or iron.

—An unnamed correspondent reporting on the destruction in Japan following the 1896 tsunami[1]

The old soldier knew it: the enemy had returned.

He quieted his breathing to listen for what he immediately identified as the booming sound of gunfire. His beloved Japanese homeland was again being invaded from the sea. His worst fear had come true, and he knew what he had to do. His duty was clear, his honor was at stake, and the respect of his ancestors depended on him fulfilling the obligation fate had handed him.

The old soldier tied his bloodred warrior's sash around his waist. He then belted on the long engraved scabbard that held his *katana,* his sword, said a short prayer to his father and his father's father, and left the small hut in the hills above the beach where he had lived for so many years. He would never see his humble home again.

Moving cautiously through the stand of trees above the beach, he could hear the booming of the enemy's guns. As he neared the beach, he could smell the salt water and he mentally prepared himself for battle. He drew his sword, grasped it with two hands as he had been taught when he was a child, and then began running down the slope that led to the beach.

He expected to meet invading soldiers, and, although he knew he could be killed, he planned on doing away with as many of the enemy as he could before he fell.

He let out a high-pitched battle cry, waved his long steel sword above his head, and ran out onto the beach.

But the old soldier stopped a few yards from the water, dumbstruck by what he saw. There were no enemy ships, or enemy soldiers in longboats rowing to shore. Instead, a giant wall of water a hundred feet high confronted him. This was what was making the booming sounds, he realized before the water came crashing down upon him, making that the last thought of his life.

After the tsunami had departed the coast and the waters had calmed down, a search party found the old man on a hill almost five miles inland.

He lay on his side with his precious sword embedded in his body, its sharp end protruding from his back, its ornate handle sticking out of his stomach. The tsunami had taken the sword from the soldier's hands, impaled him on it, and then tossed him onto this hill.

The old soldier had been right: That day he left his hut, he was meeting his final enemy.

This 1896 Japanese tsunami filled the Bay of Honshū with so many corpses, ships could not navigate through them. When the wave hit Japan's northeast coast, it was upward of 300 miles wide and 110 feet high, and it reached over 100 miles inland. (Ten and half hours after the tsunami hit Honshū, it was registered on seismic detectors in San Francisco, California.)

The wave struck the coastal towns and villages in the early evening, around 8:30 or so. In 1896, villagers in Japan went to bed very early, so many of the doomed were asleep. Their houses, with them inside in their beds, were swept out to sea in an instant. Mercifully, most died immediately the moment the massive weight of the water crashed down upon them. And perhaps it comforted all the lost souls that entire families died together, and at the same time. Many of those who were not killed by the water were soon after crushed to death under collapsing buildings and edifices; or they were impaled on debris shooting through the water at speeds of up to five hundred miles per hour.

The majority of those killed, however, were actually on the beaches when the tsunami hit. Tens of thousands of celebrants had gathered at the water's edge for a traditional ritual known as the "Boy's Festival." According to reports from those that survived the destruction, many of the festival participants had heard the rumbling and felt the quakes that preceded the tsunami. But the Japanese were used to earthquakes and none of them thought the situation serious enough to call off the festivities. There had been thousands of earthquakes in Japan over the centuries and only a tiny percentage of them had been accompanied by the giant waves.

It is estimated that close to 20,000 of the 28,000-plus that died that day were attendees at the Boy's Festival.

The tsunami brought cataclysmic destruction to the towns of Miyako, Kamaishi, Kesennuma, and Ishinomaki on Honshū. And as is always the case following a mass natural disaster, disease and injury killed many more that the water initially spared. Some of the smaller villages were completely obliterated.

The village of Hongo lost 142 of its 150-person population. Eight men survived. When the tsunami hit, they were ensconced in a hillside temple playing the ancient Japanese game of Go, in which the object is to remove the opposing player's tiles, using strategic placement of black and white playing pieces.

These eight men may have felt that the gods were playing their own game of Go by strategically placing them in a temple when the water monster came.

[1] Jay Robert Nash, *Darkest Hours*, 284–85.

34

The 79 Eruption of Mount Vesuvius

Southeast of Naples, Italy

August 24, 79

20,000 Dead

The cloud was rising from a mountain—at such a distance we couldn't tell which, but afterwards learned that it was Vesuvius. I can best describe its shape by likening it to a pine tree. It rose into the sky on a very long "trunk" from which spread some "branches." I imagine it had been raised by a sudden blast, which then weakened, leaving the cloud unsupported so that its own weight caused it to spread sideways. Some of the cloud was white, in other parts there were dark patches of dirt and ash.

—Pliny the Younger, in a letter to Tacitus describing the 79 eruption of Vesuvius[1]

The dog would not run away, no matter how difficult it became to breathe, no matter how hot it became in the house, no matter how dark the descending storm of ash made the interior of the room where he lay by his master's side. He would not abandon his beloved master. The rank, overwhelming sulfur smell completely overpowered the dog's usually keen sense of smell, so he did not know that his master had already died from suffocation. The dog lay with his head on his paws as the tears from his sulfur-burned eyes ran down the fur on his face. As the temperature rose and his chest began to burn unbearably with each breath, he started to whimper, but still he did not get up and flee the house. He involuntarily rolled over onto his back, his legs kicking spasmodically, his mouth agape, trying to get in even one small breath of clean air. But there was no clean air to be found in his master's house, and the dog died in this final position.

Today, a plaster cast of this very dog can be seen in a museum in Pompeii. When the hot ash filled his master's home, it encased the dog's body, and by the time his corpse had decayed to dust, the ash had hardened into a shell. This "sculpture by Vesuvius" was found over eighteen hundred years after the volcano erupted. Archaeologists were able to make a mold from the ash shell, capturing the dog in his final, agonizing moments, one more victim of Vesuvius.

Today, many residents of the areas around Naples pray to their personal patron saints, imploring them to protect them from the wrath of Vesuvius, the deadly volcano looming over their homes, and shadowing their lives. These faithful pray because they are keenly aware of one indisputable fact: it is not a question of *if* Vesuvius will erupt again; it is simply a question of *when.*

Since the year 1036, Vesuvius has been erupting on average every thirty-nine years. Since its first recorded eruption in 79, the average time between eruptions has been sixty-four years.

If we use the last one thousand years as the predictor, Vesuvius should have erupted in 1983. It is approximately twenty years overdue.

If we use Vesuvius's total 1,923-year recorded life to calculate the next eruption, we can expect the volcano to awaken in 2008.

How bad an eruption the next one will be is anybody's guess. What *is* known is that if Vesuvius erupts with the same intensity as it did in 79, and the towns in the Bay of Naples do not evacuate, the death toll will be hundreds of thousands this time.

Vesuvius is four thousand feet high and is, as Jay Robert Nash describes it in *Darkest Hours*, "the most consistently lethal volcano on earth."

The 79 eruption came as a surprise to the Romans occupying the land around the volcano and planting extensively in the rich soil of its sloping sides. Vesuvius had been dormant and quiet for decades and the Romans were so comfortable with the volcano that they explored its inner caverns. The Roman historian Strabo nonchalantly wrote that Vesuvius might, at one time, have been an active volcano.

Even an earthquake in 63 didn't shake up the residents of Pompeii, although it knocked down many buildings and caused enormous damage. Throughout the entire event, there was not even a puff of smoke from Vesuvius. People were even more confident that Vesuvius was dead and that they were safe. They were right—but only for the next sixteen years.

Vesuvius awoke at 1:00 P.M. on August 24, and erupted nonstop for eight straight days. This eruption consisted of a Plinian burst (the explosion of gas and rock that resembled the "pine tree" as described by Pliny) and pyroclastic flows of rock, pumice, and ash. There were no lava flows in this eruption. Millions of tons of hot ash rained down on Pompeii and Herculaneum, followed by an enormous water flow down the mountain from water trapped in a caldera (a large crater) on top of Vesuvius. The water mixed with the ash to form a scalding paste that covered everything in its path, including that dog now on display in a museum.

Thousands of people did manage to flee Pompeii, but many refused to leave their homes and their valuables.

In Ecclesiastes, it is written, "There is no new thing under the sun." In the days following the September 11, 2001, World Trade Center terrorist attack, police arrested several looters who were rummaging through the debris looking for valuables, or dead bodies they could rob. The excavation of Pompeii revealed a home owner standing on a pile of silver and gold surrounded by the slain bodies of looters.

What is most compelling about this most deadly of eruptions is the almost photographic accuracy with which the hot ash preserved the hapless citizens of Pompeii.

When the king of Naples gave permission in the eighteenth century for archaeologists to begin excavating Pompeii, they found bread in the stone ovens, drinkable wine in jugs, olives floating in still-liquefied olive oil, and even two Roman soldiers in stocks. They found skeletons holding coins and keys, armed guards still standing in position, and a mother holding her terrified daughter.

The resurrected Pompeii is now one of the most popular of all tourist attractions in Italy and on the World Wide Web are countless photos of restored buildings, columns, houses, and the amphitheater, as well as images of perfectly preserved bodies.

Vesuvius is not finished. If it ends its career with the power with which it began it, the death and destruction toll could be unimaginable.

[1] Translation © Professor Cynthia Damon of Amherst College. Used by permission.

35

Hurricane Mitch

HONDURAS, NICARAGUA, GUATEMALA, EL SALVADOR, COSTA RICA, BELIZE, MEXICO, FLORIDA KEYS

October 26–November 5, 1998

18,323 Dead[1]

This is the worst. This has no precedent in the history of the country, or even in the history of Central America.

—Delmer Urbizio, Honduras's Minister of Government and Justice

President Carlos Flores Facusse of Honduras, the Central American country hardest hit by Hurricane Mitch, said that this devastating category 5 storm erased fifty years of progress in his nation in a single day.

While visiting Honduras, Hurricane Mitch killed 14,000 people, did catastrophic damage to 21 cities, leveled hundreds of thousands of homes, and wiped out 75 percent of the country's crops. "There are corpses everywhere," President Facusse said after the storm, "victims of landslides or the waters." In Honduras, almost every one of the country's roads and bridges was damaged or destroyed by the storm.

Mitch was the most damaging Western Hemisphere hurricane in two hundred years. The last time the Americas were struck by a hurricane of Mitch's power and intensity was in 1780, when the even deadlier Great Hurricane of 1780, with its death toll of 22,000 on land alone, devastated the Caribbean. (See chapter 32.)

Mitch was precocious. Born as a tropical depression on October 22, 1998, it only needed four days to grow to a rare category 5 hurricane, a killer storm that can pack winds of over 175 miles per hour (with gusts over 200) and do what has been colorfully described in *USA Today* as "biblical"-type damage.

Central America is especially vulnerable to enormous storms, not so much because of its geography, but more because of its economy. (Although geography may have a little something to do with its vulnerability when you consider that Honduras in particular has been devastated by two of history's most gigantic hurricanes—Fifi and Mitch—in a twenty-five-year period, as well as by the Great Hurricane of 1780.) The nations of Central America—Honduras, Guatemala, Nicaragua, El Salvador, and others—are poor. The infrastructures of many of these nations, the roads, bridges, communications and transportation systems, power lines, water supplies, and so on, are, in many cases, old and fragile, and unable to withstand the beating from a storm such as Hurricane Mitch. For instance, islands off the Honduran coast have houses on stilts. As might be expected, very few of these remained standing after Mitch departed.

Mitch also brought unprecedented rains, up to twenty-five inches in some areas in the hills, which loosened the rich soil and caused mud slides and landslides that carried away entire towns, and everything—people, animals, buildings, and anything else in its path—away with it. Acres and acres of mud replaced houses, roads, farms, and other buildings. After the storm, relief workers pulled hundreds of corpses from the mud. As one worker described the scene, "It is like a desert littered with buried bodies." One rescuer suggested, perhaps only half facetiously, that the entire storm area be declared a cemetery and simply sealed off and abandoned.

Surreal scenes of madness and despair were everywhere. Parents lashed their children to trees in hopes they would not be swept away by the enormous floods. In the capital city of Tegucigalpa in Honduras, the prison collapsed and many of the prisoners used the opportunity to escape. As floodwaters raged through the streets and houses collapsed, the police started shooting at the fleeing prisoners. Banks closed, but money would not have done much good anyway because the stores were all washed away. People watched in horror as their neighbors' dead bodies floated by in the flooded streets.

Death and destruction were everywhere, and as is always the case with mass catastrophes involving thousands of deaths, disease soon became a huge problem for the governments of the affected nations as well as for the survivors. There were huge bodies of contaminated water everywhere loaded with mosquitoes that carried malaria, dengue fever, and yellow fever. Cases of cholera and typhoid started erupting, and food and water shortages were immediately critical. Also reported were respiratory problems, eye problems, and foot funguses from extended barefoot exposure to the ubiquitous mud.

There are varying reports of the number of people rendered homeless following Mitch. The numbers range from 1.5 million to over 3 million, but when there are that many people without shelter, the actual figures are secondary to the reality of hordes of people—hundreds of thousands in each city—with nowhere to live.

After Hurricane Mitch, Central America needed help in a big way, and the countries of the world responded.

The industrialized nations sent tons of food, water, and relief supplies, as well as medical workers, transportation equipment, field hospitals, and portable shelters. American helicopters brought food packets and medical supplies to small villages cut off from everything because of the collapse of bridges and the washing away of roads.

The United States and other nations that had lent money to the Central American countries also generously forgave much of Honduras's and Nicaragua's foreign debt. The aid nations realized that the hardest hit Central American countries were looking at a decades-long rebuilding effort, and that there would be no money for interest payments of loans, let alone any repayment of principles. So, in an act of global, neighborly altruism, debts were erased.

When Mitch left Central America, it headed for Mexico's Yucatán peninsula as a tropical depression. It then crossed the Gulf of Mexico, where it gained strength from the water and grew again to a tropical storm. On November 4, it descended on the Florida Keys with fifty-five-mile-per-hour winds, no longer a hurricane, but still strong enough to do serious damage. Mitch did not kill anyone in Florida, but it caused injuries, ripped roofs from houses, tore down power lines, and knocked over trees before it headed out to sea, where it finally died.

[1] This figure comprises official death tolls for Honduras (14,000), Nicaragua (3,500), Guatemala (440), El Salvador (370), Costa Rica (7), and Mexico (6), and includes those missing and presumed dead. (Official figures cited on www.honduras.com.)

36

The Chernobyl Nuclear Accident

Chernobyl, the Ukraine, the Soviet Union

April 26, 1986

31 Dead (Initially)

335,000 Evacuated

The reactor design was poor from the point of view of safety and unforgiving for the operators, both of which provoked a dangerous operating state.

—From the 1996 Nuclear Energy Agency report, "Chernobyl Ten Years On"

A nuclear accident anywhere is a nuclear accident everywhere.

—From the 2001 NEA report, "Facts, Thoughts and Lessons from the Chernobyl Accident"

Unforgiving

In the years 1990 through 1998, 1,791 cases of thyroid cancer were diagnosed in Ukrainian children living in the areas surrounding the Chernobyl nuclear power plant. Experts have attributed all of these cancers to the Chernobyl nuclear accident. More cases are expected.

Designed Flawed

The Chernobyl nuclear power plant used a nuclear reactor known as the RBMK-1000, designed and built by the Soviets, which was not then, and is not now, in use anywhere else in the world.

The RBMK-1000 uses graphite blocks in place of coolant water. It was developed for two reasons: to generate electricity, and also to provide the Soviet Union with a constant supply of weapons-grade plutonium—one of the byproducts of the graphite system. During the cold war, the Soviet Union was determined to produce weapons of mass destruction equivalent to those in the nuclear weapons program of the United States. Having an ongoing, dependable supply of plutonium allowed the Soviets to continually expand their nuclear arsenal while at the same time providing electricity for their country.

The problem with the RBMK-1000, however, as the NEA report "Chernobyl Ten Years On" states, was that it was an extremely dangerous design that did not tolerate operator error and did not have a built-in fail-safe (or fail-safer) operational routine. Put simply, in the types of nuclear reactors built and used in the United States and elsewhere, if the reactor starts losing coolant water, it begins to decrease the rate of fission (power production), thus automatically attempting to reduce the heat caused by the loss of coolant. In the RBMK-1000, if the system loses coolant water, it triggers more fission and the core becomes hotter. This is precisely the opposite of the ideal response to a loss of coolant water, and many countries tried to convince the Soviets that they were, quite literally, playing with (nuclear) fire. It is obvious that the Soviets were willing to take that risk in order to acquire plutonium.

In addition to the inherent risks in the way power was produced with the RBMK-1000 design, another problem with the reactor was the absence of a containment dome. All U.S. reactors have a concrete-and-steel containment dome that will prevent the leakage of radioactivity into the atmosphere in the event of a nuclear accident. The Soviets were also warned about this, but chose not to do anything about it.

At 1:24 A.M. on Friday, April 26, 1985, unit 4 of the Chernobyl Nuclear Power Plant exploded. There were two enormous explosions within three seconds of each other and they blew the roof off the building. Radioactive gases, debris, and materials from inside the reactor building were thrown two-thirds of a mile into the air. Pieces of the reactor's superhot fuel rods flew through the air and landed almost a mile away, setting radioactive fires that added to the exposure in the area.

Two workers were instantly killed, and twenty-nine were bathed in so much radiation that they were essentially dead from that moment on, even though most of them lingered on for a couple of weeks in the hospital, suffering through the final stages of extreme radiation poisoning. Hundreds of thousands were evacuated from the surrounding towns, countless animals were destroyed to prevent ingestion of radiation-poisoned meat, and many European countries refused grain shipments from anywhere near the Ukraine, asking their citizens to begin washing thoroughly all fruits and vegetables—even if they were native to their own country.

The Chernobyl accident happened because some workers attempted an unauthorized, low-power experiment that involved disabling the emergency coolant system. By the time everyone realized that the core was going superhot, it was too late to reverse the process (they had inadvertently allowed the heat to warp the channels in which the fuel rods were supposed to fit), and the next thing they knew, the roof was gone, two men were dead, and a deadly cloud of radioactive gas was spreading over the terrain.

Radioactivity from the Chernobyl explosion would eventually be registered as far away as the United States.

The Soviet leadership did not say a word about the explosion until two days later, on April 28, after Swedish scientists reported registering an increase in radioactivity in the atmosphere of their own country and tracing it back to Chernobyl. Even after going public with what happened, the Soviets were clueless as to how to respond to such a monumental catastrophe.

The Chernobyl reactor was eventually encased in a concrete structure called the Sarcophagus. Over six hundred thousand workers, known as "liquidators," worked on the cleanup of the reactor and the construction of the Sarcophagus. The cement enclosure was poorly built, however, and it began to leak radiation a few years after construction was completed. More work was done to ensure its integrity but there are still doubts as to its safety.

The Chernobyl nuclear accident was the worst nuclear accident of all time. Coming shortly after the Three Mile Island accident, it added muscle to the antinuclear power proponents, and spurred many countries to enact strict new safety regulations for the construction and operation of nuclear power plants.

As for the long-term health effects, the radiation exposure from Chernobyl is expected to cause hundreds of thousands of new cancers, tens of thousands of which will result in death.

The NEA report sums up the impact of the Chernobyl accident in its 2001 update to its initial report:

> The history of the modern industrial world has been affected on many occasions by catastrophes comparable or even more severe than the Chernobyl accident. Nevertheless, this accident had a significant im-

pact on human society. Not only did it produce severe health consequences and physical, industrial and economic damage in the short term, but, also, its long-term consequences in terms of socio-economic disruption, psychological stress and damaged image of nuclear energy, are expected to be long standing.

Fifteen years after the Chernobyl accident, the international community is still learning lessons, and is working to generalise these to cases of smaller accidents. Hopefully, these lessons will never again have to be applied to an accident the size and scale of Chernobyl.[1]

1 "Chernobyl Ten Years On," Nuclear Energy Agency, 1996.

37

Hurricane Fifi

Honduras, Central America

September 18–20, 1974

10,000 Dead

The banana plantations have been flattened. People are sitting on rooftops, holding tiny children in their arms and waving for help . . . The mud is eight feet deep in places. We just have no idea of how many people may be trapped. It may be weeks before we dig through the mud and find the bodies . . . People are starving, their supplies were washed away and there are no stores near their villages. They have no way to get food except from us.

—Colonel Eduardo Andino, of Honduras's National Emergency Committee, in *The New York Times*

One of the most striking photographs to come out of Honduras after Hurricane Fifi is one of a small wood frame house, typical of one of the types of handbuilt dwellings spread throughout the impoverished country. Strictly utilitarian, the house has two windows and a door, and, if there were no interior walls constructed, would consist of one, large rectangular room. The house does not have a basement, of course, and it is likely that its occupants did not enjoy either interior plumbing or running water in the house.

What is most astonishing about the photo of this house is not that the house survived Hurricane Fifi. What astounds the viewer is the location of the house. Hurricane Fifi picked up the house, carried it a distance away from its original location, and deposited it upright and intact—on the middle of a bridge.

Seeing this picture, one cannot help but be reminded of the stories told after the Johnstown Flood (chapter 47) of the floodwaters picking up a church and carrying it through the streets of Johnstown before drowning it and silencing its bell. In Honduras, though, the house on the bridge did not have a bell and was not drowned, it was carried some distance in the arms of the storm named Fifi.

In the year 2000, the unemployment rate in Honduras was 28 percent, with an inflation rate of 11 percent.

The *CIA World Factbook* calls Honduras "one of the poorest countries in the Western Hemisphere," and, as of 2001, the country was still rebuilding and trying to recover from 1998's deadly Hurricane Mitch (chapter 35).

With 53 percent of Honduran families below the poverty line, and almost half of the country's workforce employed in agriculture, it is evident that major natural disasters are especially difficult for Honduras.

In 1974, almost a quarter of a century before the country was severely wounded by Hurricane Mitch, Honduras was devastated by Hurricane Fifi.

Hurricane Fifi killed 10,000 people, left 60,000 homeless, and decimated 60 percent of the country's agricultural industry, doing extraordinary damage especially to the banana industry. Fifi did massive harm to the small city of Chomola, which sits to the north of the business center of Honduras, San Pedro Sula (which was also hit hard by Fifi). Half of Chomola's population of 6,000 perished in the storm; virtually all of Chomola's houses were leveled. In addition to those killed by the hurricane itself, many others died from drowning when a massive flood hit Chomola after Hurricane Fifi died out. Flooding deaths and damage were both extremely high from Fifi when both the Ulúa and Aguán rivers overflowed their banks.

Fifi's winds were clocked at 110 miles per hour, and it is estimated that over two feet of rain fell in the day and half Fifi spent moving through northwestern Honduras.

Hurricane Fifi may have visited Honduras for only a short time, but the damage it did to the crops—it wiped out a year's harvest, and about $150 million worth of bananas—caused widespread starvation, in a country where food was in critical shortage *before* the storm. One company, United Fruit, lost twenty-eight thousand acres of bananas. Philip Sanchez, the U.S. ambassador to Honduras at the time, summed up the situation with blunt pragmatism. "You ask how people can starve in three or four days?" he said to reporters covering the catastrophe. "These people were hungry *before* the hurricane."

The storm also left behind an enormous fear: typhoid. There were so many bodies lying in the floodwaters in the sweltering heat that followed the hurricane, health officials predicted an epidemic of typhoid. Honduras's President General Oswaldo Loez acted quickly and ordered the mass burning of corpses throughout the stricken areas. The scene was surreal: miles of devastation, crushed homes, flooded fields, and thousands of bodies piled as high as possible and set ablaze.

After the hurricane, relief efforts began, with aid coming from the United States, Cuba, Great Britain, Mexico, and other nations. The Red Cross organized vaccination and aid centers, and the Peace Corps set up camps. Recovery was slow, though, and rebuilding was somewhat hampered by alleged government corruption and misuse of charitable funds.

Hurricane Fifi should have been a lesson for Honduras. The damage the storm did should have prompted the government to put more money and effort into preparedness, conservation, watershed management, and in educating people on not building in high-risk zones.

Jon Kohl, writing in the periodical *Honduras This Week* made the point that Fifi did not seem to teach the Hondurans anything:

> On the North Coast, the Aguán River flooded big after Fifi. It is a closed basin and dumps huge amounts of water straight into the ocean. Not only did the same flooding occur with Mitch, but it carried the village of Santa Rosa de Aguán out to sea, drowning dozens. There was no effort in the headwaters to do something to avoid this repeat catastrophe.

The philosopher George Santayana wrote that those who do not learn from history are doomed to repeat it. Nowhere is this more evident than in the stories of Fifi and Mitch in Honduras.

38

The Galveston Hurricane

Galveston Island, Texas

September 8, 1900

8,000 Dead[1]

$30 Million in Damages[2]

By 8 P.M. a number of houses had drifted up and lodged to the east and southeast of my residence, and these with the force of the waves acted as a battering ram against which it was impossible for any building to stand for any length of time, and at 8:30 P.M. my residence went down with about fifty persons who had sought it for safety, and all but eighteen were hurled into eternity. Among the lost was my wife, who never rose above the water after the wreck of the building. I was nearly drowned and became unconscious, but recovered though being crushed by timbers and found myself clinging to my youngest child, who had gone down with myself and wife.

—Isaac Cline, from his National Weather Bureau report on the Galveston hurricane

The darkest horror of American history has fallen on our southern coast . . . the morning's sun rises on a scene of suffering and devastation hardly paralleled in the history of the world.

—W. J. McGee, *National Geographic*

Jake was ecstatic that he had not been killed in the giant storm, and he considered himself one of the luckiest men alive. He had survived, and even though he had lost his mother, two brothers, and his new bride, he was grateful to God that he himself had made it through in one piece.

Now, a week after that terrible day, Jake was wondering if he might not have been better off perishing with his family. Shortly after the storm, Galveston's mayor had declared martial law, and Jake had been drafted to be a member of the "dead gang." The dead gang was not for law enforcement. Hundreds of enlisted soldiers dealt with the hordes of looters that descended on the town. Over 250 scavengers were shot and killed on sight, some with pockets full of amputated fingers with rings on them. (One looter was found with twenty-three human fingers in his pockets.)

The city of Galveston was a charnel house, with dead bodies piled everywhere. There were corpses in the streets, in the houses that were still standing, on the beaches, and floating in standing water throughout the island town—perhaps a third of Galveston's population all told. The water and the heat of the sun had combined to cause rapid decomposition of thousands of bodies and city officials were extremely worried about a possible outbreak of typhoid or cholera from the many corpses strewn about. (Not to mention the appalling stench that had settled over Galveston.)

Thus, they implemented a program of immediate body disposal and drafted able-bodied men—such as Jake—to work in the dead gangs. These gangs disposed of the corpses in two ways. They piled hundreds of bodies onto barges, sailed them out to sea, and dumped them into the ocean; and they stacked up corpses in deep pits on the beach, then set them afire. The sickeningly foul smell of decomposing flesh was soon replaced by the sickeningly sweet smell of burning flesh and hair.

No attempt was made to identify or return bodies to surviving loved ones. During a health crisis, there is no time for ritual.

So Jake worked the beach crew and the only thing that kept him from bolting and heading to Houston was the free booze supplied by the city. Jake never was one to turn down a drink.

The hurricane that struck Galveston on Galveston Island, Texas, on September 8, 1900, was the worst natural disaster ever to occur in the United States.

With a death toll of at least 8,000, storm watchers remind us that the Galveston death total is higher than the number of people killed in the Johnstown Flood (chapter 47), the San Francisco Earthquake (chapter 45), the 1938 New England Hurricane (chapter 61), and the Great Chicago Fire (chapter 51) *combined*. And they're right.

The hurricane was born in Cape Verde off the coast of Africa, traveled across the Atlantic to the Caribbean Islands, then continued on its course straight for Galveston. The city was a sitting duck for an Atlantic storm of this nature, since the seaward side of the island was utterly exposed. No sea wall protected it;

no reef in the Gulf of Mexico would slow down a storm. (A seawall embankment had been proposed before the big 1900 storm but no one wanted it built, because most people thought it unnecessary. Galveston has a seawall today.)

The storm battered the island city with 120-mile-per-hour winds and five-foot waves that peaked as high as twenty feet. It is estimated that during the twenty-four hours of the hurricane, *2 billion tons* of rain fell on Galveston.

In one of the sadder losses from the hurricane, an orphanage filled with nuns and children collapsed, killing everyone inside.

Many people did survive, only to learn that their loved ones had been killed. Suicides increased dramatically following the storm.

One story about the hurricane speaks highly of the common sense of common beasts. Several Galvestonians recalled seeing a horse running through the streets. He had no saddle and was riderless. He seemed to be in a panic, but in reality, he knew what he was doing and where he was going. The horse kept running until he came to a certain house. How he picked this house we'll never know, but it was one of the homes that survived the storm. The horse ran up the front steps of the house, kicked in the front door, and ran upstairs to the second floor. He remained there for two whole days and was found later, hungry but healthy.

If this smart equine had been in charge in Galveston, the city probably would have built the seawall it so desperately needed before the great hurricane of 1900 leveled the town.

[1] 6,000 in Galveston; 2,000 in surrounding areas. Some estimates go as high as 12,000 or more dead.

[2] In 1925 dollars. This is approximately $700 million in today's dollars.

39

The London Killer Fog of 1952

London, England

December 5–9, 1952

12,000 Dead[1]

Fog everywhere. Fog up the river, where it flows among green aits and meadows; fog down the river, where it rolls defiled among the tiers of shipping, and the waterside pollutions of a great (and dirty) city. Fog on the Essex marshes, fog on the Kentish heights. Fog creeping into the cabooses of collier-brigs; fog lying out on the yards, and hovering in the rigging of great ships; fog drooping on the gunwales of barges and small boats. Fog in the eyes and throats of ancient Greenwich pensioners, wheezing by the firesides of their wards; fog in the stem and bowl of the afternoon pipe of the wrathful skipper, down in his close cabin; fog cruelly pinching the toes and fingers of his shivering little 'prentice boy on deck. Chance people on the bridges peeping over the parapets into a nether sky of fog, with fog all round them, as if they were up in a balloon, and hanging in the misty clouds.

—Charles Dickens, *Bleak House*

As Dickens so vividly tells us in this passage from *Bleak House,* London is no stranger to fog. Most of the time, it is a nuisance, nothing more, although it can be a hazard for drivers when it is exceptionally dense. Fog in London usually does not kill people by the thousands.

The London Killer Fog of 1952, however, was quite different from London's ordinary fog. It began as an ordinary accumulation of cool, condensed water vapor, quite typical for London. But in December, a mass of warm air from the North Sea parked itself above the city, trapping the fog, as well as all the myriad pollutants emanating from London's gasoline-burning motor vehicles, coal-burning factories and home chimneys, and its industrial plants where chemicals were released into the air as part of the manufacturing process. This dome of warm air served as an almost impenetrable gaseous roof over the city of London for five long days. During this period, 4,000 Londoners died—young and old alike—a death rate almost eight times the norm.

A critical factor in making this noxious air mass so deadly was its staying power. Usually, London air is buffeted by winds off the North Sea and the English Channel, which serve, in a sense, as nature's cleaning crew. The winds blow away the fog, and there are days in London when the sun shines.

Unfortunately, in December 1952, the air over London was utterly still. No measurable winds arrived to whisk away the moist blend of foul pollutants, and instead, people breathed in this vile air. There are medical reports from this deadly December week that tell of people staggering into hospital emergency rooms, gasping for breath. Obviously, some didn't even make it to the hospital.

This fog was *thick*. The airports were shut down, and the ambulances moved through the streets at five miles per hour as someone walked in front of them to lead the way. For a twenty-mile radius, visibility was approximately zero. Pedestrians had to interlock arms and grope their way through the shrouded streets. As you might imagine (and as might be expected) pickpockets had a field day. Thieves were out in full force, delighting in the natural cover the fog provided for their escapes. When the fog seeped into buildings, there were visibility problems even indoors. The fog in one London theater was so thick, the movie was visible only if you were sitting in the first row.

On December 8, the winds revisited London and blew the deadly air away, but it was much too late for the thousands who had turned blue from lack of oxygen and died, nauseous, and coughing out their last breaths.

"[This] is almost on the scale of mass extermination," said a stunned member of Parliament as the death toll mounted. Air pollution had always been a problem in London, but there had previously been a somewhat blasé attitude about it, almost as if the fog and occasionally nasty-smelling air were part of the city's character.

The Killer Fog of 1952 changed all that. In early 1953, the British government began a sweeping, comprehensive study of air quality in London, and the causes for the high levels of pollutants. This study would take four years, reveal the problems, and suggest necessary changes.

In 1956, Great Britain passed the Clean Air Act (seven years before the United States' own 1963 Clean Air Act), which drastically reduced air pollution. However, in 1962, another deadly killer fog struck London, making the point that six years was not long enough for significant changes in air quality to occur. Nonetheless, the death toll for the 1962 fog was only 136, and the vast majority of the dead were elderly victims with compromised breathing and/or heart problems. Almost a thousand people also needed medical treatment, but the overall damage was minor compared to that of 1952's killer fog.

> *It was a town of machines and tall chimneys, out of which interminable serpents of smoke trailed themselves for ever and ever and never got uncoiled.*
>
> —Charles Dickens, *Hard Times*

[1] Total deaths attributed to the killer fog are difficult to ascertain with certainty, but from average mortality rates, authorities believe 4,000 additional people died in the five days of the killer fog from fatal respiratory illnesses directly caused by the fog. According to Dr. Ernest T. Wilkins, the chief of the Atmospheric Pollution Division of England's Department of Scientific and Industrial Research, an additional 8,000 people died later from the long-term toxic effects of the fog, and its exacerbation of victims' existing respiratory and pulmonary conditions.

40

The 1928 West Indies and Lake Okeechobee Hurricane

THE CARIBBEAN ISLANDS, PUERTO RICO, THE FLORIDA COAST

September 10–16, 1928

5,000 Dead

$75 Million in Damages[1]

Expensive homes wide open and being looted. Recommend martial law for Pal Beach . . . Advise sending at once companies for guard duties.

—Clark J. Lawrence, President of the State Reserve Officers Association of Palm Beach, in a message to the governor of Florida following the 1928 hurricane

"Hurry, David! Climb!"

Jacob looked down at the lower limbs of the tree he was climbing and saw his twelve-year-old son, David, trying desperately to pull himself up to a higher branch. Jacob could do nothing but watch with desperation, as he was lodged in the fork of two tree branches with his four-year-old daughter, Rachel, on his back, her tiny arms wrapped around his neck so tight he could barely breathe. Jacob tried to catch his breath, and he prayed silently that David could make it at least up to where he waited with Rachel. Once he is with me, Jacob thought, he will make it to the top of the tree if I have to carry him under one arm and climb with the other.

The hurricane had sent the waters of Lake Okeechobee rushing into the area where Jacob had lived with his wife and their two children. Maria was dead. She had been picked up by the waters and hurled into a rock jutting up from the soil in front of their flimsy one-room house. She had hit her head on the rock with tremendous force, and Jacob saw her skull split open from the impact. He knew she was dead as soon as he saw the shiny gray surface of her brain and blood streaming from her eyes and ears. Before he could even reach her, though, a giant wall of water picked up her body yet again, and sent it hurling away at a ferocious speed. Jacob had then grabbed his two children and started running to an enormous tree a few hundred yards from his house. As he ran, he glanced behind him to see his house picked up and ripped into pieces by the water.

He made it to the tree and started climbing with Rachel on his back. David assured him he could climb by himself. Now Jacob and Rachel were about forty feet above the ground, and David was having problems.

Just as Jacob was deciding he would have to go back down and help his son, David grabbed a branch and pulled himself up with both arms.

Jacob put his hand on the back of David's neck and pulled his face to him. "Wonderful climbing, my boy. Just wonderful!" Then he kissed him on the cheek.

"Now let us get away from this bastard water demon!"

Father and son continued climbing until they were almost at the top of the tree. Beneath them, almost one hundred feet below, the water raced by, a river over land that had yesterday been dry as dust.

Jacob was relieved and knew they would survive, although they would soon be hungry and thirsty. The water would have to leave eventually, and then they would climb down and start over.

Just as Jacob was settling himself and Rachel into the crook of two branches that formed a kind of saddle, David, who had already found his own branch chair, let out a scream.

"Father! *Look!*"

Jacob looked where David was pointing and his heart froze in his chest.

Coiled in the branches surrounding him and his children were dozens of snakes. They wrapped themselves sinuously around limbs, and slid with ease along even the thinnest of branches.

Cottonmouths, Jacob thought. And in that moment, he knew that his children would soon be seeing their mother. Cottonmouths were poisonous. And there was nowhere for him and his beloved children to run.

At the moment that this thought ran through Jacob's mind, David let out a scream. Within seconds, Rachel followed suit. They both had been bitten. As Jacob twisted to look at Rachel, he felt two fangs sink into his neck. He instinctively grabbed the snake, pulled it off his throat, and threw it down into the water, but it was too late—for all of them.

Within fifteen minutes, all three had fallen out of the tree, dead from the poison of the bites.

The following day, Jacob, David, and Rachel were part of a huge raft of corpses that was pulled down the river by rescue workers to a mass pyre for cremation. After the storm, there were so many bodies floating that they had to all be tied together and moved as one.

Maria was not part of this floating cadaver raft. Her body was never found.

This 1928 hurricane that killed 5,000 people and did $75 million in damages was born in late August or early September, probably near the Cape Verde Islands off the coast of Africa. It moved across the Atlantic and slammed into Barbados on September 10; it then hit Guadeloupe on September 12, killing more than 600; and continued on to Puerto Rico, where it killed 1,000 people, left more than 250,000 homeless, and did $50 million in damages.

And still it wasn't finished.

Attacking the coast of Florida on September 16, it did $25 million more in damages and killed more than 2,500 people. Many people died from snakebites, drowning, or being impaled on or cut in two by debris shooting through the water in the grip of five-hundred-mile-per-hour winds.

Twenty-one miles of slapped-together mud dikes were flattened in Lake Okeechobee, and many of the poor, migrant workers there were killed by the storm.

In Belle Glade, Florida, all 650 residents of the town rushed to Belle Glade's two hotels, hoping to ride out the storm in the big—and with any luck, *strong*—buildings. When the storm was over, every building in town—fifty structures—had been demolished, except the two hotels. All the residents of Belle Glade survived.

The death and damage toll from this storm, and the lame attempt to prevent flooding with hand-built mud dikes, prompted federal action. In 1930, President Hoover supported funding for the building a real dike: a rock barrier eighty-five miles long, and thirty-eight feet high.

For the dead, it was too late; for the future generations living in the Everglades and Lake Okeechobee areas, it was their assurance of survival, since the hurricane of 1928 had proved quite effectively just how vulnerable the area was to dangerous, deadly storms.

[1] Total damages for the Caribbean, Puerto Rico, and Florida, in 1928 dollars.

41

The 1995 Kobe Earthquake

KOBE, JAPAN

January 16, 1995

5,502 Dead

$147 Billion in Damages[1]

I was on the fourth floor of a five-story hotel. The quake continued for 20 seconds or so, and I just lay on the floor and couldn't move. I tried the door, but it wouldn't open, so I kicked it down and barely escaped. The lower section of the hotel under the third floor had completely collapsed.

—A Japanese TV journalist who survived the quake[2]

This 7.2 magnitude earthquake in Kobe, Japan, has been called the most expensive disaster of all time. What is most impressive about its power is that this 1995 quake did all of its damage and killed thousands of unsuspecting victims in approximately twenty seconds from start to finish, at 5:46 in the morning—a twenty-second earthquake from which it would take a decade to recover.

Twenty seconds. About the time it might take the average reader to read the first paragraph of this chapter.

Twenty seconds. Such destruction in such a short time takes an emotional toll on survivors. The 1995 Kobe quake caused a cultural shift in the consciousness of the people of Kobe and its environs.

After the dust settled and it hit home to the survivors just how much damage had been done to their beloved city, a widespread depression snaked through Kobe. Some tried to help alleviate the misery by providing basic needs, such as food and shelter.

Disasters create strange bedfellows and one of the unlikeliest group of philanthropists turned out to be the organized crime gang, the Yamaguchi-gumi. Men usually more interested in taking than giving were suddenly handing out eight thousand meals a day from a parking lot. They marshaled their assets, vehicles, and manpower and worked together to feed their neighbors. One survivor, Masakazu Koga, said, "It reminds me of the time after the war. Everything is a wreck, and I don't see how we're going to rebuild it all. But the earthquake also drew us together. I've seen generosity in people that I thought had disappeared from Japan."[3]

This second largest earthquake in Japan's history caused a loss of approximately $7 billion[4] in tax revenue alone for the fiscal year 1995 in the country.

Kobe's principal industries—shipbuilding, steel production, chemical manufacturing, and food processing—were severely harmed by the earthquake and many plants were completely shut down for several days. Those that were able to reopen once electricity was restored operated at greatly reduced capacity, some at 60 percent below normal output. A staggering 90 percent of Kobe's shoe-manufacturing facilities was severely damaged by the quake, and many other smaller industries were almost completely wiped out. The cultured pearl business in Kobe was essentially out of business for almost six months.

In the days immediately following the earthquake, the basic necessities of life—food, water, shelter—were in short supply. Some people camped out at city hall; others remained in unsafe, damaged buildings. Almost a third of a million people ended up homeless. The monumental amount of damage in Kobe resulted, necessarily, in a triage response (a priority-based system) by officials, and, thus, many dangerous buildings were not cordoned off, and if they were, the barriers were, unfortunately, not enforced.

Relief supplies began coming into Kobe after a few days, including regular shipments from the Kirin Breweries, one of Japan's leading beer companies. Considering the trauma and stress the residents of Kobe were under, it would not be farfetched to imagine many of them welcoming steady shipments of beer. But this was not to be. The Kirin Breweries did ship thousands of cases of liter-sized beer bottles into the city, but had had their workers fill them with drinking water instead of beer.

As is common following major earthquakes, Kobe was also besieged by fires that erupted from broken gas mains, and falling heaters and stoves, and it is estimated that more than 1 million square meters of Kobe were burned by fires after the earthquake.

Almost 180,000 of the city's buildings were damaged or destroyed. In the Kobe harbor, more than 90 percent of the port's 187 berths were damaged. The miles-long Hanshin Expressway collapsed in several places. By January 25, nine days after the earthquake had hit, 367,000 Kobe households were still without running water.[5]

Dead bodies are an enormous problem following a major disaster, and, in Kobe, there were thousands of people who had been killed in the quake whose bodies had to be recovered, identified, and buried or cremated. Officials turned a large room in a school in town into a morgue and put a sign on the door that read The Room of Peaceful Spirits.

Influenza and pneumonia became problems as well, made worse by the cold, wet winter weather, and the lack of ready shelter.

People made do with what they had, and for over a year after the earthquake, there were huts and tents in almost every open space.

Kobe did rebuild, however, and eventually the port reopened, the bullet train began running again, the highways were repaired and cars began flowing over them, and houses were built where there had been rubble.

The 1995 quake spotlighted vulnerabilities in Kobe's building and highway construction, its public safety and fire resources, and its response to disasters. Some systems failed; many did not; some new programs needed to be implemented.

The EQE report concluded its assessment report with the following: "The Kobe Earthquake is a terribly striking example of what earthquakes can do to a modern industrialized society."[6] EQE's determination was that resources needed to be earmarked for earthquake preparedness, because all it takes is twenty seconds for a "modern industrialized society" to be reduced to anything but.

[1] EQE Risk Management *Report on the January 16, 1995 Kobe, Japan Earthquake*. This figure does not include losses of the contents of buildings, such as machinery, office equipment, and inventory of materials, which was substantial.

[2] Lee Davis, *Natural Disasters,* 65.

[3] Ibid., 66.

[4] EQE Risk Management *Report on the January 16 1995 Kobe, Japan Earthquake.*

[5] Ibid.

[6] Ibid.

42

The 1987 Collision of the *Dona Paz* and the *Vector*

110 Miles South of Manila, the Philippines, off Marinduque Island

December 20, 1987

4,386 Dead[1]

> *I was sleeping when I heard an explosion. In just two seconds, there was a big fire on the ship and I heard everybody screaming and wailing. I jumped into the water.*
>
> —*Dona Paz* survivor Paquito Osabel[2]

In Henry Wadsworth Longfellow's *The Theologian's Tale,* Elizabeth talks about "ships that pass in the night . . . Only a signal shown and a distant voice in the darkness . . ."

Had those words held sway on December 20, 1987, thousands of ferry passengers headed to Manila for Christmas might have lived to celebrate their holiday.

The collision of the ferry *Dona Paz* and the oil tanker *Vector* resulted in the largest ever peacetime loss of life at sea.

The *Dona Paz* left the port of Tacloban on the Philippine Island of Leyte. She traveled north through the Visayan Sea, into the Jintotolo Channel, then into the Sibuyan Sea, and as she approached the tiny Philippine island of Marinduque, she collided with the tanker *Vector*, which was headed for Masbate Island and was loaded with eight thousand three hundred barrels of oil.

A U.S. aircrewman remembered the *Dona Paz* incident:

> I was stationed in the Philippines at the time of the *Dona Paz* incident . . . My job there was as a search and rescue aircrewman in the SH-3G Seaking helicopter . . . The Air Force helicopters arrived on the scene, but did not locate any survivors. They did however, locate many bodies for recovery.
>
> My recollections of what I read in the Pacific Stars and Stripes that day was that the *Dona Paz* collided with a tanker around ten P.M. that Sunday evening. There was a great fireball after the collision that was seen by other ships in the area. After the collision, the tanker broke in two and sank immediately. The paper said that there were only two survivors from the tanker. The *Dona Paz,* however, did not sink immediately. It listed very badly then capsized, sinking two hours after the collision. As I remembered, there were only 24 survivors from the *Dona Paz*. For weeks, there were bodies washing ashore and some of the bodies were unsuspectingly recovered by fishermen's nets, which really upset the local populace of fishermen in the area of the incident. A friend of mine in my squadron had relatives that were onboard the *Dona Paz* when it perished. It was a very sad event . . .[3]

After the explosion described by this crewman, the *Vector* spewed thousands of gallons of oil into the sea. As soon as the flames from the explosion hit the oil, it burst into flames, turning the water into an ocean of fire.

Many of the *Dona Paz* passengers made the choice to jump overboard, rather than stay on board the burning, listing ferry. Those hapless souls jumped straight into burning oil. They instantly caught fire and even immersing themselves completely under water could not douse the flames. It is a certainty that many of those passengers chose to drown themselves as quickly as possible rather than suffer the agony of being burned alive.

Many passengers did, however, choose to remain on board the *Dona Paz*. Perhaps they harbored some slight hope that fireboats would arrive immediately, put out the fire, and safely transfer them off the ferry. These desperate dreams were a hopeless exercise, however, and all those who remained on the ferry went down with the ship. It is hoped that those who were on the ship as it headed to the bottom had earlier succumbed to asphyxiation from the billowing smoke, and were unaware of their final disposition.

Many crew members of the *Vector* also ended up in the water, and there were some who managed to stay afloat on stray pieces of timber or other debris. Approximately thirty people survived the disaster and were rescued during the night and the following morning. Some of those survivors were badly burned, however, and died later. Thousands of bodies were never recovered. Three hundred bodies did wash up on shore over the next several days. All of them, according to Philippine authorities, had been partly eaten and mutilated by sharks.[4]

To this day it is still unclear as to why the *Dona Paz* and the *Vector* collided that Christmas season night in the waters of the Philippine Islands. Sea traffic around the Philippines has always been dangerous. Whether it is from reckless disregard for maritime rules, incompetence, overcrowding of the sea-lanes, inadequate navigational and radar equipment, or hazardous vessels, the Philippine waters have a long history of tragedy.

The fact that the *Dona Paz* was allegedly grossly overcrowded may suggest the lack of respect mariners in those waters have for safety regulations. (This is probably why there has never been an accurate death toll for the accident.) This is all speculation, of course, since the crews of both ships perished in the accident, and the vessels are at the bottom of the sea.

Whatever the actual number of souls lost in the *Dona Paz-Vector* collision, it is tragic that we have to turn to wartime, battle sinkings to come up with anywhere near the number of deaths from a maritime catastrophe.

The notoriety of the *Dona Paz* collision is that it happened during peacetime, and the victims were all civilians.

[1] For a relatively recent disaster, the death toll is unreliable and cannot be confirmed. Various sources state a range of deaths, from 3,000 to 4,386. Even the number of people on board the ferry *Dona Paz* is uncertain. Some sources say well over 4,000 people crowded onto the ferry; others say as few as 1,500 were on board. Whatever the actual figure of ferry passengers, all sources are in agreement that the ship was severely overloaded with far more passengers than legally allowed.

[2] Roger Smith, *Catastrophes and Disasters,* 175.

[3] www.greatshipwrecks.com.

[4] Ibid.

43

The 1856 Rhodes Church Explosion

The Palace of the Grand Master, the Street of the Knights,

Rhodes, Greece

April 3, 1856

4,000 Dead

From lightning and tempest; from plague, pestilence, and famine; from battle and murder, and from sudden death, Good Lord, deliver us.

—Prayer Book, 1662

I beheld Satan as lightning fall from heaven.

—Luke, 10:18

The clanging of the bells was impossible to ignore.

Every bell in every church steeple in the city of Rhodes on the island of Rhodes was tolling. Usually, each church bell in town was rung twice a day: once in the morning as a call to recite the Angelus, then at noon out of custom. These twice-daily tollings were slow and stately, and the bells were silenced in less than a minute. The cacophony the people of Rhodes were hearing this night was in stark contrast to the dignified ringing of the morning and noonday bells.

The bell ringers were frantically pulling on the bell ropes from the bottom of the tall steeples. The bell ringers were, for the most part, either young boys or elderly acolytes. The heavier old men could usually keep their footing as the rope went up and down. The young boys, however, would often be lifted off the cement floor several feet in the air as they hung onto the ropes. An observer would have found such a scene quite comical, and even though these boys wore stern and solemn faces as they went about their sacred duty, most of them would admit they found it quite enjoyable to go flying up into the air as they rang the bells.

The bells were ringing because the air was filled with lightning. For centuries, European churches believed that ringing their bells furiously during lightning storms would keep away the demonic powers that were striking the earth with their lightning. In later, somewhat more enlightened years, they believed that the noise of the bells disrupted the flow of the lightning's electricity and that this would prevent strikes. As might be expected, this did not always work, and it was not uncommon for a church steeple to be struck by lightning as the bell ringer was pulling the rope, killing that hapless member of the church's flock.

In 1856, the Palace of the Grand Master, a magnificent building that had been constructed in the fourteenth century, stood on the Street of the Knights in Rhodes. The palace had its own church, the Church of St. John, and on any given day, thousands of people were in the palace as well as the church.

In 1856, Rhodes was controlled by the Ottoman Turks. Their occupying army had taken over the Palace of the Grand Master, which had large, spacious vaults in its lower levels. The Turks very quickly filled up all these storage areas with massive quantities of gunpowder. The army needed easy access to gunpowder for weapons and bombs, and the central location of the Palace of the Grand Master, along with its enormous storage facilities, worked out quite well for the invading Turks. (The native Greeks were kicked out of Rhodes when the Turks took over, and if a Greek was found in the city without permission, he would probably be beheaded.)

It was not uncommon during these times for church vaults to be used for storing the supplies of death. And the inevitable explosions of these highly flammable, deadly stores were commonplace. In 1769 in Brescia, Italy, the Italian forces stored a staggering two hundred thousand pounds—one hundred tons—of gunpowder in the vaults beneath the Church of St. Nazaire. One hot August night, a single bolt of lightning struck St. Nazaire's bell tower and set fire to the church. Shortly thereafter, the entire quantity of gunpowder instantly exploded. More than 3,000 people were killed and almost 20 percent of the city of Brescia was completely destroyed in the explosion.

The April 3, 1856, explosion at the Palace of the Grand Master took a greater toll.

The cause—a single bolt of lightning—was the same, and 4,000 people either in one of the two buildings or in the immediate area surrounding the Palace. They were all killed in the explosion. As happened in Brescia, the gunpowder stored in the vaults of the palace exploded, and the force of the detonation completely demolished the grand and enormous palace, as well as its adjacent Church of St. John. The palace had stood for over 450 years, but it was taken down by one stray bolt of lightning that, apparently, had not been cowed by the ringing bells.

This lightning strike and subsequent explosion may be the single worst lightning-caused disaster in history. Today, the old town of Rhodes is inhabited by only 6,000 people. The number of deaths from the 1856 explosion—4,000—vividly illustrates the enormous toll this bolt from the sky exacted from Rhodes.

The Palace of the Great Master was a pile of rubble for almost eighty years. In 1939, during the Italian occupation of Greece, the invading fascists determined that Benito Mussolini might enjoy living in a sumptuous place like the palace. If not Mussolini, then the King of Italy, Vittorio Emmanuele II, might find it cozy. They rebuilt and restored the palace, essentially from the ground up, being meticulous about following the original design plans for the structure.

The tourists who today tour the resurrected Palace of the Grand Master are no doubt grateful to the long-gone Italian craftsmen for giving back to Greece one of its most magnificent edifices.

44

The Bhopal Chemical Leak

BHOPAL, INDIA

December 3, 1984

3,828 Dead[1]

In the arts of life, man invents nothing; but in the arts of death he outdoes Nature herself, and produces by chemistry and machinery all the slaughter of plague, pestilence and famine.

—George Bernard Shaw, *Man and Superman*

The news was wonderful! The wealthy American company Union Carbide was planning to build a plant in a very poor section of India and had announced plans to hire eight hundred Indian workers. People were excited about the improvement to their standard of living so many jobs would undoubtedly bring about. What they did not know at the time, however, was that this precious Union Carbide plant would be the death of many of them.

* * *

Hundreds of bodies littered the streets around the Union Carbide plant on the monstrous morning of December 3, 1984. Many were covered in vomit, urine, and feces, and their skin was a purplish red color. Inhaling toxic gas had caused them to lose control of their bodily functions and to suffocate in their own fluids.

Earlier that morning, at around 1:00 A.M., forty tons of deadly methyl isocyanate gas (MIC), a chemical used to make pesticides, escaped from a tank at the Union Carbide plant when a large quantity of water was inadvertently pumped into the tank in which the chemical was stored. Water and MIC do not mix, and the tank exploded. The ensuing cloud of deadly toxic gas rose over the plant and spread across Bhopal for fifteen square miles, killing people in their beds, leaving corpses in the streets, and sending thousands of agonized Indians to hospitals that were tragically underinformed and woefully underequipped to handle such a catastrophe.

Union Carbide's official corporate position regarding workers who fled the site was stated later by Dr. Thomas Petty, a lung expert at the University of Colorado who was hired by Union Carbide to visit the injured in Bhopal. "A lot of patients could have been saved had they not panicked," said Dr. Petty. "What they did is start running, which caused them to breathe more deeply. If they just would have taken their time and sort of walked away from the scene they wouldn't have inhaled so much of the pollutant."[1]

Apparently, the fleeing, terrified, suffocating workers' deaths were their own fault.

The doctors at the local hospitals, desperate for information they could use to treat the victims, called the Union Carbide plant medical officer. What poisoned these people? How do we treat them? they wanted to know. The Union Carbide doctor said that methyl isocyanate was nothing more than a potent form of tear gas, and that all they needed to do was flush the victims with water.

Water would prove useless, of course, in treating the people who had inhaled methyl isocyanate, and the death toll quickly began to mount.

The plant was quickly shut down and Union Carbide's CEO at the time, Warren Anderson, immediately flew to India to assess the situation and initiate relief efforts. Anderson was arrested as soon as his plane set down in India. After being released on bail, he hastily returned to the United States.

Was the deadly toxic chemical leak at the Bhopal Union Carbide plant—the worst industrial accident in history—the result of sabotage by a "disgruntled employee"?

On May 10, 1988, about three and a half years after the accident, Union Carbide released a study by Arthur D. Little, Inc., which showed "with virtual certainty" that the Bhopal "incident" (Union Carbide's word) was caused by a "disgruntled employee." This allegation was not taken seriously by either the courts or the court of world opinion, mainly because of Union Carbide's actions regarding this suspect employee. If the cause of an accident that killed thousands and permanently injured hundreds of thousands was, indeed, deliberate sabotage, then the perpetrator—the biochemical terrorist—would have been hunted down and brought to justice. Union Carbide never pursued the person it believed was responsible for the sabotage, and many today believe that the leveling of such a charge was a publicity strategy to divert attention from the corporate culpability of Union Carbide.

There have been industrial accidents that have done more environmental damage (the Exxon *Valdez,* for instance—see chapter 94) but the Bhopal chemical leak alarmed the entire world and spurred calls for new legislation requiring stricter safety codes for manufacturers working with potentially dangerous substances. Why? Because subsequent investigation into the Bhopal chemical accident revealed that Union Carbide had two sets of safety rules: one for plants in the United States and another for plants abroad. When the lax safety practices in place in the Bhopal plant were compared to those in Union Carbide's West Virginia plant, it became apparent that the Bhopal plant was an accident waiting to happen. And if this could happen at one of the biggest chemical companies in the world, the thinking went, where it could reasonably be assumed that safety was a priority, what went on at smaller plants that also worked with dangerous chemicals but were less profitable and less apt to spend money on the latest equipment, safety protocols, and emergency response plans?

After five years of litigation both in the United States and in India, Union Carbide settled in 1989 with the government of India for $470 million. (With the figure of 550,000 eligible victims, this came to approximately $850 per victim. If the money were invested at 10 percent for twenty years, this figure would rise to $3.1 billion, approximately $5,600 per victim.)

This deal also immunized the company against all criminal charges. The settlement was quickly challenged in court by victims' groups, and, ultimately, the amount Union Carbide had to pay was upheld, but the immunity from criminal prosecution was overthrown. Former Union Carbide CEO Warren Anderson was immediately charged with culpable homicide by the government of India, but he went into hiding to avoid being served with the summons. Union Carbide refused to accept service on his behalf, or to inform attorneys of his whereabouts.

Union Carbide's position is that the 1989 $470 million settlement put an end to all liability on the part of the company and all its directors, and it does not acknowledge the jurisdiction of the Bhopal District Court. Interestingly, a U.S. judge, Manhattan District Court Judge John Keenan, issued a written statement ordering Union Carbide to "submit to the jurisdiction of the courts of India." So far, Union Carbide has refused to comply with the rulings of either court, and former CEO Warren Anderson is nowhere to be found.

It is estimated that 10 to 15 people a week in Bhopal and surrounding towns die from their exposure to MIC in the 1984 accident.

[1] This is the officially released total from the Indian government. The Bhopal Peoples Health and Documentation Clinic (BPHDC) claims the actual death toll to be 8,000, and that more than 500,000 people were injured during the accident and its aftermath.

The Indian government, as reported by Union Carbide in a World Wide Web release, (www.bhopal.com) "Chronology," in January 2001, states that the injury total was only 203,469, broken down as follows:

0 victims with *permanent total disability*
2,680 persons with *permanent partial disability*
18,922 persons with *permanent injury with no disability*
1,313 persons with *temporary disability from permanent injury*
7,172 persons with *temporary disability from temporary injury*
173,382 persons with *temporary injury with no disability*

The Indian government also states that there were 155,203 persons who sought a medical examination, but had no injury. www.corpwatch.org/truc/bhopal/factsheet.html

45

The 1906 San Francisco Earthquake

SAN FRANCISCO, CALIFORNIA

April 18, 1906

3,000 Dead[1]

$500 Million in Damages[2]

The Federal Troops, the members of the Regular Police Force and all Special Police Officers have been authorized by me to KILL any and all persons found engaged in Looting or in the Commission of Any Other Crime.

—Proclamation by San Francisco Mayor Eugene Schmitz following the earthquake

The street seemed to move like waves of water. On my way down Market Street the whole side of a building fell out and came so near me that I was covered and blinded by the dust. Then I saw the first dead come by. They were piled up in an automobile like carcasses in a butcher's wagon, all over blood, with crushed skulls, and broken limbs, and bloody faces. A man cried out to me, "Look out for that live wire!" I had just time to sidestep certain death.

—Earthquake survivor Sam Wolfe

Within fifteen minutes of the first huge tremors of the 1906 San Francisco earthquake, there were over fifty fires roaring throughout the city.

Gas lines had burst when the ground started undulating, and it did not take long before the flammable natural gas the pipes carried ignited.

Adding to the nightmare was the damage done to the city's water pipes. Most of San Francisco's water mains straddled the San Andreas Fault and they ruptured with the first violent vibrations.

Firefighters cannot put out fires without water, and San Francisco ultimately ended up burning for three straight days.

Desperate people will take desperate action. There are stories of Italian families pouring gallons of wine on the fire in an attempt to douse it, as well as firefighters pumping raw sewage through their hoses in place of water.

The military even implemented a plan similar to what is often done to curtail forest fires. Soldiers blew up buildings with dynamite to create firebreaks that would, they hoped, stop the fire from spreading. Unfortunately, the explosions did not work and only contributed to the inferno and made matters worse.

San Francisco sits on the six-hundred-mile-long San Andreas Fault, the gap between the tectonic plates that make up the western third of the North American continent, and which stretch from northwestern California to the Gulf of California. These tectonic plates float on the molten rock beneath them and are constantly in motion. When the enormous rock plates move against each other, an earthquake occurs. Most of the time the actual tremors of an earthquake are brief, but the resultant deaths are never forgotten, and the catastrophic destruction can take years to repair.

The 8.3 magnitude earthquake that struck San Francisco awoke the city's citizens at 5:13 A.M. on the morning of Wednesday, April 18, 1906. The first wave of tremors lasted thirty or forty seconds. There was a ten-second pause, then a second wave hit, lasting twenty-five seconds. That was it. In approximately one minute, San Francisco was decimated.

The quake took down 28,188 buildings, including the $5 million, "earthquake proof" city hall, as well as innumerable hotels, theaters, apartment houses, schools, factories, churches, thousands of individual homes, and other notable buildings. People who managed to escape from the buildings they were in after the earthquake, were then in danger of being killed by falling debris—and many were.

Neither man nor beast was safe. One of the more poignant photos from the day of the disaster shows a group of men standing over the dead bodies of a number of carriage horses killed by falling bricks. (And escaping unscathed from a falling building did not assure respite from the absurdity of the situation: landlady Agnes Zink, who managed to escape her collapsing building by shimmying naked down a drainpipe, was arrested for indecent exposure the moment her feet touched the ground.)

The earthquake, which was felt as far away as Oregon and Nevada, took out the city's electrical service, which added to the survivors' misery. Between 200,000 and 300,000 people were left homeless. Tent cities sprang up in the parks (including a few staffed by San Francisco's very industrious prostitutes).

The devastation caused by the earthquake caused problems for the public health. Corpses were removed as quickly as possible, but it wasn't quick enough to keep them away from the rats, many of whom carried bubonic plague, fed on the dead, and then bit survivors, countless numbers of whom had been forced into sleeping outdoors. Within a year of the earthquake, San Francisco also had to contend with over 150 cases of bubonic plague.

Stories of both heroism and sorrow survived the earthquake. Bank of America founder A. P. Giannini rescued all his bank's assets from the fires and, as soon as he could, started issuing rebuilding loans from his impromptu bank "branch": a board set across two barrels.

Others were not so lucky. There are many accounts of people crushed under debris, conscious but with no hope of rescue or survival, pleading with policemen to shoot them before they burned to death. Many officers obliged.

The rebuilding of San Francisco took close to three years. The city would suffer again, however. In 1989, a 7.1 magnitude earthquake that did over $6 billion in damage struck San Francisco. (See chapter 88.)

The undeniable danger of the San Andreas Fault is the price San Franciscans are willing to pay for the joy of living in the city they unconditionally love.

[1] For decades, the official death toll from the 1906 San Francisco was believed to be approximately 700 persons. New studies and new research done in the 1980s by the United States Geological Survey has shown that the actual number of deaths is closer to 3,000, and possibly higher. (This figure also includes people shot for looting after the earthquake.)

[2] In 1906 dollars.

Enrico Caruso's Account of Surviving the San Francisco Earthquake

Operatic legend Enrico Caruso was asleep in his hotel when the San Francisco earthquake struck. Caruso had sung in *Carmen* the previous night, and he provided this account for the July 1, 1906, issue of the London magazine, *The Sketch*. (After the earthquake, Caruso swore that he would never again set foot in San Francisco, and he never did.)

> You ask me to say what I saw and what I did during the terrible days which witnessed the destruction of San Francisco? Well, there have been many accounts of my so-called adventures published in the American papers, and most of them have not been quite correct. Some of the papers said that I was terribly frightened, that I went half crazy with fear, that I dragged my valise out of the hotel into the square and sat upon it and wept; but all this is untrue. I was frightened, as many others were, but I did not lose my head. I was stopping at the [Palace] Hotel, where many of my fellow-artists were staying, and very comfortable it was. I had a room on the fifth floor, and on Tuesday evening, the night before the great catastrophe, I went to bed feeling very contented. I had sung in *Carmen* that night, and the opera had one with fine éclat. We were all pleased, and, as I said before, I went to bed that night feeling happy and contented.
>
> But what an awakening! You must know that I am not a very heavy sleeper—I always wake early, and when I feel restless I get up and go for a walk. So on the Wednesday morning early I wake up about 5 o'clock, feeling my bed rocking as though I am in a ship on the ocean, and for a moment I think I am dreaming that I am crossing the water on my way to my beautiful country. And so I take no notice for the moment, and then, as the rocking continues, I get up and go to the window, raise the shade and look out. And what I see makes me tremble with fear. I see the buildings toppling over, big pieces of masonry falling, and from the street below I hear the cries and screams of men and women and children.
>
> I remain speechless, thinking I am in some dreadful nightmare, and for something like forty seconds I stand there, while the buildings fall and my room still rocks like a boat on the sea. And during that forty seconds I think of forty thousand different things. All that I have ever

done in my life passes before me, and I remember trivial things and important things. I think of my first appearance in grand opera, and I feel nervous as to my reception, and again I think I am going through last night's *Carmen.*

And then I gather my faculties together and call for my valet. He comes rushing in quite cool, and, without any tremor in his voice, says: "It is nothing." But all the same he advises me to dress quickly and go into the open, lest the hotel fall and crush us to powder. By this time the plaster on the ceiling has fallen in a great shower, covering the bed and the carpet and the furniture, and I, too, begin to think it is time to "get busy." My valet gives me some clothes; I know not what the garments are but I get into a pair of trousers and into a coat and draw some socks on and my shoes, and every now and again the room trembles, so that I jump and feel very nervous. I do not deny that I feel nervous, for I still think the building will fall to the ground and crush us. And all the time we hear the sound of crashing masonry and the cries of frightened people.

Then we run down the stairs and into the street, and my valet, brave fellow that he is, goes back and bundles all my things into trunks and drags them down six flights of stairs and out into the open one by one. While he is gone for another and another, I watch those that have already arrived, and presently someone comes and tries to take my trunks saying they are his. I say, "No, they are mine"; but he does not go away. Then a soldier comes up to me; I tell him that this man wants to take my trunks, and that I am Caruso, the artist who sang in *Carmen* the night before. He remembers me and makes the man who takes an interest in my baggage "skiddoo" as Americans say.

Then I make my way to Union Square, where I see some of my friends, and one of them tells me he has lost everything except his voice, but he is thankful that he has still got that. And they tell me to come to a house that is still standing; but I say houses are not safe, nothing is safe but the open square, and I prefer to remain in a place where there is no fear of being buried by falling buildings. So I lie down in the square for a little rest, while my valet goes and looks after the luggage, and soon I begin to see the flames and all the city seems to be on fire. All the day I wander about, and I tell my valet we must try and get away, but the soldiers will not let us pass. We can find no vehicle to find our luggage, and this night we are forced to sleep on the hard ground in the open. My limbs ache yet from so rough a bed.

My valet succeeds in getting a man with a cart, who says he will take us to the Oakland Ferry for a certain sum, and we agree to his terms. We pile the luggage into the cart and climb in after it, and the man whips up his horse and we start.

We pass terrible scenes on the way: buildings in ruins, and everywhere there seems to be smoke and dust. The driver seems in no hurry, which makes me impatient at times, for I am longing to return to New York, where I know I shall find a ship to take me to my beautiful Italy and my wife and my little boys.

When we arrive at Oakland we find a train there which is just about to start, and the officials are very polite, take charge of my luggage, and tell me go get onboard, which I am very glad to do. The trip to New York seems very long and tedious, and I sleep very little, for I can still feel the terrible rocking which made me sick. Even now I can only sleep an hour at a time, for the experience was a terrible one.

46

The September 11, 2001 Terrorist Attacks

New York City, Washington, DC, Pennsylvania

September 11, 2001

3,036 Dead[1]

> *We calculated in advance the number of casualties from the enemy, who would be killed based on the position of the tower. We calculated that the floors that would be hit would be three or four floors. I was the most optimistic of them all . . . due to my experience in this field, I was thinking that the fire from the gas in the plane would melt the iron structure of the building and collapse the area where the plane hit and all the floors above it only. This is all that we had hoped for.*
>
> —Osama bin Laden, November 7, 2001

On September 11, 2001, the unthinkable happened in New York City, and America and the world have been thinking about what happened ever since.

Two fully loaded and fully fueled jet liners were hijacked out of Boston and deliberately crashed into the twin towers of the World Trade Center, killing everyone on board both planes (including the suicide terrorists), as well as 2,673 people who could not escape the burning buildings before they collapsed to the ground. This number included firefighters and police officers who rushed into the building as soon as they arrived on the scene and were trapped in the upper stories when the buildings collapsed.

The devastation spread over sixteen acres in lower Manhattan. The cleanup and recovery of remains continued through 2002, and the owners of the property have vowed to rebuild on the site. Although human remains were found every day, it was believed by forensic experts that many people were completely incinerated by the flaming fuel oil, or crushed to dust under tons of concrete and steel. Hundreds of people's remains will never be recovered.

Within six months after the attack in New York, it was learned that the burning of glass, office equipment, paint, and insulation, and all the other chemical-laden items that fill a modern office building, had polluted the air in lower Manhattan. Many workers were complaining of breathing difficulties and other toxic inhalation–related health problems. It is still too early to know the long-term health effects of the burning of the World Trade Center.

The instantaneous effect of this attack was so profound and unprecedented that cable TV stations cut off their regular broadcasts immediately following the collapse of the towers, and either put up a condolence message, or carried a feed from CNN or one of the other news networks covering the tragedy.

This was the worst terrorist attack on United States soil. President George W. Bush immediately declared war on the perpetrators and vowed that justice would be served.

At the same time that the planes were crashing into the World Trade Center, a similarly loaded plane was being crashed into the Pentagon. A fourth plane, believed to have been headed for either the Capitol or The White House, was taken over by passengers and crashed into a field in Pennsylvania.

The attacks were immediately linked to Saudi expatriate Osama bin Laden and his Al Qaeda terrorist network. Bin Laden was already on the FBI's most wanted list for his connection to the August 7, 1998, embassy terrorist bombings in Dar es Salaam, Tanzania, and Nairobi, Kenya, as well as his involvement with other terrorist bombings around the world. Following the September 11 attacks, a $25 million reward was offered for information leading to the apprehension and conviction of bin Laden.

The Al Qaeda headquarters was thought to be in Taliban-ruled Afghanistan and the United States began a military campaign against the Taliban and the Al Qaeda operatives holed up in the country's many secret caves. By mid-November, 2001, the Taliban had lost sway in Afghanistan.

The Anthrax Attacks: An Al Qaeda Connection?

On October 4, 2001, with the nation still reeling—emotionally, economically, politically, and militarily—from the September 11 attacks, the United States was faced with another possible threat. A sixty-three-year-old man in Florida was diagnosed with inhalation anthrax. Florida's Lt. Gov. Frank Brogan, speaking to the media, acknowledged that, while some countries had developed anthrax as a biological weapon, there was no evidence that this case was a bioterrorist attack.

In less than a week, however, after two more Floridians tested positive for anthrax infection, government officials reported that they believed the strain of anthrax that had infected the Florida victims was manufactured, not natural.

A day later, an NBC employee in New York tested positive for anthrax contamination. She had opened a letter that had been dusted with anthrax powder.

Now there was no doubt. America was under attack again.

The question immediately and repeatedly asked was "Is this a foreign terrorist attack, or is it a domestic attack?"

Many experts and government officials believed that Iraq was involved in the anthrax mailings.

A CIA source quoted in Britain's *Guardian* newspaper in October 2001, said, "Making [anthrax] powder needs repeated washings in huge centrifuges, followed by intensive drying, which requires sealed environments. The technology would cost millions. They aren't making this stuff in caves in Afghanistan. This is prima facie evidence of the involvement of a state intelligence agency. Maybe Iran has the capability. But it doesn't look likely politically. That leaves Iraq."

That said, though, others did look to Osama bin Laden and his Al Qaeda terrorist network and the anthrax mailings as the second phase of a concerted, targeted terrorist attack on America.

The anthrax mailings were responsible for 18 cases of anthrax infection: 11 through inhalation, and 7 through skin. Five people died from the disease.

Postal authorities continue to offer a $2 million reward for information leading to an arrest in the anthrax-by-mail cases.

[1] This figure, which is accurate as of September 5, 2002, is broken down as follows:

NEW YORK: 2,803

(Note: This figure includes the hijackers as well as the passengers and crew on the two hijacked planes: American Airlines Flight 11: 92; United Airlines Flight 175: 65.)

WASHINGTON: 189

At the Pentagon: 125

Aboard American Airlines Flight 77: 64 (hijackers, passengers, and crew).

PENNSYLVANIA: 44

Aboard United Flight 93: 44 (hijackers, passengers, and crew).

JOHNSTOWN AS LEFT BY THE FLOOD.

47

The Johnstown Flood

JOHNSTOWN, PENNSYLVANIA

May 31, 1889

2,500 Dead

$17 Million in Damages[1]

Seen from below, the dam looked like a tremendous mound of overgrown rubble, the work of a glacier perhaps. It reared up 72 feet above the valley floor and was more than 900 feet long. The dam wall had over the years become pock marked with brush and trees growing in the cracks of the rock wall. From below there was no indication that the lake was being held back by this man-made creation.

—David McCullough, *The Johnstown Flood*

Such an avalanche of horrors never slipped upon any American city. Horrors piled on horrors, woe augmenting woe; bankruptcy, orphanage, widowhood, childlessness, obliterated homesteads, gorged cemeteries and scenes so excruciating it is a marvel anyone could look upon them and escape insanity.

—New York World

Forewarned is forearmed, so the saying goes, but the warning must be taken seriously so the arming can occur.

In the case of the catastrophic 1889 Johnstown, Pennsylvania, dam burst and flood, almost everyone in Johnstown and its environs who knew of the Johnstown dam knew of its problems and its potential hazards to the town and its people. Small floods in the area were common and "the dam has bust, take to the hills!" was a running joke in Johnstown and surrounding towns. As is often the case, however, the "dam doomsayers," no matter how restrained their warnings, were painted as alarmists, fools, or cowards, and dismissed or mocked by those Johnstownians to whom they voiced their concerns.

The stories from the Johnstown flood, many of which are recounted in David McCullough's seminal account of the disaster, *The Johnstown Flood*, as well as in Jay Robert Nash's comprehensive *Darkest Hours,* are almost too incredible to believe, and yet these things did happen; these nightmares were real.

The Methodist church of Johnstown was completely lifted up off its foundation *in one piece* and sent hurtling down the valley. There are many accounts of people hearing the church's bell clanging as it was carried away.

The floodwaters picked up thirty-seven locomotives, each weighing forty tons, and carried them away as though they were model trains.

One woman was trapped among a dozen corpses, buried under deadly wreckage all night. Throughout the dark, overnight hours, the hair of a dead woman floated across her face and she was unable to stop it. When she was finally rescued, she had completely lost her mind from the "water torture" and the grimness of her night.

Tons of debris piled up at the junction of the Little Conemaugh and Stony Creek rivers, and burning stoves that had been swept away by the waters ignited flammable materials in the wreckage. Everything caught fire and 80 people who had survived the flood were burned alive in a tangled trap of wire, rocks, wood, and corpses, both human and animal. Imagine dying like that: being picked up by a wall of water, dragged through the streets wrapped in barbed wire and pelted by rocks, being submerged, only to surface again and again and perhaps have your face slashed open by a piece of metal swirling in the water, and then to be trapped in a mountain of churning water and deadly metal and rock. And then be burned alive in this torture chamber.

The force of the deluge was so powerful that entire houses were picked up by the waters, carried away and then piled up on top of each other—people's homes casually stacked one on top of the other, like a child's toys.

Rescuers found survivors unclothed, yet uninjured. Many told stories of the waters ripping every piece of clothing from their body, yet leaving them unscathed.

Incredibly, after the flood, the body of a resident of Johnstown was found in Steubenville, Ohio, a distance of *one hundred miles away.*

* * *

The Johnstown dam was built between 1838 and 1853 by the state of Pennsylvania as part of its canal system. By the time the dam was finished, though, the railroad had made canals obsolete and the dam was never used for its intended purpose.

The state of Pennsylvania sold the seventy-two-foot-high, and nine hundred-foot-wide dam, to the Pennsylvania Railroad, which later sold it to Altoona, Pennsylvania, congressman John Reilly, who afterward sold it at a loss to the South Fork Fishing and Hunting Club. This was when neglect and bad decisions set the stage for the disaster that followed.

The dam needed a great deal of work. The South Fork Club did do some repairs, but it spent only around $17,000, a ridiculously inadequate amount for what was needed.

The dam created a 3.5-mile-wide, 1.25-mile-long, 100-foot-deep reservoir lake, which was completed in 1852 and called Lake Conemaugh. The lake was stocked with fish and used for boating and other recreational water activities by members of the elite club. (Steel magnates Andrew Carnegie and Henry Clay Frick were members.) Beautiful cottages were built along the lake's shore and the area was a popular resort for South Fork Club members.

The head of the South Fork Club, Colonel B. F. Ruff, wanted his members to be happy—and to catch fish. Subsequently, Ruff ordered the dam's spillway channels blocked so that fish could not get out of the lake into the surrounding rivers. This left only a flume made from boards for water overflow from the top of the dam.

Many engineers and even just plain townsfolk had told the club for years that the dam was in trouble and that it needed repairs, but Ruff refused to spend any more than the $17,000 already put into the dam. A report by the Army Corps of Engineers after the flood cited the following as the causes for the dam break: "the lowering of the crest, the dishing, or central sag of the crest, the closing of the bottom culvert, and the obstruction of the spill-way,"—all of which were done on Ruff's orders.

After heavy rains, the dam broke at 3:10 P.M. on the day after Memorial Day. The floodwaters hit Johnstown fifty-seven minutes later, at 4:07 P.M. The 40-foot-high, half-mile-wide flood wave ripped up fifty feet of earth as it made its way down the valley toward Johnstown.

Twenty million tons of water—4.5 billion gallons—traveled at forty miles an hour down the valley to Johnstown. Upon its arrival, it wiped out the city, including 1,600 houses and 280 businesses. Over 2,000 people died immediately, and most authorities have estimated the final death toll at around 2,500 people. Some sources cite a much higher figure.

As is often the case with major disasters, the tragedy brought out the best and the worst in people. There are many heroic stories of rescuers braving the deadly floodwaters and risking their own lives to save others. And there are also stories of ghoulish looters hacking off the fingers of dead women to get their rings. Some of those looters were caught and subjected to a swift form of trial and verdict: they were immediately lynched.

A memorial to the victims of the Johnstown Flood now stands in town; there is also a museum. The story of the Johnstown Flood continues to fascinate people of all ages, some of whom were born a hundred years after the waters raged.

Some descendants of flood survivors have a constant reminder within their families of the toll the flood took: two Johnstown babies born prematurely during the flood were named Flood.

[1] In 1889 dollars.

48

The 1917 *Mont Blanc* Explosion

Halifax Harbor, Canada

December 6, 1917

1,635 Dead

$35 Million in Damages[1]

Houses were simply indistinguishable masses where they had not been devoured by the flames that rise and fall, that roared and seethed and made the place like a smelting oven.

—*Montreal Daily Star*

Although the explosion of the French munitions ship *Mont Blanc* happened during World War I, and the scope of this book does not include disasters resulting from military or wartime activity (the Holocaust, Hiroshima, and so on), the *Mont Blanc* disaster is included because it was the largest accidental explosion of all time, its wartime occurrence notwithstanding. This explosion also stands as the largest man-made explosion before the atomic bomb was dropped on Hiroshima in 1945. The deaths and damage caused by the *Mont Blanc* explosion were cataclysmic.

The Great War was always on the minds of the people of Nova Scotia. They were constantly reminded of what was going on in Europe by the steady stream of ships in and out of their harbor, headed for the war, or returning for resupplying before heading out again.

On the morning of Thursday, December 6, 1917, the French freighter *Mont Blanc* entered six-mile-long Halifax Harbor from the north Atlantic to meet with the British warship *High Flyer.* The *Mont Blanc* had sailed from France to New York, where she had picked up an enormous cargo of high explosives. On board were thirty-five tons of the flammable liquid benzene, two thousand three hundred tons of wet and dry picric acid (a chemical used in explosives), two hundred tons of TNT, ten tons of gun cotton, and three hundred rounds of ammunition. The plan was for the *High Flyer* to escort the *Mont Blanc* back to Europe, where French troops were eagerly awaiting the munitions and explosives she carried.

The *Mont Blanc* began moving through the mile-wide harbor channel, slowing somewhat as she began to pass through the short half-mile-wide section of the waterway known as "the Narrows."

At the same time, the Belgian relief ship *Imo* was heading out of the channel. The *Mont Blanc*'s pilot suddenly became alarmed to see that the *Imo* was heading straight for his ship. The pilot blew the *Mont Blanc*'s horn, and the *Imo* then signaled with whistles that she was maneuvering to port, her left, which meant that she would end up in the same lane as the *Mont Blanc*. The *Mont Blanc* was staying to her right and her captain hoped that the *Imo* had inadvertently given the wrong signal and that she would actually stay to her starboard, her right, which would keep her clear of the *Mont Blanc* and on the Richmond side, the south side of the channel.

The *Imo* continued heading straight for the *Mont Blanc*, however, and even though the *Mont Blanc* attempted evasive maneuvers, the *Imo* was on a collision course with the heavily loaded munition ship. Seeing the inevitability of a crash, the *Mont Blanc*'s captain turned his ship so that the *Imo* would avoid hitting the section of the hull beneath which the dynamite was stored. This maneuver worked in that the *Imo* did not strike the TNT, but she did rip open the hull where the picric acid, benzene, and huge quantities of highly flammable gun cotton were stored. Twenty-five barrels of benzene broke open and mixed with the acid, and a fire broke out immediately.

At first, the crew of the *Mont Blanc* tried valiantly to put out the fire, realizing the potential danger if it spread to the dynamite. However, their efforts were to no avail and after a few minutes, the captain gave the "abandon ship" order. His men boarded lifeboats and rowed frantically for shore. Meantime, the blazing *Mont Blanc* drifted aimlessly and the *Imo* made for the channel's northern shore and the city of Dartmouth. Within minutes after the crew abandoned her, the *Mont Blanc* brushed against a pier and set it on fire. The Halifax Fire Department responded and the noise and commotion prompted dozens of people, including many children, to run to the docks to witness the spectacle. Big mistake.

At 9:05 A.M., twenty minutes after the collision of the two ships, the *Mont Blanc* exploded. The blast was so huge, that the suburb of Richmond and everyone in it was destroyed. More than 1,600 people were instantly killed; 325 acres were leveled; flying glass blinded 1,000 people; injuries were in the thousands, and fires broke out everywhere.

As for the *Mont Blanc*, one of her gun cannons was hurled three miles from where she exploded.

In addition, two-thirds of the crew of every ship in Halifax Harbor were killed. The explosion was heard and broke windows sixty miles away.

Once the world learned about the disaster, relief workers, trainloads of supplies, and dozens of medical personnel swarmed to the area. Many of the injured were beyond help. Complicating matters was a blizzard that covered Richmond and Dartmouth a few days after the explosion, seriously hampering rescue efforts as the smoking rubble became covered with snow. Many who could have been saved died from exposure and complications from being lost beneath the rubble for too long.

The states of Maine and Massachusetts were especially resolute in their relief efforts. The Canadian paper *The Globe* made note of their generosity, compassion, and altruism in a front-page story titled "Splendid Help from Our Ally" the day after the catastrophe.

The entire crew of the *Mont Blanc* survived, although one man did die later from wounds received in the explosion. Seven crewmen of the *Imo* perished; the ship was rebuilt, renamed, and put back into service. She sank five years later after running into a reef off the coast of the Falkland Islands.

Today, Halifax regularly commemorates the lives lost in the enormous explosion caused by someone whistling the wrong notes.

[1] In 1917 dollars.

49

The Sinking of the *Sultana*

The Mississippi River, North of Memphis, Tennessee

April 27, 1865

1,547+ Dead[1]

> *When I got about three hundred yards away from the boat clinging to a heavy plank, the whole heavens seemed to be lighted up by the conflagration. Hundreds of my comrades were fastened down by the timbers of the decks and had to burn while the water seemed to be one solid mass of human beings struggling with the waves.*
>
> —A *Sultana* survivor[2]

The *Titanic.* The *Sultana.* It is one of the ironies of nautical life that more people died on a river than in the middle of the north Atlantic.

The Civil War was finally over. General Lee had surrendered on April 9, 1865, and thousands of Union soldiers were immediately set free from Confederate prisons.

Many of these men were not in the best of shape; the conditions in the

Southern prisons had, in many cases, been terrible. At the Cahaba Federal Prison in Alabama, for example, the five thousand Union soldiers had had to use water that flowed more than two hundred yards from an artesian well, and this running water was used for human waste, dirty dishwater, the contents of spittoons, and other filth before it got to the soldiers.

Illness was commonplace, and by the time these men were released in April 1865, many were debilitated, malnourished, gaunt, and sick. Their only thought was to get back home—to get back up North. Their physical appearance bespoke the miseries they had endured. Their bandages were filthy; some had lost arms and legs; some were blind.

The 1,720-ton Mississippi side-wheeler steamboat *Sultana* set out from New Orleans for Cincinnati on April 21, 1865. She had a legal passenger capacity of 376, and when she left New Orleans, she carried approximately 100 passengers and 80 crew. The *Sultana* also carried a large cargo of casks of sugar, plus one hundred horses, mules, and pigs, and one ten-foot-long alligator in a cage.

The *Sultana* stopped in Vicksburg, Mississippi, where the ship's engineers discovered that one of the boilers was leaking. They quickly repaired it, and while in port at Vicksburg, the *Sultana* took on close to two thousand four hundred released Union prisoners as well as another eighty civilian passengers. No official roster was kept, and one report claimed that the ship was so full that there was not even room for one more human being.

When the *Sultana* set out from Vicksburg, she was carrying more than six times the legal limit of passengers.

The steamship continued on up the Mississippi for two days, arriving in Memphis, Tennessee, at 7 P.M. on April 26, 1865. The boiler was leaking again, and it was again repaired. Some people got off the *Sultana* in Memphis and, for one reason or another, never got back on. They were the lucky ones. The *Sultana* took on coal at Memphis, and then set out for Cincinnati.

At 2:00 A.M. on the morning of April 27, the *Sultana*'s twice-repaired boiler exploded.

The blast was huge and hundreds of bodies were blown into the air from the force. Many came down into the water in bloody pieces. The explosion awakened the captain, who opened his state room door to be met with smoke and flames. The fire raced through the ship and immediately hundreds of people began jumping overboard. Water is a safe haven from fire, except many of the Union soldiers aboard the *Sultana* could not swim, and the panicked nonswimmers pulled under many of those that could, thus drowning all.

The *Sultana* burned mightily in the night. For almost an hour, a group of seven hundred soldiers huddled en masse at the front of the enormous ship watching the fire consume the decks. Then the wind shifted and blew the inferno toward the terrified, emaciated soldiers. They all ended up in the water, and very few survived.

One Union soldier, a Private Summerville, fortuitously survived the initial blast. He was thrown some distance away from the ship while he was sleeping, and awoke to find himself in the water. Summerville saw people all around him, grabbing desperately at anything that could float. One of the horses was seen with ten men hanging on to him. The terrified animal could not take all the weight and remain afloat, and men and horse all drowned. Summerville later recalled seeing one man paddle by him on a barrel. The man had no face. It had been burned away in the fires, and yet the man was not screaming or crying. He was just paddling along.

Several ships, including the *Bostona*, the *Essex*, and the *Tyler*, raced to the scene to rescue whomever they could, but over half of the people on board perished. Bodies washed up on shore along the Mississippi for days after the tragedy.

The sinking of the *Sultana* was one of the worst shipping disasters of all time, eclipsed only by the collision of the *Dona Paz* and the *Vector* (chapter 42) and the *Mont Blanc* explosion (chapter 48).[3] Media attention to the tragedy was almost nonexistent, however, because all attention was on the end of the war between the states, and the assassination of Abraham Lincoln, only twelve days before the *Sultana* disaster.

Today, descendants of survivors and victims of the *Sultana* maintain contact and try to keep alive the memory of the great steamship and the people lost on April 27, 1865.

[1] This is the official death toll, and it is believed to be *fairly* reliable, but it is possible that the number of people killed could actually be significantly higher if the number of unauthorized Union soldier passengers was higher than believed by authorities. Some sources use the figure 1,700 dead. Whatever the true figure, it is certain that more people died in the *Sultana* disaster than on the *Titanic*.

[2] *American Heritage* magazine, October 1955.

[3] We did not consider military disasters for this book. Though it is true that the majority of the *Sultana*'s dead were soldiers, the *Sultana* disaster is included here because it was not a wartime sinking, and the explosion of the boiler and the drastic overloading of the ship were the causes of the multitude of deaths.

50

The Sinking of the *Titanic*

THE NORTH ATLANTIC

April 15, 1912

1,512 Dead

Carpathia reached Titanic position at daybreak. Found boats and wreckage only. Titanic sank about 2:20 A.M., in 41.16 N; 50.14 W. All her boats accounted for, containing about 675 souls saved, crew and passengers included. Nearly all saved women and children. Leyland Liner Californian remained and searching exact position of disaster. Loss likely total 1800 souls.

—The text of the *Titanic* "Death Message" sent by the RMS *Olympic* on Monday, April 15, 1912

Unsinkable.

That was the word used to describe the RMS *Titanic.*

The possibility of the *Titanic* sinking was such a nonissue with its builders that, for cosmetic reasons, they skimped on the number of lifeboats on board, wholeheartedly believing that they would never be needed. It is likely that the designers begrudged the lifeboats even the deck space they were allotted, such was the arrogance of the shipbuilding community at the time, and the total confidence in the ship's invincibility.

The *Titanic* was constructed so that she could remain afloat if three and, in some cases, four of her sixteen belowdecks watertight compartments were breached and flooded. The ship was not, however, designed to handle *six* of her compartments filling with water. No one involved in the design and construction, nor anyone on the crew, gave even the remotest credence to the possibility that more than three compartments would flood in any imagined accident.

Therefore, the *Titanic*'s sinking was unthinkable. Yet, on the moonless night of April 14, 1912, on her inaugural voyage, the unthinkable happened. The *Titanic* hit an iceberg, broke in two, and sank in the northern Atlantic in the early hours of April 15.

Recent ultrasound imaging has revealed some startling information about the gash in the *Titanic*'s hull where she scraped the iceberg. The damage was actually much smaller than had been previously believed. The total area damaged was between twelve and thirteen square feet, about the size of a refrigerator or a human body. There was no long, gaping breach, as had been surmised for years.

The critical flaw in the *Titanic*'s design was not extending the separating walls between the watertight compartments all the way to the top of the compartments. If the walls had been solid, instead of having had an open space at the top, the incoming water from the gash would have filled a compartment and then gone no farther. What happened instead was that the water poured over the top of the wall and began flooding adjacent compartments. The cumulative effect was the relentless filling of one compartment after another, until the front of the ship became so heavy that it began to sink, raising the rear half out of the water, resulting in the ship splitting in half and plummeting to the ocean floor.

Another major problem, only recently discovered through advanced testing, was the steel used to build the *Titanic.* Tests have shown that it was inferior, even for the standards of the time; and yet, while important, this may have been, essentially, irrelevant. The *Titanic*'s "sister ship," the *Olympic,* was built at the same time as the *Titanic,* and from the same materials, and she sailed successfully for almost twenty-five years.

The bolts used to rivet the *Titanic*'s plates in place have been examined and found also to be made of inferior steel, containing a dangerously high amount (9.3 percent) of slag, which would make them extremely brittle in cold water. Again, the same rivets were used on *Olympic,* and her hull did not rupture in cold water, nor did her rivets pop out of the plates when stressed.

After I studied the *Titanic* event carefully for my 1998 book, *The Complete Titanic,* it is my conclusion that the single most important factor in the sinking of the *Titanic* (other than striking the iceberg, of course) was the short walls separating the watertight compartments. If we reenact the event exactly the way it happened, changing only one thing—extending the watertight compartment walls to the ceilings—the *Titanic* would not have sunk. None of the other problems—insufficient lifeboats, inferior steel, brittle rivets, bad communication, and so on—would have mattered if the water had been stopped in the first two compartments.

The reason the sinking of the *Titanic* is one of the worst disasters of all time is not because of the death toll. Many disasters have resulted in more deaths. Instead, it is because the sinking of this great ship, on her very first voyage, was a dramatic and powerful wake-up call for the world. The sinking showed that man cannot for a single moment believe he has outsmarted the powers of nature. The builders of the *Titanic,* along with her crew and passengers, were blasé about everything having to do with *Titanic*'s transatlantic crossing. The span of ocean, the presence of icebergs, the deadly cold, the limitations of communications, none of these factors was considered threatening or insurmountable. Nature had other plans, however, and all the millions of dollars and man-hours that went into *Titanic* were nonchalantly undone by a slow gliding iceberg that was probably eons old by the time it met the unsinkable *Titanic.*

The wreck of the *Titanic* was discovered in 1985 by explorer Robert Ballard. Salvage missions to retrieve items from the*Titanic*'s debris field have been going on ever since. Cameras have penetrated the ship itself, but there is an international agreement that nothing is to be removed from the ship's deck or interior. It is believed that there are probably skeletons in the deepest recesses of the wreck.

The ship is decaying at a rapid rate and will ultimately collapse. Regular expeditions to *Titanic* chronicle the wreck on film and artifacts from the ship recovered from the ocean floor are preserved and exhibited for the public. James Cameron's monumentally successful 1997 film *Titanic* sparked new, passionate interest in the *Titanic's* story among people all over the world.

51

The Great Chicago Fire and Peshtigo Forest Fire

Chicago, Illinois	**Peshtigo, Wisconsin**
October 8–10, 1871	October 8, 1871
300 Dead	1,502 Dead

A terrible calamity is impending over the City of Chicago! More I cannot say; more I dare not utter.

—Author George Francis Train, lecturing in Chicago the night before the fire started

Some of the scenes from the Great Chicago Fire were truly horrifying, including some moments that must have scarred the psyches of the survivors for life.

One story, as related by Chicago visitor Alexander Frear, in Jay Robert Nash's *Darkest Hours,* is abominable. A little girl runs screaming down the street, her long blond hair trailing behind her; her tresses completely on fire like a long cape of flame. As she passes by the Sherman House Hotel, a man whose intentions were surely noble and good, thought to douse the fire by throwing a full glass of liquor on the little girl. The alcohol ignited (of course) and in an instant, the hapless child was covered from head to toe in a bright blue flame. Frear did not stay to watch her burn to death.

The fire drove some people insane; it drove others to robbery and looting. One woman tossed a bundle of clothes out her second-story window only to see a stranger catch it and run away. The woman's baby was in the bundle. The woman and her sons chased the man through the fire but could not catch him. Leaning on a bridge railing and screaming in emotional agony, she looked down and saw her child on a pile of cotton bales where the robber had hastily tossed him. Mother and child were later reunited, and survived.

The Great Chicago Fire started in the barn of Mrs. Patrick O'Leary on DeKoven Street on Chicago's West Side around 9:00 P.M. on Sunday, October 8, 1871. Although the story of Mrs. O'Leary's cow kicking over a coal oil-filled lantern has become part of American mythology, it has never been confirmed that the fire started in this manner. Several stories circulated after the fire about how it had begun and that was only one of them. Smoking hobos carelessly discarding their cigarettes were blamed, as was a visitor to the O'Leary home going to the barn for fresh milk and accidentally dropping a candle.

Whatever the real cause, the fire began to spread immediately, and, within minutes, several houses were burning. It was not long before the entire West Side of Chicago was engulfed in flames.

This devastating fire ended up burning for two days. It consumed almost four square miles of Chicago, killed upward of 300 people, left 90,000 people homeless, burned to the ground almost eighteen thousand buildings, and did close to $200 million in damages—in 1871 dollars. Sixty insurance companies ultimately went bankrupt from the claims.

There are several reasons why the fire spread so quickly and did such an enormous amount of damage, not the least of which is that almost everything in Chicago was made of wood. Even the sidewalks. One survivor recalled seeing the entire ground aflame, and described it as a "sea of fire." Strong winds fed the flames and allowed the inferno to move quickly from building to building, block to block, until it seemed to Chicagoans that the whole world was on fire.

Another factor was the lack of water, the woefully inadequate fire-fighting equipment, and the fact that there were only two hundred firefighters for the entire population of Chicago. The main water-pumping station for the North Side was destroyed by the fire, thus rendering the fire trucks that were available useless. There was always the lake, but there was not enough time, and it was too far away.

Thousands of people immersed themselves in the lake, however, to escape the searing, three-thousand-degree heat roasting the city alive.

Finally, early in the morning of the tenth, the wind died down and it started to rain. The fire eventually died out and the survivors walked among the ruins, dazed and in shock. Some were never right again. There was unimaginable destruction and thousands of burn victims everywhere. One of the most horrible fires in American history was over, but the scars would last for centuries.

In one awful instant a great flame shot up in the western heavens, and, in countless fiery tongues, struck downward into the village, piercing every object that stood in the town like a red-hot bolt.

—A Peshtigo survivor

On the same day as the Great Chicago Fire, Peshtigo, Wisconsin, was devastated by a forest fire that would go down in history as the worst of all time. Some historical sources suggest that cinders and sparks from the Chicago fire started the Peshtigo forest fire, but the area had been extremely dry for quite some time and small fires had been breaking out for most of the fall. Railroad workers who were clearing land to lay track may have started the conflagration.

The Peshtigo fire burned to the ground 1.28 million acres of forest and did close to $200 million in damage—the same amount as done by the Great Chicago Fire (again, in 1871 dollars). The fire incinerated seventeen towns and the blaze was so intense that some survivors described it as a "fire tornado." Everything burned, including bricks and lawns. The ambient temperature in Peshtigo during the fire was so high that some people actually burst into flames and even houses exploded. As in Chicago, a heavy wind fanned and spread the flames. In one impossible sight, a house was lifted one hundred feet off the ground by the heavy winds, then exploded into flames above the heads of the people staring incredulously up at the astonishing spectacle.

Peshtigo did not get the attention it deserved in 1871, and it has not gotten the attention it deserves during the past 130 years. Even its federal aid was delayed, with almost all resources going to Chicago for rebuilding and cleanup. Michigan's governor had to plead with his own citizenry not to send money and supplies to Chicago, but to send it to him to help the Peshtigo survivors.

The Chicago Fire was caused by reckless construction practices, inadequate fire-fighting personnel and equipment, and bad luck. The Peshtigo fire, which took place on the same day and at almost at the same time, was likely caused by bad weather and, apparently, carelessness with fire.

They both resulted in incredible devastation but Chicago rebuilt itself and now thrives. Reportedly, the woods of Peshtigo are still what Nash describes as a "barren wasteland." There is a Peshtigo Fire Museum located in a former church building. It is open from nine to five daily after Memorial Day; admission is free.

52

The Sinking of the *Toya Maru*

HAKODATE HARBOR, JAPAN

September 26, 1954

1,155 Dead

I felt a terrific lurch. The floor listed about 45 degrees and water began pouring into the ship. In the dark, everyone was thrown together. Some were pushed over, some were stepped on. They were screaming and shouting in the dark. It was like a hell on earth.

—Kaichiki Yamakazi, a *Toya Maru* survivor

The *Toya Maru* is Japan's *Titanic*, except that, unlike the *Titanic*, the Japanese train ferry did not sink in the middle of the ocean, but rather in a harbor; and it wasn't an iceberg that sank her, but an even more powerful force of nature, a typhoon.

The death toll of the *Toya Maru* disaster—1,155—is only slightly less than that of the *Titanic*'s 1,512, and it ranks as one of the worst ship disasters of all time.

The Tsuguru Strait separates the Japanese islands of Honshū and Hokkaidō and there is busy ferry traffic between Aomori on Honshū, and Hakodate on Hokkaidō. The *Toya Maru* was a train car and passenger ferry that shuttled across the seventy-mile-wide Tsuguru Strait. The ship was a big, boxy vessel that could hold nineteen fifteen-ton boxcars (there were twelve on board the day she sank), plus 1,209 passengers and 163 crew and support personnel, for a total of 1,372 persons (1,394 when the ferry carried sleeping cars).

The *Toya Maru* was a workhorse vessel whose design and weight made her somewhat prone to listing, even in calm seas. She was definitely not built to withstand a typhoon. In addition, the ferry was designed so that there was no way to prevent water from storms and high waves from entering the train deck of the ferry, adding instability and contributing to her tendency to list in rocky waters.

The typhoon that sank the *Toya Maru*, christened by the Japanese authorities Typhoon No. 15, was born either in the Pacific Ocean or the East China Sea. It hit the southern tip of Japan's southernmost island, Kyūshū, at 1:00 A.M. on September 26, 1954. It moved beyond Kyūshū, traveling northeast along Japan's western coast, past Hiroshima, Toyama Bay, and the small island of Niigata, speeding along at forty miles per hour, covering the one-thousand-mile distance from Kyūshū to Japan's northernmost island, Hokkaidō, in just under a day. Typhoon No. 15 arrived at Hokadate harbor at midnight, approximately five and half hours after the *Toya Maru* had set sail from Hokadate, heading for Aomori on Honshū.

The *Toya Maru*'s master (captain) had been informed of the arrival of the typhoon and yet made the decision to leave berth, almost fully loaded with trains and passengers. An investigation into the accident determined that this decision was "professional negligence in seamanship."

The ship launched with 1,314 persons on board. Only 159 were rescued and survived. Of the 1,155 that died, 1,041 were passengers, 73 were crew members, and 41 were other people on board at the time. Several hundred bodies washed ashore; hundreds more were lost in the water and never recovered.

Shortly after leaving her berth at around 6:40 P.M., the *Toya Maru* was battered by gale-force winds and high waves. It was obvious to the master that it was too dangerous to sail, so he made the decision to drop anchor and ride out the storm on the water rather than attempt to return to Hokadate harbor. He dropped anchor a minute past seven. This turned out to be a bad decision, although, by that time, it is doubtful that the ship would have been able to return safely even if the master had tried.

The violent waves caused some of the train cars to break loose from their moorings, slide across the deck, and crush several passengers. While the ship was anchored in the harbor, water got into the lower decks compartments and rendered the engines inoperable. The captain had been attempting to maintain some semblance of stability using the engines and the rudder, but once the water shut them down, there was nothing anyone could do to save the *Toya Maru*.

The ferry began to take on water, which weighed down the vessel and caused her to touch the bottom of the harbor.

A short time later, the *Toya Maru* capsized.

Included in the passenger death toll were more than 50 Americans. These included members of the United States 1st Cavalry Division transferring from Hokkaidō to Honshū, along with members of their families. Also lost were an executive with the Max Factor Cosmetics company and a YMCA secretary from Ohio.

Throughout Japan, 1,130 vessels were damaged, destroyed, or sunk by Typhoon No.15. Several other cargo ferries out of Hakodate sank, including the *Tokachi Maru*, the *Kitami Maru*, the *Hidaka Maru*, and the *Seikan Maru No. 11*. These sinkings resulted in the deaths of 275 crew members, in addition to the death toll from the *Toya Maru*.

In an official investigation, the Hakodate Local Marine Accidents Inquiry Agency determined that the master had been guilty of negligence, and it also acknowledged that the design of the ship, with its inability to shut out incoming water on the train decks, was a contributing factor to the disaster.

53

The 1906 Courrières Mine Explosion

Courrières, France

March 10, 1906

1,099 Dead

He that diggeth a pit shall fall into it. —Ecclesiastes 10:8

Only thirty-nine days after this most tragic of disasters, the eyes of the world would turn to San Francisco, California, and that city's devastating 8.3 magnitude earthquake, leaving to the people of Courrières, France, the burden of mourning the 1,060 miners and 39 others lost in their terrible mine explosion.

The coal mines of northern France stretch the length of that country's Pas de Calais region, the area that lies near the borders of Belgium and Germany. These mines are deep and widespread and they lie beneath the soil of France like subterranean warehouses of millennia-old riches. The French have worked for decades tunneling out these deposits, and there are mine entrances scattered throughout the Pas de Calais region, as far north as Lens, and as far south as Verdun.

Mining coal is one of the most dangerous endeavors of man. As an occupation, it is dirty, exhausting, and perilous, as well as being able to turn deadly in seconds.

One of the biggest worries of miners (after a tunnel collapse, of course) is a coal dust explosion.

A 1992 report, published by the United Nations University Press titled *Industrial Pollution in Japan,* stated the following regarding coal dust explosions:

> [C]oal-dust explosions . . . present a particular problem, because coal dust is something that is produced at every point in the mining process and accumulates, through the movement of air and the transportation of coal, on the floors, walls, and ceilings of the mine, all the way from the mine entrance to the deepest shafts. Therefore, when a small explosion occurs somewhere in the mine, it is followed by a chain reaction fuelled by the coal dust, and the resulting explosion envelops the entire mine infrastructure.
>
> [C]oal-dust explosions are the worst type of explosion because there is a great amount of carbon monoxide produced . . . Coal dust, being a solid rather than a gas, does not burn completely, and high-density coal-dust clouds can be formed. This prevents adequate air circulation, contributing to the production of carbon monoxide. Even if a coal-dust explosion does not spread throughout the length and breadth of the mine, the resulting carbon monoxide gas does in fact spread in this way and all the workers are poisoned.[1]

The morning shift started early in the mines; by seven o'clock, the men were already in the tunnels. The roster of men heading below ground for the day's work was enormous: 1,795 men, each in a hard hat, and each never expecting that this day might be his last in the mines. Almost as though fate stayed its hand until all the men were underground, shortly after seven, there was an enormous coal dust explosion at the entrance to the mine in Courrières.

What caused the explosion? Even now, almost a century later, there is no definitive answer. Was it an electrical short? Some kind of spark that ignited the flammable dust? No one knows. What is known is that the explosion blew heavy coal cars and equipment out of the mouth of the tunnel, belched enormous flames, and blew the roof off the duty shack nearby. Anyone in the path of these deadly missiles was killed, including 98 horses.

The reason for the explosion, however, was the last thing on the minds of both the trapped workers and their families, who quickly became desperate for news. Some of the workers who were not too far down the tunnel at Courrières were pulled from the debris, but many of these men were gravely burned and did not survive. Others, who were near entrances elsewhere in the tunnel complex, managed to flee to safety.

At Courrières, the digging began immediately. Progress was slowed greatly by the accumulation of deadly carbon monoxide gases that was building up following the explosion. Nonetheless, those on the surface worked feverishly to save those they could. A total of 735 men survived; 60 percent of that day's crew perished.

The scene was madness. More than a thousand family members and friends had gathered at the Courrières site to wait for word on their loved ones. The police had to be brought in to keep everybody back so the rescue teams could work.

One man, Sylvestre, was having none of it. His brother was a miner and he broke through the lines of police officers and raced into the mine to look for his brother. Sylvestre and his brother both died that day, but it is not known if they died together.

The efforts to rescue everyone turned out to be futile. One of the mining supervisors determined that it would take at least a week to dig out the tunnels enough to rescue the many hundreds of men trapped below. A week in a cave filled with carbon monoxide fumes and no food or water was an unequivocal death sentence. And thus it was for the 1,060 men lost that day.

Carbon monoxide poisoning is deceptive. In the United Nations University Press report, it states that the poisonous carbon monoxide gas replaces the oxygen in the blood which, if not halted, can lead to death. If a victim is placed in fresh air, the body will replace the lost oxygen, but only if the body does not use it up for other activity. "Therefore," the report states, "the most basic rule in mine rescue work is to prohibit walking and other bodily exercise, and this means that very careful attention must be given to people who look as if they are perfectly healthy."[2]

One mine worker who managed to escape returned fourteen times into the mine, each time bringing out an injured coworker. He seemed fine, and yet the carbon monoxide was doing its sinister work and the strenuous exertion of carrying out miners was depleting any new oxygen his body was making. This finally took its toll, and on his fifteenth trip into the mines, the heroic man died of asphyxiation from carbon monoxide poisoning.

The Courrières explosion was the worst mining accident in France's history and one of the all-time worst industrial accidents in history.

[1] Jun Ui, *Industrial Pollution in Japan,* ch. 5, sec. III.

[2] Ibid., ch. 5, sec VII.

54

The Sinking of the *Empress of Ireland*

The St. Lawrence River

May 29, 1914

1,024 Dead

Empress of Ireland was stopped off Father Point in the fog. She was struck amidships by the collier Storstad. Ship gone.

—Capt. Henry Kendall, R.N.R.

The Empress of Ireland and her sister ship, the *Empress of Britain,* were both built by Fairfield Shipbuilding & Engineering in Glasgow, Scotland, in 1905. The *Empress of Ireland* was officially launched for service and made her maiden voyage on January 10, 1906.

The *Empress* weighed 14,191 gross tons, and measured 570 feet by 66 feet. She was about two-thirds as long as the *Titanic* (chapter 50).

She bore quadruple-expansion twin screw engines that had a maximum speed of between eighteen to twenty knots, and she regularly made round-trips between Quebec and Liverpool for the Canadian Pacific Line.

Her passenger capacity was 310 in first class, 350 in second class, and 800 in third class. The *Empress of Ireland* had lifeboat capacity for 1,968 persons. The ship's maximum capacity of passengers and crew was 1,860, which gave her an excess lifeboat capacity of 108.

The *Empress of Ireland* set sail from Quebec for Liverpool on May 28, 1914, at 4:27 P.M. with 87 first-class, 253 second-class, and 717 third-class passengers, for a total of 1,057, along with a crew numbering 420. A total of 1,477 persons were on board for her final voyage. She also carried one thousand one hundred tons of cargo and she was commanded by Captain Henry Kendall.

The *Empress* headed down the St. Lawrence River, and all was fine until sometime after one in the morning. At that time, the passenger liner passed Father Point, and the crew, on lookout with binoculars, could see lights ahead at a distance of approximately six miles.

The lights belonged to the Norwegian collier *Storstad*, commanded by Captain Thomas Andersen and carrying eleven thousand tons of coal. Almost immediately after they sighted the collier, a dense fog rolled in and completely obscured visibility. Neither crew could see what was directly ahead, and yet both ships proceeded on course without hesitation, although Captain Kendall did slow his forward speed.

At approximately 1:30 A.M., Captain Kendall suddenly saw the *Storstad* directly in front of them in the fog. The collier was dead ahead in the *Empress of Ireland's* path.

Kendall acted quickly, but it was to no avail. He shouted through his megaphone to Captain Andersen to go full speed astern. He then ordered his own helmsman to go full speed ahead, helm hard aport. He obviously was trying to steer both ships out of each other's path, but it was too late for such maneuvering. The *Storstad* struck the *Empress* at midships, tearing a huge twenty-five-foot-high by fourteen-foot-wide hole in her side. Water started rushing into the *Empress* at the extraordinary rate of sixty thousand gallons a second.

Captain Kendall then ordered his ship full speed ahead, hoping to beach her before she sank. He also ordered the passengers roused and the lifeboats readied. The ship was now listing heavily, though, from the forward thrust of the *Storstad*. Even if all the passengers had managed to make it on deck, the lifeboats would have been useless.

All of Captain Kendall's attempts to salvage his ship failed, and fourteen minutes later, the *Empress of Ireland* lay on the bottom of the St. Lawrence River.

Ship gone.

A total of 1,024 passengers and crew were lost. There were 453 survivors. Captain Kendall survived, as did Captain Andersen and all of the *Storstad's* crew.

The tragedy of the *Empress of Ireland*—one of the worst ship disasters of all time—was almost immediately forgotten. She had not had many famous people on board; she had been in service for eight years (unlike the *Titanic*, who had been on her maiden voyage); and the horrors of World War I, which began the same year, distracted the public from the *Empress* disaster.

Twenty days before the *Empress of Ireland* sank, her captain received the following letter from his employer:

From: Manager-in-Chief Of Ocean Services
To: Captain Henry Kendall
Date: May 9, 1914

Dear Sir:

In handing over the command of this vessel to you, I desire to particularly call to your attention to the importance of your command and to the value of the ship. I emphasize to you the instructions of the company relative to the care of your vessel and the lives of your passengers.

It is to be distinctly understood that the safe navigation of the ship is to be in all instances your first consideration. You must run no risk which by any possibility might result in accident; you must always bear in mind that the safety of the lives and property entrusted to your care is the ruling principal [sic] *by which you must be governed in the navigation of your ship. And that no saving of time on the voyage is to be purchased at the risk of accident.*

I cannot sufficiently emphasize my desire that these instructions shall be carried out to the letter. It is expected that all officers of your ship will bear this in mind, and will be specially cautioned by you, and, furthermore, that everyone on board will do their utmost to please and to gratify the company's patrons.

The *Empress of Ireland* still lies on the bottom of the St. Lawrence River in 150 feet of water.

Postscript

Is the *Empress of Ireland* cursed?

There is a true story about a diver who, a year after the sinking, made the 150-foot dive to the wreck in an attempt to score some of the reputed $1 million in passengers' jewelry cached in the captain's safe.

The diver managed to make it to the ship and swim all the way into the captain's quarters, where the safe still sat, undamaged and unopened. While trying to get the safe open, the diver's equipment was tangled up in the wreckage and he ended up trapped and unable to free himself. He drowned.

Did the spirits of the passengers of the *Empress of Ireland* do away with this cold-blooded grave robber? No one knows for sure, but the passengers' riches still sit undisturbed at the bottom of the St. Lawrence River.

[1] Gavin Murphy "St. Lawrence River Swallows Empress in Just 14 Minutes," 2000. www.nepeanmuseum.on.ca/empress.html

55

The Fire on the *General Slocum*

THE EAST RIVER, NEW YORK, NEW YORK

June 15, 1904

1,021 Dead

It is absolutely impossible to describe the horrible scene on the Slocum. The flames spread so rapidly and it seemed only a second before the whole craft was ablaze from end to end. Women and children jumped in the wildest manner to their death, while the efforts of mothers to save their little ones was the most heartrending spectacle I have ever witnessed.

—*General Slocum* survivor Reverend Julius G. Schulz, in *The New York Times*

No one thought to ask the woman's name. The deck was bedlam, and flames surrounded the small group of women who had formed a circle around the young woman who had chosen a rather inopportune time to go into labor. The soon-to-be-mother grunted and panted as she pushed out her new baby into what was looking increasingly like one of the circles of hell as so vividly described by Dante.

A couple of older women, both mothers, helped the birth along, nervously watching as the flames closed in, and as fellow passengers, some of them on fire, ran past them in panic.

Finally the baby was out, but there was no time for even cleaning her off. The new mother rose off her back, picked up her newborn infant, wrapped her in her shawl, and ran to the edge of the *General Slocum*'s deck. Looking around one last time, she then leaped off the burning deck into the churning waters, clutching her child to her with all her strength.

The new mother without a name had obviously believed she and her child would be better off in the East River than on a burning ship on which there would soon be not a square foot of deck that was not ablaze.

She made a choice. It is difficult, if not impossible, to know if it was the right choice. After the September 11, 2001, terrorist attack, people trapped in the upper stories of the World Trade Towers chose to jump to their deaths rather than be burned alive by flaming jet fuel. They knew they would die, but they chose the easier death.

Did the new mother make the same decision? Or did she really think she and her child might survive? We will never know, for the woman and her child were never seen again.

The steamship *General Slocum* was named for an American army officer who commanded part of the Union line at Gettysburg and later served as a U.S. representative from New York.

The *General Slocum* story, when told in sequence, sounds impossible. How could a ship that can be seen from two shores burn out of control, resulting in the deaths of 1,021 passengers?

Couldn't people have just swum to shore? Perhaps, if all the passengers had known how to swim, and if the majority of them had not been women dressed in cumbersome skirts and carrying young children.

A popular excursion steamship, the *General Slocum* was loaded with over thirteen hundred passengers—mostly women and children, all of whom had eagerly come on board one bright sunny Wednesday for a celebratory annual Sunday school outing sponsored by their church, St. Mark's Lutheran Evangelical.

As the ship set out into the East River, her big paddle wheels and high decks could be seen from both shores.

An hour into the journey a fire broke out midship belowdecks. It is believed today that a deckhand threw a cigarette into a closet where paint and hay were stored together. A crew member investigating the smell of smoke opened the door; thus creating an enormous back draft that quickly fed the flames. The fire spread rapidly. People begin to scream, and the crew, who had never been through a fire drill, decided that running through the decks screaming "Fire!" was the smart thing to do.

The crew reportedly immediately told Captain William Van Schaick about the fire, but he did nothing about it and continued his course down the river. People on the shore watched helplessly through binoculars as the fire engulfed women and children, driving many of them to leap into the water, where they quickly drowned or were grabbed by one of the ship's enormous paddle wheels and then mangled and crushed to death.

The captain still did not stop and, instead, ordered full speed ahead. He could have beached his vessel on Sunken Meadow Island, allowing people to flee the burning ship to safety. Instead, he stayed in the water and headed for North Brother Island, a few miles from the point where the ship caught fire. (The captain later claimed he was afraid he would bring the fire ashore and jeopardize lives and buildings if he beached early.) The *General Slocum* continued on, and the steady movement through the river fanned the flames and turned the ship into a floating furnace. New York City firefighters brought their equipment to the 138 Street pier, expecting the captain to berth the ship. We can imagine their shock when the *General Slocum* just paddled on by, her decks on fire, her passengers screaming and leaping to their deaths.

Some boats in the water tried to get close to the steamship, but within a short time, there were too many bodies in the water—living and dead—to approach safely.

On board, there was no hope of putting out the fire. The nylon hoses were either split open or clogged; the metal hose couplings were all rusty; there was no water supply with which to fight the fire; the life preservers crumbled when touched. The weak railings could not take the pressure of hundreds of people, and the thin wood broke, sending people into the water, to drown or be crushed to death in the paddles.

Finally, the *General Slocum* crashed into rocks off North Brother Island (the captain missed the beach) and some of the remaining passengers managed to get off safely. Later, the public and investigators were shocked to learn that every member of the crew, including the captain, had gotten off the ship and all had survived. Captain Van Schaick was arrested the moment his feet touched the shore, and accusations of neglect and callous indifference to their passengers rained down relentlessly on the captain and his crew.

Captain Van Schaick, who was blinded in the fire, was eventually convicted of negligence and sentenced to ten years in Sing Sing. President Taft commuted his sentence after a few years, but Van Schaick lived with the notoriety of being the captain who was responsible for the worst disaster on water in New York's history.

56

The 1888 New York City Blizzard

NEW YORK, NEW YORK

March 12–13, 1888

800 Dead

$7 Million+ in Losses[1]

Light snow, then clearing. Fair and colder.

—March 12, 1888, weather forecast for New York City

This is an occasion when money won't make the mare go.

—Wall Street businessman, in *The New York Times*

Snow for sale! Come early and avoid the rush!

—Graffiti seen following the blizzard of 1888

You call this a blizzard?

—A visitor from Texas during the blizzard of 1888

The show must go on. This is the sacred rule performers live by, and that included German opera star Ludwig Barnay.

He had been looking forward to his Monday evening appearance at the Academy of Music in New York. American audiences responded with enthusiasm and passion to his voice and he knew that the performance would be memorable.

Ludwig had walked to the Academy of Music from his hotel because it had been snowing heavily in New York since early that Monday morning and the horse-drawn carriages could not make their way through the snow. He did not mind the walk. He just made sure he kept his throat tightly wrapped and warm as he trudged through the snow to the theater.

Ludwig Barnay went straight to his dressing room and began preparing for his performance. He noticed that the backstage crew was smaller than might be expected for such a major production, and it occurred to him that perhaps the snowstorm was bigger than he had at first believed. True, the phones were not working and he had heard a rumor about a ferry being stuck in the frozen waters of New York Harbor, but he had seen people shoveling their sidewalks and some (but only a few) of the stores were open.

No matter, Ludwig mused. The show must go on, and tonight I will sing so gloriously, my audience will pay no attention to the ghastly, howling wind.

The stage director kept his hand raised above Ludwig's shoulder. When he was given the signal from the director, he gently tapped Ludwig twice on his left shoulder, his cue to take the stage.

Ludwig Barnay strolled proudly out onto the stage of the Academy of Music, in full costume, ready to sing. He reached center stage, turned and faced the audience . . . and the notes froze in his throat.

The auditorium was empty. Was this some sort of sick American joke? Ludwig asked himself. But then Ludwig heard applause—the sound of two or three people clapping—and he saw that there were actually a dozen or so people in the concert hall, scattered among hundreds of empty seats.

Ludwig just stood there a moment, looking at the row upon row of vacant seats. He heard his musical cue but did not begin singing. Instead, he bowed once, turned and walked off the stage. The hearty dozen New Yorkers who had managed to make their way through the thick snow to hear Ludwig Barnay sing were left, instead, with nothing but the sound of the ghastly, howling wind of the blizzard of 1888.

Rain changed to snow and began falling in New York shortly after midnight on Monday, March 12. There was over ten inches of snow on the ground by seven in the morning, and New York's snow total, on March 13, when the storm finally ended, was just under twenty-one inches.

When the snow at last stopped and the cleanup began, dead bodies were found frozen beneath the snow. Political boss Roscoe Conklin, who almost died in the storm but was found in time, gasped to his rescuers, "It's death out there . . . people are dying everywhere . . . I saw bodies sticking from the snow." A bread delivery man froze to death during his rounds. New Yorkers were stranded in paralyzed elevated trains until enterprising citizens found ladders and charged passengers twenty-five cents each to get them out of the trains. Equally enterprising New Yorkers sold stranded passengers homemade sandwiches *The New York Times* described as "indifferent" for another twenty-five cents each. Houses were buried; horses died in the streets; total paralysis throughout the place the Algonquin Indians called Mahatta (later, Manhattan) was the order of the day.

The 1888 blizzard was enormous, powerful, and in no hurry to leave. It stretched from Maine all the way down the east coast to Washington, DC, and extended west from New York City all the way to the Ohio border. It packed seventy-mile-an-hour winds and dumped massive quantities of snow. Connecticut and Massachusetts saw fifty inches; drifts were forty to fifty feet high; ships sank in the harbor; telegraph operators in New York had to cable London to reroute messages to cities in New England and elsewhere in the United States. Fire alarm systems failed. Electricity was cut off. The East River froze. Children stayed home from school. Businessmen headed off for work, turned around after a few minutes in the storm, and returned home to spend the rare weekday workday with their families.

The New York Times evocatively described one scene from the blizzard of 1888:

> *By 3 o'clock in the afternoon the Grand Central Station and its vicinity, which is usually so full of activity, presented a most dismal and melancholy appearance. The interior of the station and the yard immediately outside, where the hissing of steam and the clanging of bells is heard day and night, were as silent as the grave. Clouds of snow were driven into the immense station, whirled up to the transparent ceiling, and again fell softly on the long lines of trains, covering them with white palls and giving them the appearance of immense coffins of giants laid out and awaiting burial. No sound was audible in the great structure save that of the moaning of the wind.*[2]

The death toll from the blizzard of 1888 is estimated at 400 directly from the storm (freezing to death, heart attacks, fatal accidents) plus another 400 or so post-blizzard deaths. It was one of the worst blizzards in history and the inability at the time to forecast its arrival and strength led to more deaths and damage than would likely result today.

[1] In 1888 dollars.

[2] *The New York Times*, March 13, 1888.

57

The 1981 India Rail Accident

The Bagmati River, Bihar, India

June 6, 1981

800+ Dead

Beautiful Railway Bridge . . .
Alas, I am very sorry to say
. . . lives have been taken away . . .
Which will be remember'd for a very long time.

—William McGonagall

India's sixty-seven-thousand-mile railway system has fourteen thousand trains that carry more than thirteen million people each day. Many trains are illegally overloaded, or transporting passengers traveling without tickets. With this level of traffic, it is not surprising that India's railways suffer approximately 400 accidents each year, over 250 of which are caused by human error.

There have been many serious rail accidents in India, including derailments, head-on collisions with other trains, equipment failures, fires, and collisions with cars and buses.

In 1981, an accident in the northern Indian state of Bihar claimed the distinction—still unchallenged—of the worst rail accident of all time.

India, unfortunately, has a long history of tragedy and misfortune. Epidemics and famines are common in India, and natural disasters and bad weather, including earthquakes, floods, hurricanes, droughts, cyclones, and typhoons, are ubiquitous events on the roster of India's hardships.

On June 6, 1981, it is generally believed that bad weather and bad luck combined to cause the rail disaster in which more than 800 people died, some from the crash, some from drowning. However, there is still controversy today as to the actual cause of the accident and the actual number of deaths.

The Bagmati River snakes through northern India into Nepal and there are several railroad bridges along its length. On the day of the accident, a ten-car train was crossing a bridge over the Bagmati River in Samastipur, India, when a cyclone, or at least very high winds, struck the train and sent seven cars hurling off the bridge into the river below. The engine and two cars were all that was left on the bridge tracks.

Many authorities give credence to the cyclone story, although shortly after the accident, other versions of how the tragedy occurred surfaced, including a statement from the region's rural development minister. In the most commonly repeated alternate tale, the train's seven cars flew off the bridge after the conductor applied the brakes much too suddenly so as to prevent hitting a water buffalo that was sitting on the bridge's tracks.

Railway historian David Fry dismisses this theory:

> It is unlikely however that braking alone would cause such a derailment. The distribution of the forces incurred in braking a passenger train is fairly even. Each of the vehicles is individually braked and they are of similar weights. The explanation would hold more credibility if it had been applied to a goods train . . . with adjacent wagons possibly having widely differing axle loads and/or braking abilities. But with a passenger train . . . [each car] in the train is individually braked.[1]

Whatever the cause for the train's plunge into sixty feet of water, it is certain that many hundreds of people died, and that many bodies were never recovered. The terrain and the river itself made recovery extremely difficult, and Indian military divers, after an entire day working in the submerged wreckage, were able to bring up only 50 bodies. After five full days of retrieval efforts, the recovery total was only 212 bodies. Nonetheless, the train had been packed with passengers and many believe that the figure of 800 is probably very close to the actual number, and perhaps even a little low.

In the past two decades, India has worked to improve rail safety, yet the accident rate is still inordinately high. In 1995, 395 people died when two passenger trains collided. In 1999, 200 died in yet another head-on collision. Part of the reason death tolls are so high in Indian rail accidents is because passengers regularly overcrowd compartments and then come up with innovative ways to get extra room: they hang out of windows or ride on the roofs of the cars.

Another contributing factor to the high accident and death toll is the age of India's trains. Many engines date to when India was controlled by the British and some of the tracks and bridges are equally old and in need of repair.

India holds the notoriety of being the country where the worst train accident of all time occurred. Considering the rate of accidents in India caused by human error, added to the accidents caused by equipment failure, it is likely that if the death toll from the 1981 Bihar accident is ever exceeded, it will be in another rail accident in India.

[1] Quoted on danger-ahead.railfan.net/accidents/samastipur/home.html.

58

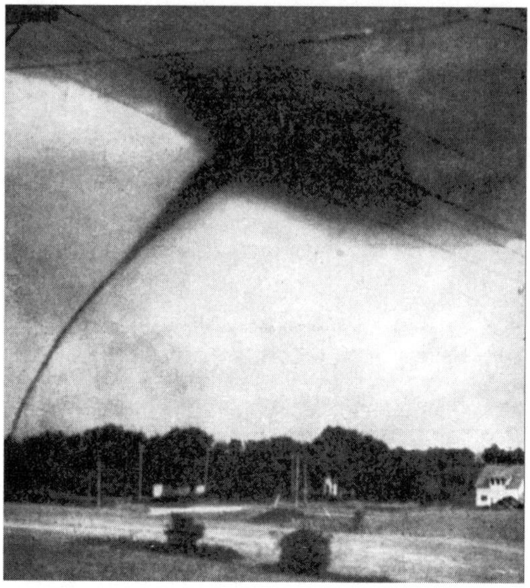

The Tristate Tornadoes

MISSOURI, ILLINOIS, INDIANA

March 18, 1925

689+ Dead[1]

$500 Million+ in Damages[2]

Guess it's gonna storm, Jim.

—Railroad worker T. H. Phillips, to his helper Jim

"Boy, this apple pie is good," Lemley thought to himself as he took another bite. He was seated on his favorite stool in his favorite restaurant in Poplar Bluff, Missouri, having a piece of apple pie after lunch. He hated to rush his dessert, but he wanted to get back to work before it started raining. The sky had looked a little funny when he went into the restaurant, and he figured they'd be getting some rain, and possibly a thunderstorm, in fairly short order.

Suddenly, just as Lemley lifted a piece of pie to his mouth, the roof of the restaurant flew off into the sky in one single piece. Before Lemley could even register what a bizarre experience it was to be sitting in a roofless restaurant with a slab of apple pie suspended in front of his mouth, all four walls of the restaurant vanished—just flew away, looking like giant playing cards hurled by a Goliath—and he was knocked to the floor. Lemley could see the front wall of the restaurant fly away to the east, the double glass doors banging open and closed a few times until the glass shattered from the stress.

Then there was nothing but the wind blowing through the suddenly naked restaurant. No one was injured, and, amazingly, all the tables were unmoved. Lemley got up off the floor and walked out to his truck. People were beginning to gather in the restaurant's parking lot. Lemley got in his truck and drove home where he spent the next six hours in his basement. He figured if he survived, he'd go back and pay for the pie later. He did, and he did.

Later, he spoke to a reporter about his ordeal. "The roof went off first," he recalled, "and then all four sides were swept away. I was left sitting . . . with nothing around me and a slab of apple pie in my hand. Then I got out."

The Tristate Tornadoes, believed to be the most damaging and powerful tornado system in America's history, were a series of at least eight deadly F5 tornadoes that raged at up to seventy-three miles per hour across a 219-mile path in three states in five hours, killing hundreds, injuring thousands, and leveling cities.

This storm was like something out of a horror movie. One schoolhouse filled with children literally exploded from the force of the wind. All the children inside were completely torn apart by the explosion.

The main tornado came to life in the early afternoon of March 18, 1925, in Ellington, Missouri. It traveled to Annapolis at seventy miles per hour, destroying 90 percent of the town upon its arrival. It then left Missouri, still traveling at over sixty miles per hour, and entered Illinois, where it hit Gorham, which was completely wiped out; Murphysboro, which was 40 percent destroyed; DeSoto, 30 percent destroyed; West Frankfort, 20 percent destroyed; then into Parrish, 90 percent destroyed. From Gorham to Parish, 541 people died, and 1,423 were seriously injured in a span of forty minutes. In West Frankfort, the Orient Mine, the second largest coal mine in the world, was caved in and destroyed. In Princetown, Indiana, the Heinz pickle factory was leveled.

The tornado then struck Griffin, Indiana, destroying it completely, before moving to the town's outskirts, where it completely obliterated 85 entire farms. On its way toward Indianapolis, it died out and did no further damage.

After the tornadoes passed through the towns in their paths, all communication was wiped out, water mains were broken, and all electrical power was cut off. Hundreds of people were buried alive and rescue efforts would not take place quickly enough to prevent many of them from dying in the rubble. Fires that broke out after the tornadoes also did enormous damage in some areas, finishing the destruction that the storms had begun.

Since these massive tornadoes had struck completely without warning, there was no time whatsoever to prepare or take shelter (as Lemley's story so dramatically illustrates), and because communication, water, and power were nonexistent after the devastation, relief and rescue efforts were difficult and, in some locales, impossible. Many of the bodies of the dead went unclaimed because the next of kin had also been killed. An especially poignant scene took place outside a grammar school that had been destroyed. The bodies of all the children who had been killed were laid out on tiny mattresses as the principal, who survived, tried to identify them. None of the parents came to claim them because they had also been killed in the storm.

The Tristate Tornadoes did unspeakable damage to three states in a very short period of time and once again dramatically illustrated the deadly, speedy, and indiscriminate power of the forces of nature.

[1] This is the official death count, but scores were also reported missing, never found, and presumed dead.

[2] In 1925 dollars.

59

The 1903 Iroquois Theater Fire

CHICAGO, ILLINOIS

December 30, 1903

602 Dead

Dead Fill Restaurant

The scenes in Thompson's restaurant, adjoining the theater, were ghastly beyond words. Few half hours in battle bring more of horror than the half hour that turned the place into a charnel house, with its tumbled heaps of corpses, its shrieks of agony of the dying, and the confusion of doctors and nurses working madly over bodies as they strove to bring back the spark of life.

Bodies were everywhere piled along the walls, laid across tables, and flung down here and there. Some were charred beyond recognition, some only scorched, and other black from suffocation. Some were crushed in the rush of the panic.

The continuous tramp of the detachments of police bearing in more bodies, the efforts of the doctors to restore life, and the madness of relatives and friends who poured in through police

> *lines to ransack piles of bodies, made up a scene of horror of which the reader has no conception.*
>
> —*The New York Times*, Thursday, December 31, 1903

The brand-new Iroquois Theater sat between Dearborn Avenue and State Street in downtown Chicago. The area was bustling this winter afternoon with an enormous crowd excited about seeing the famous song-and-dance man Eddie Foy in *Mr. Bluebeard.*

Children were everywhere. This day, December 30, was the day before New Year's Eve, and schoolchildren were on their Christmas vacation.

After everyone filed in, there were 1,830 people in the Iroquois audience, in a theater that had precisely 1,602 seats. More than 225 people stood in the aisles and in the back of the theater. It is believed that 1,000 of the 1,830 people in the theater were children. In addition to the paying audience, there were also 275 crew, cast, and workers in the theater, for a total of 2,105 people in the building.

The Iroquois Theater was thirty-eight days old, and there was still construction going on between shows. The theater's owners had all the proper certificates and papers needed to open, however, even with such egregious hazards as fire escapes with no stairs or ladders, no suitable fire extinguishers, no fire alarm, a sprinkler system that did not work, thirty fire exits of which twenty-seven were padlocked, seats stuffed with extremely flammable hemp, no asbestos fire curtain for the stage, and not even a single fire drill for the theater staff.

Yet even with all these perils, the Iroquois Theater shamelessly advertised itself as "absolutely fireproof." This was done deliberately to calm the nervous Chicagoans who were still alive thirty-two years after the Great Chicago Fire of 1871. It did not matter if it was true or not; it seems that as long as the people believed the theater was fireproof, that was all that mattered to the theater owners and managers.

The first act of *Mr. Bluebeard* went smoothly. The second act began with a group singing "In the Pale Moonlight," a song that required a lighting effect that gave the stage a blue glow. The electric arc light started sparking and the sparks ignited a hanging piece of gauze scenery. The fire was visible from the audience, but it was small and no one seemed to be bothered—at first. Stagehands tried hitting the blaze with sticks, which served only to fan it and make it grow. When the fire began to spread, more people noticed it and the tension level began to rise.

The production's star, Eddie Foy, who was backstage awaiting his cue, knew that a panic could break out if anyone shouted "Fire!" or began running toward an exit, so he ran out on stage half-dressed in his costume and addressed the audience. "Don't get excited," he shouted to the crowd. "Don't stampede; it's all right."

Foy then shouted to the crew to lower the asbestos fire curtain onto the stage. Since there was no asbestos fire curtain, the stagehands lowered a piece of painted scenery that got stuck halfway down. It was then that almost the entire cast fled the theater through a backstage emergency exit. The opening of this door created a draft that sent a blast of air to the fire, causing a blowtorch of flames to fly out from under the half-dropped piece of scenery, right over the audience's heads.

This started the panic.

Everyone began running toward the exits and the fire escapes. Ultimately, only 200 people actually died from asphyxiation or burns. The other 402 died from being crushed to death in the stampede for the exits, and the piling-up effect of the single staircase feeding into one small lobby area.

The fire department arrived very quickly, but there was little they could do when bodies were piled six high in front of the doors and in the lobby.

The fire was eventually put out. Then began the grisly job of removing the bodies. It is estimated that fire and rescue workers pulled two or three bodies per minute from the theater nonstop for almost three hours. Ten bushel baskets of money and jewelry were recovered from the bodies. Hundreds of the dead were children, and the Iroquois Theater fire would ultimately rank as the worst theater fire in U.S. history.

At first the owners tried to blame the audience for their own deaths, saying it was because they panicked and stampeded that so many people died. The theater was safe, they insisted, but violations and evidence of inferior materials began surfacing, following investigations by both the police and the media. The owners and managers were indicted but no trial ever took place, and it wasn't long before allegations of graft and malfeasance began surfacing regarding the Chicago building inspector, police and fire departments, and other government personnel and agencies. It is hard to imagine that a theater so obviously unsafe would be allowed to open unless somebody (and perhaps *a lot* of somebodies) was being paid.

As is always the case with mass disasters, the Iroquois Theater fire attracted those execrable exploiters without a conscience or a heart who descended upon the burning building pretending to be rescuers, and ran into the burning theater to steal from the dead. Deservedly, many of these thieves died in the theater, either from smoke inhalation, burns, or in the crush of panicked people trying to flee the building.

The Iroquois Theater fire caused a massive inspection of all theaters nationwide, as well as new, stricter safety, building, and fire codes. In an editorial, the *New York Herald* claimed that a fire of the enormity of the Iroquois Theater fire could never take place in New York. After the fire, however, half of all New York theaters had to be shut down for safety code violations.

And speaking of editorials, an editorial cartoon in the *Chicago Daily Tribune* on January 1, 1904, showed a drawing of a theater exit door with a huge steel hasp padlocked across it and cobwebs covering the top half of the door. No words were necessary.

The Iroquois Theater did not reopen under the same name. In 1904, it opened as the Colonial Theater, and operated until 1925, when it was torn down. Three years later, in 1928, the Oriental Theater opened on the same site and operated until 1998. Today, the building is home to the Ford Center for the Performing Arts, Oriental Theater. The Ford Center meets all fire regulations and safety codes.

60

Hurricane Georges

Antigua, Anguilla, Barbuda, St. Kitts, Nevis, Guadeloupe, Hispaniola, U.S. Virgin Islands, British Virgin Islands, Puerto Rico, the Dominican Republic, Haiti, Cuba, the Bahamas, Florida, Louisiana, Mississippi, Alabama

September 20–30, 1998

602 Dead

$5.9 Billion in Damages

When the eye passed over, it was silent. And then you could hear it coming again. It sounded like a tractor-trailer running down the highway.

—Puerto Rico Georges survivor Frank Vega

We're sleeping in trees like our animals.

—Haiti cattle rancher Clovis Daniel, who lost his entire herd to Georges

Ernest Hemingway's 150-year-old Banyan tree came down, a victim of Hurricane Georges.

However, all the descendants of Hemingway's six-toed cats survived the storm on Islamorada unscathed.

In early October 1998, the Associated Press reported on a group of schoolchildren in Key West, Florida, at Poinciana Elementary School, who shared their stories of making it through Hurricane Georges alive. One of the students remarked that the howling of the wind of the enormous storm made him think it was Halloween. Halloween is over in one night, however; the damage and deaths caused by Georges would be remembered in the Florida Keys and the Caribbean Islands for years to come.

Hurricane Georges was one of the most destructive hurricanes of all time, and also one of the longest lived. In fact, the National Weather Service, which is famed for its unemotional, matter-of-fact reports and forecasts, frustratingly dubbed Georges "the hurricane that just won't die."

Georges was born on September 13 as a storm off Cape Verde, Africa. Within forty-eight hours it had become a tropical depression, a tropical storm shortly after that, and then a hurricane on September 17.

It attacked the Caribbean Islands of Antigua, St. Kitts, and Nevis, first, then moved on to Puerto Rico, where it did major damage. Then it savaged the Dominican Republic and Haiti, hit the Florida Keys, and moved up into Louisiana, Mississippi, and Alabama. Georges wreaked havoc for ten straight days before dying out on the Gulf Coast.

Of the almost $6 billion in hurricane damage from Georges, $1 billion of the damage in the United States was insured, and approximately $1 billion of the damage in the Caribbean. The remaining damage consisted of losses that had to be funded either by the damaged city or through relief donations, or not repaired or replaced.

Georges made a lot of people homeless, including more than 100,000 in the Dominican Republic, at least 18,000 in Haiti, at least 17,000 in the U.S. territory of Puerto Rico, and 3,000 in St. Kitts.[1]

In addition, Georges did serious damage to the crops on the islands it attacked, and it almost devastated the tourist business in some places. In tourism and agriculture are how many of the people on the Caribbean islands make their living, so Georges's impact was catastrophic. On June 11, 1999, the Associated Press noted that "island nations [hit by Georges] had to come to grips with lost harvests, wrecked government buildings, lost tourist income and sudden populations of newly homeless."

There was over $1 billion in damage in the Dominican Republic, where 70 percent of the country's bridges and 90 percent of its crops were destroyed.

Puerto Rico was the hardest hit, with $2 billion in damages. A staggering 3 million people lost their power and water, and FEMA estimated that 33,113 homes were destroyed, and 50,000 more damaged. Puerto Rico's coffee crop was

75 percent destroyed; its plantain crop was 95 percent destroyed; 65 percent of its chicken population was killed in the storm.

On Haiti, bodies were still being found a month after Georges hit. Most of the deaths on Haiti were due to flooding and mud slides. For ages, it has been common practice for Haitians to cut down trees on the mountain slopes in the hills where they live and make charcoal with the wood. This may give them a livelihood, but it also sabotages nature's very effective system of having the foliage and trees soak up enormous amounts of rainfall. With the hills of Haiti so despoiled, Georges's torrential rains created deadly mud slides that swept people away and buried them alive before drowning them in mud. There were also $300 million in lost crops in Haiti from Hurricane Georges.

In Cuba, Fidel Castro made a conscious effort to spin the damage done to his country in a positive way. AP reported that "Fidel Castro seemed relieved in Cuba, where only five people were killed after evacuations to safe zones. 'The first victory was to reduce the losses,' Castro proclaimed." Yet, Cuba lost 3,481 homes and 60,475 homes were damaged. A total of 20,000 homes were completely flooded; there was major crop damage throughout the country; and 200,000 people were evacuated during and after the storm.

The United States had its share of misery from Georges. In general, the rainfall from Georges was between twenty and thirty inches wherever it visited in the southern states.

In the Florida Keys, there were ninety-mile-per-hour winds for ten hours. Almost a quarter of a million people were evacuated; three-quarters of a million people lost their electricity.

In the Keys, 340 police officers, supplemented by 700 National Guardsmen, were placed on duty to prevent looting and vandalism, and to assure hesitant tourists that everything was fine, so "Come on down, we need those tourist dollars." In the Keys, 1,536 homes were damaged and Georges spawned twenty-eight tornadoes.

Alabama experienced eighty-five-mile-per-hour winds, and twenty-five-foot waves on the immediate coast. There was severe flooding in southern Alabama and 177,000 people lost electricity.

Hurricane Georges was a category 4 hurricane that showed the people in the area it hit what living in a real horror story feels like.

Nevertheless, Hemingway's cats made it through just fine.

[1] Associated Press.

61

The Great New England Hurricane of 1938

LONG ISLAND, NEW YORK; THE NEW ENGLAND STATES

September 21, 1938

600+ Dead

$400 Million+ in Damages[1]

The facilities of this bank are available to those who suffered loss through the recent great storm. The First National Bank of Boston.

—Ad on the front page of the *Boston Evening Globe* the day after the New England hurricane

Man's New Best Friend

In Stony Point, New York, dams built by sixty beaver colonies saved three upstate New York highways from flooding in the aftermath of the Great New England Hurricane of 1938. The beavers even went so far as to cut down trees the night *of* the hurricane to strengthen already-built dams that were holding back rivers that would have wiped out U.S Highway 6, Johnstown Road, U.S. Highway 9W, and Route 17.

> In the forests of Vermont, New Hampshire, and northern Massachusetts the trees have been slaughtered as if by a mile-high giant hand plunging crazily through them and slashing with a half-mile scythe . . . Today the place is a grotesque waste of prostrate broken trunks, green tops and upturned roots flung about in wild confusion . . . The loss is officially put at 5,000,000,000 board feet.[2]

Depressed No More

Two million trees are a lot of trees, yet, the Great New England Hurricane of 1938, a.k.a. the Long Island Express, destroyed two *billion* trees[3] in eight hours on Long Island and in the New England states where it struck on September 21 of that Great Depression–era year.

Speaking of the Great Depression, this devastating hurricane effectively ended that economic crisis for much of New England. The storm did so much damage that it resulted in innumerable people being put to work to rebuild and repair, and it helped bring about a new era of growth and economic health. Depression-era wages before the hurricane were maybe $2 a day; they started rising after the storm as federal damage relief funds were sent to the affected states. The amount of work, for a time, exceeded the available workers, in a classic supply and demand paradigm.

The damage to the region's 20,000 miles of telephone lines and telephone switching equipment was enormous, and it took two thousand seven hundred Bell Telephone workers to repair or replace them all. The Work Project Administration (WPA) in Massachusetts immediately suspended government construction projects and put all eighty thousand laborers to work in the Boston area on repair and cleanup duty.

The Great New England Hurricane of 1938 was born on September 4 in the Cape Verde Islands off the coast of Senegal. It tracked west across the Atlantic at an unhurried pace for a couple of weeks, ending up slightly north of Puerto Rico on September 18. It then began to move much more quickly, reaching speeds of sixty miles per hour, a record for forward speed for an Atlantic hurricane.

The storm skirted the Bahamas and the coast of Florida on September 19 and 20, and arrived off the coast of Cape Hatteras ("the Graveyard of the Atlantic"), North Carolina, on the morning of September 21. It continued its northward trek, hit Long Island like a sledgehammer around noon that same day, and laid waste to Fire Island and the Hamptons. It then crossed Long Island Sound and struck Milford and New Haven, Connecticut, stretching as far north in the Nutmeg State as Hartford. It eventually moved north into Canada, but not before leaving behind a trail of death and destruction that is remembered to this day in Long Island and the New England states. (As often happens after cataclysmic storms, it wasn't long before the looters arrived. The night of September 21, after the storm had departed, Long Island citizens patrolled their streets and beaches, armed with clubs. The storm had done enough damage—they were not going to allow thieves to do more.)

The time the Great Hurricane took to get to New England seems long enough for reports and warnings to have been issued to people in the path of the storm. Radio stations did not give weather reports that day, however, as the hurricane approached. Most radio stations were broadcasting a speech by Adolf Hitler. The Czechoslovakians had recently invaded Germany and Hitler was making a bombastic speech demanding the return of the occupied area, the Sudetenland, to Germany. Radio stations felt it more important to broadcast Hitler than to warn of an impending major storm.

This storm was an unwelcome visitor to New England, and the stories of its power are astonishing.

As the storm passed New York City, its winds were so strong, it made the Empire State Building actually sway.

The storm surge from the hurricane picked up the Providence, Rhode Island, lighthouse and carried it away.

Mr. and Mrs. Livingston Gibson of Westhampton Beach, Long Island, climbed onto the roof of their house to escape the rising waters. However, the house itself was picked up by the enormous surge and carried across Moriches Bay, dumping the Gibsons unceremoniously on the Westhampton Golf Course. Mr. and Mrs. Gibson, three rats, and a snake all survived the trip.

Estimates as to the total damage vary, but the National Weather Service did publish a summary of the damage wreaked by the storm, and the numbers are staggering.

- 8,900 homes, cottages, and buildings destroyed
- 15,000 homes damaged
- Over 2,600 recreational boats sunk or destroyed
- Over 3,300 boats damaged
- 2,605 fishing vessels sunk or destroyed
- 3,369 fishing vessels damaged
- Over 600 deaths and more than 1,700 injuries

What is chilling about these damage figures is that they are low. Low, that is, when compared with the damage that would occur if a storm the size of the Great Hurricane hit Long Island today. Many professional storm watchers believe that if a storm the size and strength of the hurricane of 1938 struck in the same places today, it would result in the single greatest disaster in the history of the United

States. Long Island was very underdeveloped in 1938 and yet the damage was still over $400 million in 1938 dollars. Today such a storm would redefine the term *catastrophic.*

[1] In 1938 dollars. Damages would be over $18 billion in 2000 dollars.

[2] Michael Wynn Jones, *Deadline Disaster,* 123.

[3] This figure is from Arthur A. Francis, "Remembering the Great New England Hurricane of 1938," *Salem Evening News,* September 21, 1998.

62

The 1977 Tenerife Runway Collision

Los Rodeos Airport, Tenerife Island, Canary Islands

March 27, 1977

583 Dead

We are now at take-off.

—KLM Flight 4805 Captain Jacob van Zanten

There he is . . . look at him! Goddamn . . . that son-of-a-bitch is coming! Get off! Get off! Get off!

—Pan Am Flight 1736 First Officer Bragg, just before the collision

This deadly collision between two Boeing 747 jumbo jets was the worst commercial aviation disaster in history, and even though fog and bad pilot judgment were major contributing factors to the tragedy, this accident can also justifiably be blamed on terrorism.

Was there a terrorist or a terrorist bomb on board either of the two planes that collided?

Were either or both planes somehow sabotaged by terrorists?

Were either or both planes hijacked and then piloted into each other?

No to all.

But it was a terrorist's bomb that caused the collision nonetheless.

On March 27, 1977, a terrorist bomb exploded in a flower shop in the Las Palmas Airport terminal in the Canary Islands, injuring eight people, one seriously. At the time, KLM Flight 4805 was on its way to Las Palmas from Amsterdam; Pan Am Flight 1736 was on its way there from Kennedy Airport in New York, where it had stopped for refueling and boarding after taking off from Los Angeles. After the bomb went off at Las Palmas, and following the threat of a second bomb, the airport was closed and both planes were diverted to Los Rodeos Airport in Tenerife in the Canary Islands, landing within forty minutes of each other.

After a delay of approximately four hours, Las Palmas reopened, and both planes mistakenly taxied for takeoff at the same time. The KLM plane lifted off and the Pan Am pilot and crew saw it heading straight for them about nine seconds before impact. Even though the Pan Am pilot tried to turn left out of the KLM plane's path, and also applied full power to try and lift off out of its path, by the time he acted, the collision was inevitable.

The KLM plane left the ground and its landing gear and an engine immediately collided with the Pan Am plane. The KLM plane continued to climb another one hundred feet before the pilot lost complete control and the plane crashed and burst into flames about 250 yards down the runway from where it had lifted off. The Pan Am plane never left the ground, broke into several pieces, and burst into flames upon being struck by the KLM plane.

There were no survivors from the KLM flight. Sixty-one people out of the 335 on board the Pan Am flight survived the collision. (Seventy people on the Pan Am flight actually survived the collision but 9 were gravely injured and died later.) The total dead from both flights was 583, the worst plane accident in aviation history.

A lengthy investigation into the cause of this tragic accident concluded that KLM Flight 4805's Captain Jacob van Zanten was solely to blame for the collision. According to the final official accident report, van Zanten took off without being cleared; he did not obey the tower's "stand by for takeoff" command, and he did not abort his takeoff when he discovered that the Pan Am 747 was still taxiing on the same runway. Van Zanten was in a hurry to get back in the air: If he had waited much longer, he would have exceeded his allowable flight time and the flight would have been delayed or held over, causing great inconvenience for his passengers and problems for his airline.

There were several additional factors contributing to the accident, not the least of which were significant ground fog and the heavy Spanish accent of the Los Rodeos air traffic controller, which resulted in a misunderstanding, on both sides, of some words and phrases. The planes were given taxiing instructions that had them facing each other at opposite ends of a runway. The Pan Am flight was supposed to turn off the runway at an exit, but the captain could not see the turn because of the fog.

The result of all these mistakes and misjudgments led to one of the most horrible accidents imaginable. The only thing that might have made this worse was if the collision had occurred in the air.

The way it claimed hundreds of lives resulted in the development of new rules and regulations regarding air traffic controller language usage, taxiing instructions, and runway configuration.

As is often the case with cataclysmic man-made disasters, the precautions came too late for the 583 killed in Tenerife in 1977.

63

The 1947 Texas City Harbor Explosion

Texas City, Texas

April 16–17, 1947

552 Dead

$100 Million+ in Damages

For God's sake, send the Red Cross! The city has blown up!
—A Texas City telephone operator

"What if someone finds out?" the husband nervously asked his playful wife.

"How will anyone know? You don't plan on taking your shoes off for anyone, do you?"

The husband shook his head. Satisfied, his wife continued painting her husband's toenails with bright red polish. "You better not," she said teasingly. "I don't want you barefoot around anybody but me."

The husband smiled and nodded as he silently wondered where he might be able to discreetly buy a bottle of nail polish remover.

* * *

Rescue workers cleared a path as four men carried a torso into the morgue. The morgue was actually McGar's Garage, the only standing building large enough to hold the dead. The men carried the torso to a table and set it down gently. The hairy chest told them that it was the body of a man, but he was missing his head, arms, and legs. And buried in his chest, but visible, was a car key.

The garage/morgue was filled at this time with survivors trying to identify the bodies of their loved ones. It was not an easy task, since most of the corpses were terribly burned and mangled, making identification almost impossible in some case.

A woman approached the table where the torso lay and her eye fell on the key. It somehow looked familiar.

"Could you get that for me?" she asked a young man wearing a bloody apron.

"Certainly, ma'am." The attendant grabbed a scalpel and dug the key out of the man's chest. He handed it to the woman who looked at it quizzically. "I'll be right back," she told the young man.

The woman was found later sitting in her car in the driveway of her house, sobbing hysterically. The car was running and the key she had asked for was in the ignition. The headless torso was her husband.

"Look at this one," Janet's sister Amy said.

Janet looked down and saw a corpse with his face half blown away and the other half burned black. Janet was not the least bit shaken by the grisly sight. She had seen far too much in the past few days to get upset anymore.

"No, that's not Peter."

Amy started walking away when she suddenly heard a piercing scream. She looked back and saw Janet down on her knees, bending over the burned corpse's feet. When she lifted her head, Amy could see that the corpse's toenails were painted bright red.

On Saturday, April 12, 1947, the French freighter *Grandcamp* pulled into the Texas City harbor, carrying cotton, twine, equipment for oil wells, and peanuts. The *Grandcamp* had stopped in Texas to take on two thousand three hundred tons of ammonium nitrate fertilizer, a highly flammable and potentially explosive compound. Two berths over from the *Grandcamp* sat the U.S. freighter *High Flyer.* She was also in Texas City to take on ammonium nitrate fertilizer.

The *Grandcamp* was loaded over a four-day period without incident, but on the evening of Wednesday, April 16, a fire broke out somewhere belowdecks on the French ship, most likely from a carelessly tossed cigarette. At first, the fire was relatively small and the crew was hesitant to use too much water. Almost all of the cargo on board would be ruined if it was saturated, and since the cargo was their payday, they inadvertently let the fire get out of control. When the sun came up the following morning, a thick column of black smoke could be seen rising above the *Grandcamp*. By then, the port authorities had grown concerned, since there was a Monsanto chemical plant fewer than seven hundred feet from where the *Grandcamp* was berthed. Concerned about the fire spreading to the plant and its flammable chemicals, the fire department was called, and, as is procedure for a harbor fire, the *Grandcamp* was ordered towed out of port to a safe distance from the shore.

It was the right idea, but the decision was made *much too late.*

While waiting for the tugs that would hook it up for towing, the freighter exploded with such force that it registered on an earthquake seismic detector in Denver, Colorado, a thousand miles away. The explosion was actually heard 160 miles away, and all of the 227 people who had come to the docks to gawk at the fire were killed instantly. All the windows in Texas City shattered, as did half the windows in Galveston ten miles across the bay. Thirty-two city blocks were erased by the blast, and 2 planes flying a thousand feet above Texas City were torn apart, killing the 4 people onboard, including John Morris and Fred Brumley of Pelly, Texas.

But this was not the end of the disaster. In fact, the explosion of the *Grandcamp* was only act one of a terrible three-part tragedy. Within minutes of the freighter's explosion, the second act occurred when the Monsanto chemical plant exploded, along with three (full) oil tanks nearby.

The combined force of the explosive ammonium nitrate, the flammable chemicals in the plant, and the fuel oil in the tanks was described by one expert as akin to a low-yield nuclear bomb. Hundreds of cars were flattened in seconds, many with people in them. Metal was hurled away from the plant and the ship with such deadly speed that people were decapitated and dismembered if they were unfortunate enough to be in the path of one of these lethal missiles. Four brothers were crushed by a railroad car that had been picked up and sent flying.

Fire and rescue personnel, and military troops sent by President Truman, arrived in Texas City quickly and began doing what needed to be done—helping the wounded, picking up the dead, picking up the body parts scattered everywhere, and maintaining order.

But Texas City still had to contend with act three of this macabre play.

The day after the explosion of the *Grandcamp*, the Monsanto plant, and the oil tanks, the U.S. freighter *High Flyer* exploded, its ammonium nitrate cargo detonating from fires caused by the inferno of the day before.

This added to the nightmare and many Texas City residents fled the city. Some never came back.

It took years, and more than $100 million to rebuild Texas City, but rebuild it did, and today, when natives mention "the explosion," everyone knows what they're talking about.

64

The 1944 Italy Train Tunnel Suffocation Disaster

The Armi Tunnel, Balvano, Italy

March 2, 1944

521 Dead

. . . a reeking little tunnel . . . and every poisonous element of death . . .

—Charles Dickens
Bleak House

Early morning, some would call it the middle of the night, in Salerno, Italy.

A train station at four in the morning.

Though the sun had not come up yet, there was tremendous activity at the station as freight was loaded, passengers boarded, and the devious waited.

The majority of the legal passengers on this train were military personnel.

There was a war on, and Europe was manic with troop movements and cargo shipments, in addition to the bustle of routine civilian endeavors and travels.

At five o'clock, the forty-nine-car train—forty-seven boxcars and two steam engine locomotives—chugged slowly out of the Salerno station. (Salerno is on the southwestern coast of Italy, near the site of another massive tragedy, the eruption of the deadly volcano Mount Vesuvius—see chapter 34.)

The freight train was crowded when it left the station; within minutes, it was overcrowded. Hundreds of people without tickets climbed onto the train outside of the small town of Balvano as the train began its steep climb up Mount Armi. The train was supposed to be carrying mostly goods and supplies, but ultimately close to six hundred people also crowded into the cars.

Civilian and military passengers filled the cars, pulled by the steam locomotives powered by coal. The coal was extremely low grade, since all of the top-grade coal was being used in the war effort. It had large amounts of dust in it and did not burn cleanly, or efficiently. However, it was all the trains could get at the height of the war.

The train began its ascent of Mount Armi, huge columns of black smoke belching from its smokestack. The engineers knew there was a problem and that the extra weight of the passengers who had sneaked onto the train was making it very difficult for the two steam engines to pull the heavy cars up the steep hill.

The train reached the Armi Tunnel and managed to make it partway through before the engines failed to handle the load. The train's wheels began to slip and then the train came to a full stop in the middle of the tunnel.

What to do? What to do? The two Italian engineers immediately began arguing about the best course of action.

One wanted to stoke the engines with enormous amounts of coal and try to steam their way up the incline through the long tunnel. Once they made it to the top of the hill, he probably figured, the downhill leg of the trip would be simple.

The second engineer did not believe the engines could pull the overweight cars up the remaining miles of the slope, no matter how much coal was frantically shoveled into the furnaces. He wanted to shut down the engines completely and allow the train to roll back down the hill, using the brakes to stop it once it reached level ground. His plan was probably to then toss off the extra passengers who had caused the problem in the first place.

As this debate was going on, the furnaces of the train were still ablaze, and the train's smokestacks were continuing to belch prodigious amounts of thick black smoke—inside the tunnel.

This smoke was loaded with carbon monoxide.

The official definition of carbon monoxide is a colorless, odorless, tasteless, and toxic gas produced as a by-product of combustion. Carbon monoxide inhibits the blood's ability to carry oxygen to body tissues, including vital organs such as the heart and brain. It can do serious damage to human beings and, at high levels, can kill within minutes.

It is believed that the 521 passengers who suffocated to death in the Mount Armi tunnel that March day during World War II died within minutes. Some reports say within seconds.

From all reports, we can conclude that the carbon monoxide concentration in the air inside that tunnel was probably immediately somewhere between 10,000 and 12,800 parts per 1,000,000 (PPM). This is the level that can cause death within one to three minutes of exposure. Given this, as well as the fact that the tunnel was quite long, thereby severely limiting any possibility of ventilation, the people in the trains probably did not even know what hit them. Of the almost 600 people on board, fewer than 100 survived, only because they were in the farthermost rear cars, some of which were still out in the open air when the train stalled inside the tunnel.

Lower concentrations of carbon monoxide bring a slew of identifiable physical symptoms, including severe headaches, fatigue, dizziness, nausea, vomiting, and even convulsions. At the twelve thousand plus parts per million level, the passengers probably felt an overwhelming dizziness and an inability to breathe, followed by their passing out and dying almost instantly. Since it was very early in the morning and many of the passengers were overworked military men, it is a certainty that many of the people on board were sleeping when the train stalled inside the tunnel. For these people, death came as they slept, and they probably never woke up or were aware of what was happening.

The news of this disaster—one of the worst railway tragedies in European history—did not make it into the papers. Wartime censorship kept this terrible story quiet until after the war ended.

65

The 1985 Japan Airlines Flight 123 Crash

Mount Otusaka, Japan

August 12, 1985

520 Dead

Ah, it is hopeless. —Flight 123 Captain Masami Takahama

They did not know how much time they had, but they knew that they were doomed. The violent shaking, the terrifying ascents and plunges, the rows of dangling oxygen masks, the panicked looks on the faces of the flight attendants all added up to one thing: The plane was going down and it was possible that no one might survive the crash.

Of the 524 people onboard, only 4 did survive. They were found following a nightmarish search on a wooded mountain slope littered with smoldering wreckage and bloody body parts.

Many who didn't survive left behind final letters to their loved ones, words from those who knew they were going to die and who wanted to say one last good-bye to their family and friends.

It is amazing that the letters survived the crash, but many of them did—tiny, fragile pieces of paper that somehow managed to be there waiting for the team of white-suited workers carefully accumulating the belongings of the dead. How can one write a heartfelt farewell in a gyrating plane, the screams of the doomed a horrible reminder of what is about to happen?

We don't know how the writers did it, but they did. They found their final voice. Love is apparently deaf to the sounds of death.

For seven years, the aft pressure bulkhead on this 747 withstood 12,319 takeoffs and landings, flew through wind and rain, and endured the cold air as high as eight miles above the surface of the earth. For seven years, it handled the stresses of flight, and no one noticed the cracks. The rear tail fin of this bulkhead had been damaged in a bad landing in Osaka, Japan, in 1978 and Boeing, the plane's manufacturer, had repaired it and proclaimed the plane safe for flight.

Except that it wasn't.

Investigations revealed that the repair job did not even meet the standards of Boeing's own repair manuals. The faulty repair put too much stress on the metal skin of the bulkhead and it began to crack. And no one noticed.

It would take seven years for the truth to be learned, but Boeing's blatant disregard for proper repair procedures would ultimately claim 520 lives in what must be considered a preventable accident.

Boeing Flight 123 had 524 people—509 passengers and 15 crew members—on board when it took off uneventfully on August 12, 1985, at 6:12 P.M. from Tokyo-Haneda Airport in Tokyo, headed south to Osaka.

Twelve minutes into the plane's flight, at 23,900 feet and at a speed of 345 miles per hour, the crew felt an unusual vibration and heard a loud noise. The aft pressure bulkhead had finally given up and had completely ruptured, taking out all of the plane's navigational hydraulic pressure with it. From the cockpit recorder:

CAPTAIN: All hydraulics failed.
COPILOT: Yes, sir.
CAPTAIN: Descend.
COPILOT: Yes, sir.

Fifteen seconds go by.

CAPTAIN: Hydro [hydraulic] pressure is lost.
COPILOT: All lost?
CAPTAIN: All lost.

As the crew lost control of the plane, it plunged to 6,600 feet, with its speed dropping to a very dangerous 124 miles per hour, putting the plane at risk of stalling in midair. Using engine thrust, the captain managed to climb back up to 13,400 feet, but then it started to fall again, this time almost vertically.

As the plane plunged toward the ground, it first hit a ridge on a mountain, but did not crash into this first wooded crest. At this point, the captain can be heard on the cockpit recorder frantically giving orders: "Raise nose, raise nose, raise nose . . . Flap up, flap up, flap up, flap up, flap up . . ."

Three seconds after the plane brushed the first peak of the mountain, it crashed into the forest of Mount Otusaka. The plane was sixty-two miles from Tokyo, and the crash occurred forty-five minutes into the plane's fateful final flight.

Rescue teams were not able to get to the site until the following morning, because of its isolation and the fact that Flight 123 crashed at around sunset. Visibility at night in the mountains is almost zero, so the wreckage—and the plane's four survivors—had to wait until morning.

The scene at the crash site was horrific. Bodies and body parts were strewn all over, and corpses were found in trees yards away from the crash.

The four people still alive—Yumi Ochiai, an off-duty stewardess; a twelve-year-old girl who was found in a tree; and a mother and her eight-year-old daughter—had all been seated in the rear of the plane and had somehow survived the impact, as well as a night in the forest, with broken bones and other injuries.

The crash of Flight 123 was the worst single airplane accident of all time; and the second worst passenger airline accident. The Tenerife collision is the only accident in which more lives were lost, but that disaster involved two planes. (See chapter 62.)

Boeing admitted that the cause of the accident was its faulty repair seven years before the crash and accepted full blame. By doing so, the airline manufacturer prevented the survivors from taking it to court, and Boeing's insurance company handled financial settlements. Japan Airlines, Flight 123's operator, also accepted part of the blame—they agreed to an 80/20 liability split—for improper inspections and negligence.

66

The 1942 Cocoanut Grove Fire

Boston, Massachusetts

Saturday, November 28, 1942

492 Dead

If only those within had waited patiently at their tables and filed out in orderly fashion, there would have been few if any deaths, the officials declared, since the fire itself was not a serious one. The firemen at the scene described it as a "flash fire" in the decorations of the nightclub and they could have extinguished it quickly if they had been able to get at it.

—*The New York Times*, November 30, 1942

Stanley Tomaszewski survived the Cocoanut Grove fire, even though it was his match that had started it.

It was ten o'clock on a Saturday night and the sixteen-year-old had been working for several hours in the crowded, noisy, smoky nightclub, Boston's

Cocoanut Grove. This was one of the club's busiest times and the place was jam-packed this Thanksgiving weekend evening with World War II soldiers home on furlough, celebrating before being shipped off to Europe; locals out for a night on the town; fans who had attended the hotly contested Holy Cross–Boston College football game; and even visiting celebrities, including Western movie star, cowboy Buck Jones.

The legal capacity of the Cocoanut Grove was 460 people. This night, close to 1,000 people crowded into the block-long nightclub. No one, it seems, was turned away.

The Cocoanut Grove was decorated to resemble a tropical paradise. There were paper palm trees, plastic bamboo groves, cheap tropical wallpaper, cloth wall hangings and ceilings, fake leather booths, hanging loops of silk, and other clutter everywhere. Almost all of it was intensely flammable.

There were thirteen ways to get in and out of the Cocoanut Grove—in theory. There were twelve small doors scattered throughout the building, as well as the main revolving door at the front entrance. Nine of the twelve doors were always locked, however; and one door was completely blocked, leaving two small doors and the glass revolving door for egress. The building's windows were boarded over.

Shortly before ten, busboy Stanley Tomaszewski was told by bartender John Bradley to replace a lightbulb that had been removed by a patron in the downstairs Melody Lounge. The intimate downstairs lounge was dimly lit, but it apparently wasn't dark enough for the man who removed the lightbulb. Removing the bulb, he had plunged the corner of the lounge where he and his date were seated into total darkness. Stanley Tomaszewski had to light a match to see what he was doing as he attempted to install the new bulb.

That single match resulted in the deaths of 492 people. Within seconds, a nearby fake palm tree ignited and a wave of flame raced across the Melody Lounge's ceiling. The fire was then sucked upstairs via the cement staircase into the overflowing, crowded main room of the nightclub. Just as the bandleader raised his baton to strike up "The Star-Spangled Banner," a woman with her hair ablaze screamed "Fire!" and the panic began.

Since most of the club's doors were permanently locked to prevent people from entering without paying the cover charge, the majority of the people upstairs swarmed for the revolving doors, which quickly jammed with the masses of bodies all trying to get through at the same time. Firefighters later reported finding burned and mangled bodies six high and six deep when they removed the revolving door. While many people were burned alive or died from smoke inhalation (from the toxic smoke billowing off the flame-retardant booths), many were also trampled to death by hordes of panicking people.

We now know that the Cocoanut Grove was a death trap. In addition to its being severely overcrowded, there were a number of hazards in the club that contributed to the high death toll and resulted in new, stricter safety and occupancy laws being enacted in Boston.

The fire completely destroyed the interior of the club in just under fifteen minutes. By the time the firefighters arrived at 10:20, the entire building was a raging inferno.

Victims were brought to several nearby hospitals, strongly taxing the medical resources of the area. Emergency supplies of blood and sulfa had to be flown in from Washington, DC, and New York. Severely burned victims were placed on gurneys in hospital hallways until they could be treated. Very little treatment of the Cocoanut Grove's almost 200 burn victims was done on the scene. It is believed that airway restoration, fluid administration, and pain management at the scene (all standard protocols in use today) would have reduced the mortality rate of the Cocoanut Grove fire victims by at least 50 percent. The Cocoanut Grove fire changed the way burn victims are treated by emergency personnel.

The victims who were admitted to the hospital suffered from burns of varying severity, and smoke inhalation. The majority of the burn victims had burned body surfaces of approximately 13 percent, with the range being as high as 70 percent, with most of the damage on the face and hands. Hospital stays ranged from 1 to 143 days, with the average hospital stay being approximately a month.

By Sunday morning, all of the dead and injured had been removed from the nightclub. Tables, chairs, glasses, and personal effects of the victims lay strewn on the sidewalk in front of the club, washed there by the force of the firefighter's hoses.

In the ensuing days, Boston police also had to contend with the conscienceless vultures who descended upon the gutted building to loot the pocketbooks, wallets, and any other valuables remaining in the burned-out husk of the club.

An inquiry into the Cocoanut Grove fire revealed many fire law and safety violations. Club owner Barney Welansky, and others involved, ultimately went to prison for their culpability. (Welansky was sentenced to forty-two years in prison.)

The Cocoanut Grove was torn down in 1945; a hotel parking garage now stands in its place. A memorial plaque commemorates the lives lost on the spot.

67

The 2002 Egyptian Train Fire

Reqa Al-Gharbiya, Egypt

February 20, 2002

373 Dead

The smoke was coming at us and we started screaming and knocking on the doors and at this point the fire broke into the carriage, so we opened the door and jumped while the train was in motion.

—Survivor Mounir Gerges, to CNN

In chapter 22 of Genesis, God instructs Abraham to sacrifice his son, Isaac, on a burning altar as a tribute.

"Take now thy son, thine only son Isaac, whom thou lovest," God said to Abraham, "and get thee into the land of Moriah; and offer him there for a burnt offering upon one of the mountains which I will tell thee of."

Did Abraham balk at God's unspeakably cruel command? Quite the contrary. He got up early the following morning, saddled up his donkey, and rode off into the mountains to the land of Moriah with his son, Isaac.

Upon arrival, Abraham told the two young men who had accompanied him and Isaac on the journey to wait with the ass. "I and the lad will go yonder and worship," he told them.

Abraham then loaded a pile of wood on his son's back, lit a torch, and they headed off.

On their way to the place of sacrifice, Isaac, who was clearly no fool, decided to speak up. "Behold the fire and the wood, but where is the lamb for a burnt offering?" he asked his father.

Don't worry, his father told him. God will provide the lamb for the offering.

When they arrived at the spot God had spoken of as being perfect for a human sacrifice, Abraham built an altar, stacked wood around it, tied up his son, and placed him on the sacrificial pyre. Abraham then pulled a knife to thoughtfully kill his son before he set him on fire. Just as he raised the knife, God finally spoke up and told him to stop. "Lay not thine hand upon the lad, neither do thou any thing unto him," God commanded, "for now I know that thou fearest God, seeing thou hast not withheld thy son, thine only son from me."

God then provided a ram for Abraham and Isaac to sacrifice instead, and Abraham went home and was fruitful, for part of God's reward for Abraham's obedience was to multiply his seed.

This story is the basis for the Islamic holiday of Eid al-Adha, or the Feast of the Sacrifice, a four-day celebration. It is one of the most important holidays on the Islamic calendar.

On Wednesday, February 20, 2002, more than 3,000 Egyptians crowded onto a train in Cairo to make the three-hundred-mile trip to Luxor to celebrate the religious holiday with their families. The train's eleven passenger cars were designed to hold 150 people each, but reports from the police at the scene indicate that there may have been as many as twice that number of people in each car.

A fire on board killed 373 people in the worst train disaster in Egyptian history in 150 years.

The packed train left Cairo around 11:30 Tuesday night, February 19. About an hour and a half into the journey, a cooking gas cylinder exploded and sent flames racing through seven cars. The train did not have a dining car or any other facilities for cooking on board, and it was common practice for passengers to bring small stoves with them and brew coffee and tea during trips.

The blazing train continued flying down the track for two and a half miles, finally stopping at a small town about forty-five miles south of Cairo. It is likely that the failure to apply the emergency brakes as soon as the fire was detected contributed to the fire spreading as the air rushing into the moving train fed the flames. It was later reported that the the engineer had been completely unaware that a fire had broken out on board.

Once the train stopped and firefighters and police arrived on the scene, it took several hours to extinguish the fire.

The scene inside the train cars was grim.

Dozens of bodies were burned beyond recognition and piles of bodies were found to have melted into each other from the intensity of the flames. Corpses were burned into the seats—the clothes, seat fabric, and human flesh creating one enormous charred conglomeration.

Some people, perhaps as many as 40 or more, died when they leaped from windows of the burning train to escape the flames. Even that method of escape was barred for some, though. Many corpses were found trapped behind screens and bars blocking some of the train's windows. One twenty-two-year-old construction worker, Said Fuad Amin, leaped from a window when he saw a woman running through his car with her clothes on fire. Amin survived with only a broken hand and a possible concussion. The train had still been moving extremely fast when Amin decided to jump. "I thought I was going to die anyway," he later told Reuters, "so I jumped."

Some 65 people were hospitalized or treated for injuries.

The Egyptian government announced that it would immediately pay approximately $650 in emergency assistance to the survivors and the families of the victims.

More than one thousand three hundred trains crisscross Egypt, and for many of the nation's poor, trains are the only affordable way to travel. Tourists and the wealthy usually travel on high-speed, air-conditioned trains; the poor use older, slower trains that are often packed well above capacity.

There is a tragic irony in the fact that many of the dead were traveling to commemorate a religious holiday celebrating Isaac being saved from a death by fire. The 373 who died were not so fortunate.

68

The 1907 Monongah Mine Disaster

MONONGAH, WEST VIRGINIA

December 6, 1907

362 Dead

As fast as the bodies are removed from the mines they are being taken to the morgue and prepared for burial. After being placed in coffins, they are taken to an adjoining room, where a steady stream of people file by all day long. When a body is recognized by relatives or friends the information is at once given to Coroner E. S. Amos, who has been on duty since the first body was brought from the mines.

—John F. Cowan, *West Virginia Dispatch*

Of the 362 men killed in this, the worst mining disaster in U.S. history, only 1 man was not a miner.

A gentleman wearing a business suit and carrying a satchel filled with paperwork and cigars was found dead among the miners and their gear, buried in the tunnel along with everyone else.

The man was an insurance salesman and the papers he was carrying were life insurance policies he had been trying to sell to the miners on the morning of December 6, 1907.

One of the divisions of the Department of Labor is OSHA—the Occupational Safety and Health Administration. OSHA monitors workplace conditions and enforces safety regulations to help keep workers safe. Similar in focus and function is MSHA—the Mining Safety and Health Administration—the Department of Labor's unit that monitors the many mines in the United States.

Back in 1907, mining was a much more dangerous occupation than it is today, and workers were at a much greater risk of injury or death than they are today.

The West Virginia State Archives, in a report titled "West Virginia's Mine Wars," notes that "West Virginia fell far behind other major coal-producing states in regulating mining conditions. Between 1890 and 1912, West Virginia had a higher mine death rate than any other state. West Virginia was the site of numerous deadly coal mining accidents, including the nation's worst coal disaster."[1]

The following is from MSHA's contemporary study and summary of the Monongah Mining Disaster of 1907.

> At 10:20 A.M., December 6, 1907, explosions occurred at the No. 6 and No. 8 mines at Monongah, West Virginia.
>
> The explosions ripped through the mines at 10:28 A.M., causing the earth to shake as far as eight miles away, shattering buildings and pavement, hurling people and horses violently to the ground, and knocking streetcars off their rails . . . The mines were connected underground and were considered model mines, the most up-to-date in the mining industry.
>
> Electricity was used for coal cutting machinery, locomotives were used to haul coal, and the largest areas of each mine were ventilated by mechanical fans.
>
> For a time pandemonium reigned. Every local mine official was missing. It was impossible to fathom the nature and extent of the catastrophe, or to tell whether either mine was on fire or full of gas.
>
> Soon after the explosion, four miners emerged through an outcrop opening, dazed and bleeding but otherwise unharmed. The stunned survivors could tell nothing of the fate of the others still underground.
>
> Frantically, [volunteers] cleared away the wreckage at the entrance and tried to force their way into the mine. They soon began to succumb to the toxic mine air and had to be rescued themselves. The explosion filled the mine with "black damp," an atmosphere in which no human being could live. It blocked the main heading with wrecked

cars and timbers, and demolished one of the fans, which greatly restricted ventilation. Choking coal dust, rubble, and wrecked equipment impeded the progress of volunteer rescue teams. The No. 8 mine's huge ventilation fan had been destroyed, and a smaller fan was used to ventilate both mines.

At 4:00 P.M., moaning was heard near a crop hole, and a rescuer was lowered through the hole on a rope. About 100 feet below, he found miner Peter Urban sitting on the shattered body of his brother, Stanislaus, staring glassy-eyed into space as he sobbed uncontrollably. He was the last survivor of the Monongah disaster.

Exhausted volunteers found conditions in the mines almost unbearable, heat was intense, and afterdamp caused headaches and nausea.

In some headings, ventilation materials and bodies had to be hauled 3,000 feet over massive roof falls and wrecked machinery, mine cars, timbers, and electrical wiring.

The stench of death was barely tolerable, and became overpowering as the search dragged on. Searchers never lost sight of the fact that there might possibly be some men in the mine alive.

[Immediately,] embalmers [began working] around the clock in shifts. Caskets lined both sides of the main street. The bank served as a morgue. Churches conducted funeral services several times a day as dozens of men dug long rows of graves on nearby hillsides.

Disputes flared over identification of victims, and more than once, a body was claimed by two families. The 362 casualties of Monongah's coal mine disaster left more than 1,000 widows and children.

The Marion County Coroner's Jury, after hearing from numerous witnesses, concluded the victims of the disaster died from an explosion caused by either a blown-out shot or by ignition and explosion of blasting powder in Mine No. 8.[2]

It was later learned that an eighteen-car train filled with coal somehow snapped off a coupling pin, which caused the chain of cars to roll backward down a slope and crash into an electrical power line. The accident caused a short circuit that began sparking and subsequently ignited the highly flammable coal dust, resulting in an explosion. A similar accident, in which coal dust was ignited, resulting in an explosion, had happened the previous year in France (chapter 53), causing an accident that killed 1,099 men.

The Monongah Mine produced four million tons of coal a year, and as the MSHA narrative notes, the mine was "state of the art" for its time. The day of the catastrophe, the mines had been inspected by 5:00 A.M. and declared safe for work. And, truth be told, they were. But accidents happen, and it will never be known why the coal train broke a coupling. Was the coupling loose? Were the coal cars overloaded? Was someone not paying attention?

Regardless of the truth, the reality is that the coal train did break the coupling and 362 men died in this tragic, record-breaking accident.

[1] The West Virginia State Archives, the West Virginia History Center.

[2] Department of Labor, Mining Safety and Health Administration, part of a mining disaster exhibit found online at www.msha.gov. See the Web site for the complete exhibit.

69

The 1996 Saudi-Kazak Midair Collision

The Indira Gandhi Airport, New Delhi, India

November 12, 1996

349 Dead

I've never seen anything like this—so much death . . . I could not react. People were just too shocked to react.

—Rakesh Agarwal, a college student from Charkhi Dadri, in *The Washington Post*.

There is an old adage that says that much of what man does is either for God or money. Wars are fought in the name of God; lives are committed to the pursuit of money. Spirituality and material gain are powerful motivators. And sometimes they seal someone's fate.

On Tuesday, November 12, 1996, a Saudi Boeing 747 took off from Indira Gandhi Airport in New Delhi, India, loaded with over three hundred passengers who were traveling to Saudi Arabia to make a pilgrimage to an Islamic holy site, or to start a new job. God or money.

The Saudi plane took off early in the evening and was told by an Indian air traffic controller to ascend to fifteen thousand feet. At the time that the Saudi plane was climbing, a Kazak freighter carrying thirty-seven passengers and crew, was approaching the airport and was given instructions to descend to fourteen thousand feet.

The separation standards for flight are universal around the world: one thousand vertical feet and five miles trailing distance for all planes. Thus, the Saudi and Kazak plane would have been within the vertical separation requirements—barely—but the equipment in the Indira Gandhi Airport was not able to tell the controllers that the two planes were in the same flight path and headed straight for each other. The radar equipment the tower was using was outdated and did not include a transponder, which would have provided the controllers with this critical information.

An Indian official quoted on CNN.com (who declined to have his name made public) said, "It would have been better to have a transponder. If two aircraft are closing in on each other, it can't be seen on traditional radar."

At the time of the accident, the American company Raytheon was installing new radar equipment in the Indira Gandhi Airport that would allow air traffic controllers to be able to tell the altitudes of planes passing each other. The United States had not cleared the system for use at the time of the collision, however, and all communications and instructions were dependent on the equipment in use at the time.

After the crash, the government of India said that even though the new equipment had not been operational, its existing equipment was adequate and in good working condition. It blamed pilot error—specifically the Soviet pilot—for the accident. There was talk that the Soviet pilot had an inadequate command of the English language, and since English is the official air traffic controller/pilot language throughout the world, a communication problem could have easily contributed to the tragedy. The Kazak airline bristled at this suggestion and assured the world that its pilots were fully qualified and spoke fluent English.

In a six-month period in 1994 and 1995, the skies above India experienced three in-flight, near-miss midair collisions. The Indian Commercial Pilots' Association investigated the near misses and determined that the blame was due to out-of-date and inadequate air traffic equipment. On CNN.com, it was reported that "the pilots' association had recommended installation of state-of-the-art radar systems, such as transponders, VHF communications equipment and CAT II equipment, to aid landings. But the government had not done so, the group said. Indian Civil Aviation Minister C. M. Ibrahim denied that India's air traffic control systems and its equipment were outdated . . ."

Another issue raised was the fact that all Russian-built aircraft used metric measurements; Western-built planes used feet. This begs the question as to why there is no standard on something equally as important as the English language requirement.

The Saudi plane with 312 onboard was airborne for only seven minutes when it collided with the incoming Kazak freighter, with 37 aboard.

Investigations revealed that the Saudi pilot survived the initial impact and was able to somewhat control the plane's death dive. There was evidence that he deliberately steered the plane away from a village, crashing it in an empty field instead. "It's the pilot's mercy that he ensured the villagers were not harmed," said Jeet Ram Gupta, a lawyer from Charkhi Dadri, who witnessed the accident.[1]

Debris, bodies, cargo, and luggage from the two planes covered a six-mile area.

The Saudi plane dug a trench 180 feet by 15 feet deep in Indian farmland. There were dismembered limbs and body parts scattered all over the field, which was fallow but commonly used for chickpeas.

The two planes landed seven miles apart, and no one on the ground was injured in this, the worst midair collision in history.

A thirty-year-old United States Air Force pilot flying in supplies for the U.S. embassy in New Delhi witnessed the crash from a height of twenty thousand feet. "We noticed out of our right-hand [side of the plane]," he told *The Washington Post*, "a large cloud lit up with an orange glow, from within the clouds. The glow intensity of the cloud became dimmer and the two fireballs descended and became fireballs on the ground."

Following the fiery crash, firefighters, police, and people from surrounding villages rushed to the two sites, hoping to find and rescue survivors. Instead, all they found was flaming debris and body parts.

There were no nearby morgue facilities, so bodies were brought back to the airport and placed on blocks of ice in the hangars, pending identification.

S. S. Sidhu, a former secretary general of the International Civil Aviation Organization, told CNN that "internationally speaking, 75 percent of the cause of air accidents is human error. Mechanical or systems failures are only 25 percent."

This seems to be true in the case of this cataclysmic midair collision, although inferior equipment surely contributed to the catastrophe.

[1] *Washington Post,* Nov. 13, 1996, A01, and on www.WashingtonPost.com.

70

The 1974 Turkish Airlines DC-10 Crash

ERMENONVILLE FOREST, FRANCE

March 3, 1974

346 Dead

I didn't know it was a dead body . . . I thought it was something else falling from the explosion . . . It was a woman, although I could not be sure that it was a woman because she was completely smashed, completely broken . . . Her head was here, her brains were here . . . Then I ran to another one, and I saw the other woman . . . One breast had been torn off. She was dead, too, and completely broken.

—A French farmer, witnessing the DC-10 disaster[1]

Completely Broken

Of the 346 passengers and crew members who died in this tragic—and preventable—crash, there were probably no worse deaths than those of the first 6 to die.

The other 340 on board died instantly in a fiery explosion when the plane hit the ground outside of Paris at 475 miles per hour. Trees were severed and those remaining upright dangled with shredded clothes and dismembered human limbs. A hand was found holding a Paris restaurant guide. A single shoe stood upright on one of the plane's wheels. The parents of a young woman were told that their daughter's identity had been confirmed because the search team had found half of her head, but only half. Everything else of their daughter was gone.

The first six victims were subjected to the horror of falling from the sky and dying on impact, and they also had to experience a nightmarish free fall, still strapped to their seats, fully conscious and uninjured as they plummeted to earth.

This Turkish Airlines DC-10 was approximately twenty-five miles northeast of Paris and 12,500 feet in the air when a rear cargo door with a defective lock popped open during flight. The rear cargo bay immediately decompressed, which caused the floor of the plane's rear passenger compartment to buckle and quickly rupture. When the floor ripped open, six passengers, still strapped into their seats, were sucked out of the rear of the plane and sent plunging to earth. They were all probably aware of at least part of their final fall.

The fates of the passengers and crew of the Turkish DC-10 were likewise sealed, but they would remain in the plane.

When the rear passenger compartment floor was torn out of the plane, it ripped out all of the cables that controlled the plane. The plane was instantly transformed into a $20 million dead weight that was no longer able to negate the effects of gravity.

The plane crashed into the Ermenonville forest and ripped a path of death and devastation a half mile long and three hundred feet wide. The plane broke into several pieces; the people on board were savagely torn apart by the impact. The crash was so powerful, recovery and cleanup teams found only 4 intact bodies out of 346 people killed—and they were found three miles away from the site of the crash. The retrieval of body parts and the identification process was one of the most grisly and horrific in the history of aviation. Some of the workers were unable to deal with such a surreal and macabre sight and left after only a short time. The forest was drenched with blood and littered with human body parts over an enormous area. It is understandable that some people would not be able to handle working in such a charnel house.

The DC-10 Flight 981, had originated in Istanbul, Turkey, and was headed for London. The plane had stopped at Orly Airport in Paris for a brief layover. As mentioned earlier, this tragic accident was preventable. Two years before this crash in France, the rear cargo door of a DC-10 headed from Detroit to Buffalo had flown off during flight over Winslow, Ontario, in almost the identical manner as the door had on the Turkish Airlines plane. Luckily for the passengers and crew, the control cables, although severely damaged, had not been severed or ripped out when the door flew off. Through piloting that goes beyond the word *skillful*, the pilot was able to land the plane in Buffalo with no fatalities. All sixty-seven onboard survived the accident.

An investigation revealed that the door flew off the plane because of a faulty door lock. McDonnell-Douglas decided to replace the locking mechanisms on all identical DC-10s with a safer system, install a viewing port that would allow visual confirmation that the lock was in place, and post informative notices instructing airport personnel on how to properly engage the lock.

Nothing was done to the DC-10s except to post the instruction sheet. Moreover, unfortunately for the people on board the Turkish Airlines flight out of Orly Airport, the worker who closed the rear cargo door of the plane was Algerian and could not read the English language poster.

McDonnell-Douglas ultimately claimed that the locking mechanism on the door should have worked fine if Turkish Airlines had not been negligent in maintaining its equipment. Turkish Airlines denied the allegations and in 1975 a great number of lawsuits were quietly settled out of court, thereby preventing a full disclosure of who was to blame for the catastrophe. Granted, Turkish Airlines had a terrible safety record at the time of the crash, but the private settlements kept their maintenance and repair records out of the public eye.

The DC-10s were finally fixed, but only after the Federal Aviation Administration issued a directive that the locks be repaired properly. An FAA directive requires mandatory compliance; a bulletin from the manufacturer to airlines that owned and operated DC-10s (which is what was issued after the first accident) does not require compliance in order for the airline to continue to operate the plane, and is viewed as more of a suggestion. Until 1974, McDonnell-Douglas's suggestion to fix the door locks on the cargo doors of the DC-10 was apparently ineffective.

[1] Jay Robert Nash, *Darkest Hours*, 573–74.

71

The L'Innovation Department Store Fire

BRUSSELS, BELGIUM

May 22, 1967

322 Dead

$23 Million in Damages

[O]ne man was transformed into a living torch before my eyes as he hesitated to leap from a high window.

—Fireman Jacques Mesmans[1]

It was like a scene from a movie, although twenty-two-year-old Catherine Seydel had not expected to be starring in her own personal horror film simply by walking into a department store to try on some new clothes.

L'Innovation Department Store on the Rue Neuve in Brussels was one of the biggest stores in the country, towering five stories above the closely packed streets in one of the older sections of the city. In May 1967, the store was festively decorated with American flags, red, white, and blue bunting, and travel posters for American cities. If not for the employees and shippers speaking French and Dutch, the store could have been any American department store. On July 22, 1967, L'Innovation had scheduled a big promotion of American goods and manufacturers, which it had been touting for weeks.

Two months before the extravaganza was set to begin, at around noon on May 22, 1967, a fire broke out on the fourth floor of the store, and the panic began immediately. Shoppers started rushing toward the elevators, knocking people down, desperate to escape the fire. The fire apparently started when a gas cylinder exploded somewhere on the store's upper levels, but there was an immediate suspicion of arson, a charge that has never been proven. Fire broke out in two more places in the store almost immediately after the initial explosion.

L'Innovation Department Store was huge. At the time the fire started, there were at least two thousand five hunded people shopping, plus another one thousand five hundred employees, on the store's five floors. With this number of people, the number of deaths from the fire is blessedly small, considering how high it could have been. Yet "even" at only 322, the L'Innovation fire is the worst retail department store fire of all time.

The first shoppers to become aware of the fire were on the third floor; Catherine Seydel was in a dressing room trying on clothes. The shoppers could hear the commotion on the floor above them and quickly began to swarm toward the exits. Unmindful of what was going on, Catherine Seydel left her dressing room, probably to look at herself in a full-length mirror. That was precisely when her own personal horror movie started.

As she stepped out of the dressing room, she was carried off—swept away is another way of describing it—by a stampeding mob. The blouse she had tried on was ripped off her body, and she was unable to do anything but hope she would be able to escape.

The crowd took Catherine to an outside wall of the third floor where there were several windows, all of which, unfortunately, were locked. Another shopper smashed the windows open with his bare hands, and Catherine was able to climb out onto the ledge, where she waited, terrified and thinking she was going to die, until she was rescued by the fire department.

L'Innovation did not have a sprinkler system. It did have a fire alarm, and the store employed fifteen full-time firemen, but only two responded when the fire broke out and they tried to put out the blaze with small, hand-held fire extinguishers. They were not very successful.

As we have seen in many high-rise fires, when exits are blocked and elevators are inoperable, people climb out onto the ledges of the building. This happened in the Winecoff Hotel Fire (chapter 84); and during the World Trade Center catastrophe (chapter 46), people leaped from windows because there were no ledges on the building.

During the L'Innovation fire, many of the customers and employees did climb out onto the ledges, and many of them jumped. There were cars parked along the Rue Neuve and many of the people aimed for the roofs of the vehicles, hoping to break their fall. The ones that hit the cars did survive, although they were injured, some seriously. The ones that missed the cars and landed on the sidewalk died, choosing death from a fall over being burned alive, a decision many have to make in situations like these.

Some people were able to climb onto the roofs of the adjoining buildings and escape before those structures burned to the ground. Some hung on and waited until firefighters stretched out their safety nets, and then jumped to safety.

As the fire raged, it spread to the roof of the building, where L'Innovation had stored a large quantity of tanks of butane gas for camping. It probably figured they were safest on the roof, away from people.

The fire found the butane and all the tanks exploded, which was the catastrophic finale for the building and for many of those who died in the tragedy. The fire department was working to control the blaze, a classic urban conflagration, when exploding butane tanks were thrown into the mix, a development that proved beyond any fire department's capabilities.

The store was utterly destroyed, as were several buildings nearby on the street.

As in many disasters, there was heroism at the L'Innovation fire. One man who had escaped the inferno realized that there had been several children in the store who had not gotten out. He summoned the necessary courage, dashed back into the burning building, and, miraculously, made it back out again—leading and carrying several small children.

When the fire was over, the damages were estimated at around $23 million. This included the merchandise lost in the fire, as well as the structure itself.

It is likely that investigators and rescue personnel saw, lying in the cinders among the rubble and the burned bodies, many traces of red, white, and blue.

[1] Jay Robert Nash, *Darkest Hours,* 335.

72

The 1974 Midwestern Tornadoes

Indiana, Kentucky, Ohio, Mississippi, Alabama, Tennessee, Georgia, North Carolina, Michigan, West Virginia, Virginia, Canada

April 3–4, 1974

315 Dead

$600 Million+ in Damages

I went into the house and just then I felt the wind kick. We—there were seven of us—got down on the floor of the kitchen . . . then all the windows went all at once, you could hear them breaking all over the house. Then all I could hear was the wind. Mud and glass were flying around and hitting everybody. The rushing wind went on and on. All you could hear was the wind.

—A Xenia, Ohio, survivor[1]

The old woman sat in her rocking chair and stared straight ahead, looking nowhere and everywhere, perhaps remembering her younger days, perhaps not remembering anything at all. An Ohio National Guardsman crouched in front of her, his gun slung over his shoulder, his helmet under his arm.

"Ma'am?" he said softly. "Are you injured? Are you all right? Can you tell me your name, please?"

The old woman just stared at a spot on the Guardsman's collar, her eyes glazed and unfocused. She did not say a word, and her body moved, almost imperceptibly, just enough to make her rocker swing back and forth every so slightly.

The National Guardsman gave up, stood up, and put his helmet on. He looked around the immediate area and saw a Red Cross doctor a couple of houses over.

The Guardsman pulled a bright silver whistle out of his shirt pocket, blew a piercing note, and then repeated it three times, with shorter notes. The doctor looked up upon hearing the signal and the Guardsman waved him over.

The doctor picked up his bag and started walking toward the spot on the block where the old woman's house had been. As he neared the lot and got a closer look, he realized precisely what had happened. The old woman's house had been blown apart around her, the walls and the roof carried away by a tornado, the interior of the house reduced to mounds of rubble. In the middle of the debris sat the old woman in her rocking chair. She had been sitting in that very chair when the tornado descended on her house, and she sat there still, seemingly uninjured.

The doctor shook his head as he pondered the shock-trauma the woman was now experiencing and he wondered how he should treat her. Her house had disappeared around her as she sat in her rocking chair. No wonder she was unable to speak.

The doctor stepped gingerly over the broken dishes, furniture, picture frames, and all the other memorabilia that had once graced her home.

He walked up to the woman, crouched down as the Guardsman had, and looked into the woman's eyes. Nothing.

"Ma'am?" he began. "Can you stand up for me? Can you tell me your name?" Nothing but the slow, small rocks of her chair.

Later that night, the rocker remained where it stood, only now it was empty. The woman was in a hospital, hooked to an IV, and on a monitor.

All she had done for the past five hours was shake her head.

The series of tornadoes that devastated eleven states in April 1974 was the type of storm cycle that is just plain unfathomable. There is no better word for what struck the Midwest and South that spring and it is easy to imagine a resident of any of the affected states looking at the sky, shaking his or her head, and exclaiming, "This is a nightmare!"

A total of 148 tornadoes struck eleven states and Canada in an eighteen-hour period, the worst tornado outbreak in those states in half a century. More than 100 tornadoes assaulted these states in the first eight hours, and five states—Alabama, Kentucky, Ohio, Indiana, Tennessee—were so severely damaged they were declared disaster areas by then President Richard Nixon.

The storms began in Decatur, Alabama, at approximately 4:40 P.M., and ended in Winslow, Ontario, eighteen hours later, leaving behind cataclysmic destruction and a record for the books. The 148 tornadoes' path stretched two thousand five hundred miles south to north, and some towns were less fortunate than others were.

Xenia, Ohio, was one of the hardest hit cities in the Midwest; the tornadoes leveled almost three-quarters of the town. Guin, Alabama, also took the full brunt of the tornadoes, and when it was over, 100 percent of Guin was gone. Winds in these killer tornadoes were clocked at an astonishing 260 to 320 miles per hour. A typical F1 tornado usually carries winds of around 75 to 100 miles per hour. (See "Tornado Scale" chart.)

The people who survived the 1974 tornado disaster were either extremely lucky, or had done what they could to prepare for major tornadoes beforehand (which, admittedly, is very little) by building a storm shelter cellar either in their house or on their property, and going to it as soon as the storms struck.

Many of these survivors surfaced after the storm to find themselves in an unimaginable landscape of rubble and devastation.

The 1974 tornadoes were not the first to hit the area, and they certainly were not the last, but they definitely were the worst.

F4 and F5 Tornadoes on April 3, 1974

F5 Tornadoes[2]

Location	***Killed***	***Injured***
Indiana, Kentucky, and Ohio	3	210
Mississippi and Alabama	30	280
Kentucky and Indiana	31	270
Ohio	34	0
Indiana	6	76
Alabama	28	260

SOURCE: National Weather Service.

F4 Tornadoes

Location	*Killed*	*Injured*
Tennessee and Kentucky	5	6
Georgia and North Carolina	3	40
Alabama and Tennessee	22	250
Tennessee	22	271
Ohio	2	39
Kentucky (8 tornadoes)	24	623
Indiana (6 tornadoes)	36	702
Georgia (2 tornadoes)	15	84
Alabama	3	178

SOURCE: National Weather Service.

An additional 120 F1–F3 tornadoes were recorded in the United States and Canada, in addition to these the F4s and F5s.

[1] Frances Kennett, *The Greatest Disasters of the 20th Century,* 132.

[2] In the 1996 Helen Hunt movie, *Twister,* F5s were dubbed "the Fingers of God"—and for good reason.

73

The 1964 Lima Soccer Riot

National Stadium, Lima, Peru

May 24, 1964

318 Dead

In countries where soccer is one of the few diversions and emotional releases for a poor and restless mass, the game takes on the proportion of a kind of controlled warfare.

—Robert Lipsyte, *The New York Times,* May 1964

Sports.

People who are not sports fans cannot understand the fanaticism manifested by hardcore devotees of teams, players, and individual sports in general. Everyone knows someone who has his favorite team's logo on almost everything he owns; someone who schedules his life around his team's season schedule; someone who gets depressed if his team's performance is not up to snuff.

Sports.

Since following sports is an interest people indulge in in their spare time, it is considered entertainment, and yet players, coaches, and fans elevate what is, in essence, the professional playing of a game, to something more akin to a noble, heroic quest, much more than merely a way to wile away a few hours.

Sports have the trappings of a science: statistics are followed intensely; sports has its own branch of medicine—"sports medicine"; predictions and forecasts for game results are arrived at using complex formulas and calculations.

Military imagery (as in the epigraph) is often used by sportswriters, such as describing a game between two teams as a "grueling battle"; describing the winners as the "victors" and "victorious"; calling the playing field a "battlefield"; and perceiving a team's coach as something akin to a general leading his troops into battle. In fact, serious sports fans are insulted by the dismissive admonishment, "It's only a game." The most recent in-your-face example of the deliberate elevation of sports to something more than just a game, was in the Friday, March 22, 2002, issue of the newspaper *USA Today*. The NCAA Tournament ("March Madness") was in full swing, and the front page of the newspaper proclaimed (*above* the fold, of course), in bold, enormous type, "Just a game? Hardly."

Sports.

None of this makes any sense to those who are not into sports one whit; yet all of this is incredibly important to those who live for sports, and consider them one of the most exciting and fulfilling facets of their lives.

Such passion can turn incendiary. Such passion can cause otherwise rational people to lose their minds, if only briefly. Such passion can result in a riot in which 318 people are killed, a tragedy that is ranked as the worst sports disaster of all time.

Lima, Peru. National Stadium. Close to forty-five thousand soccer fans filled the stands to watch Peru take on Argentina in an Olympic-qualifying match. For the entire game, the crowd was loud and rambunctious, but relatively orderly, and, most important, people remained in their seats.

Two minutes were left in the game, and Argentina led Peru, one to nothing.

The crowd was almost completely made up of Peru fans, so the mood, not surprisingly, was hair-trigger tense.

Suddenly, the popular Peruvian winger Lobatón scored a goal and the crowd went wild. The game was now tied, one to one, and it seemed that overtime was a certainty.

But then the referee, R. Angel Pazos, from Uruguay, voided the Peru goal for unruly play by the Peruvian team, and the crowd exploded in rage. Its fury could be heard in people's screams and stomping, and Pazos called off the game and ordered the players into the locker rooms for their own safety.

With the players gone and the game seemingly over, all restraint of the crowd vanished. Matia Rojas, a heavyset local known as the Bomb, rushed onto the field and attacked Angel Pazos. Forty police officers and two attack dogs descended on Rojas, in full view of the tens of thousands of enraged spectators, and beat him into submission.

As the Bomb was dragged off, the crowd broke down the fence surrounding the stands and stormed onto the field. Such a mass of humanity was a force unto itself, and people at the bottom of the swarm who could not move fast enough or get out of the way were crushed to death by the maniacal sports fans.

The crowd was at a fever pitch and people lit fires in the stands and broke every window in the stadium. The ridiculously outnumbered police were terrified and reacted by lobbing tear gas grenades into the stands and firing live rounds over the heads of the mob. This not only further infuriated the thousands of angry fans, it also caused a mindless panic, which resulted in even more people being crushed to death or being suffocated in the massive throng of rioters.

Thousands rushed the iron doors leading out of the stadium, but, as is the custom during play, they were all locked. An eighteen-month-old girl was crushed to death when her father lost his grip on her. Others choked to death on the thick cloud of tear gas.

The doors were finally broken open and the crowd stormed onto the streets of Lima. Thousands of people then marched to the home of the Peruvian president, Fernando Belaunde, demanding that the game be officially declared a draw. The deaths, injuries, terrible violence, raging fires, and the people desperately choking mattered little to an insane mob that was fixated on only one thing: the Peru soccer team must not be judged the loser in the match that had just taken place.

The crowds raged through Lima throughout the night, and the following day, many returned to the stadium to vandalize it further and steal the trophies on display.

The Peruvian government declared a state of emergency for the entire nation, and the hospitals and morgues in Lima were overloaded with the bodies of the dead and the injuries of the wounded. Corpses were laid out under sheets on the lawn outside the Lima hospital for family identification.

A total of 318 people died that day, and over 500 more were injured, some seriously.

The government passed legislation providing benefits to widows, and an official mourning period lasting one week was declared shortly after the disaster. Fifty people were ultimately arrested for rioting and looting (some had even robbed the dying).

The Lima soccer riot is not the only sporting disaster resulting in many deaths. It is the worst, however.

Perhaps the serious fans' inclination to use "war" analogies for sporting competitions is not that farfetched after all.

74

The 1979 American Airlines DC-10 Crash

CHICAGO O`HARE INTERNATIONAL AIRPORT, CHICAGO, ILLINOIS

May 25, 1979

273 Dead[1]

The left wingtip hit first, and the aircraft exploded, broke apart, and was scattered. Flight 191 struck the ground in left wing-down and nosedown attitude into an open field and a trailer park. The disintegration of the aircraft structure of the wreckage was so extensive that little useful data were obtained from postimpact examination . . .

—From the National Transportation Safety Board's official report on the crash

This 1979 DC-10 American Airlines crash epitomizes everything that sends fearful air travelers into paroxysms of terror.

The possibility of being hijacked, of being in a midair collision, of having to subdue a crazed shoe-bomb terrorist, of coming down with a raging case of food poisoning, and many other fears of the "flight experience" are often in the minds of air travelers, even though they know that the odds of any of these things happening are extremely slim.

What is almost always taken as a given, however, is that the airplane itself is well built, properly maintained, and, God help us, *safe*. Americans build most of the world's airplanes, and thus they are the best. Or at least we want to believe so.

In the vast majority—the *overwhelming* majority—of cases, this is absolutely true.

The DC-10 that crashed on May 25, 1979, had been built by McDonnell-Douglas, one of the biggest and most respected aircraft manufacturers in the world. That said, however, the problem that caused that crash was none of the myriad flight nightmares people have. It was, instead, bad design and the neglect of routine maintenance.

On May 25, 1979, the DC-10 taking off from Chicago's O'Hare Airport with 271 people on board crashed and burned because the plane's left engine fell off.

From the December 1979 NTSB report:

> Witnesses saw white smoke or vapor coming from the vicinity of the No. 1 engine pylon. During rotation, the entire no. 1 engine and pylon separated from the aircraft, went over the top of the wing, and fell to the runway. Flight 191 lifted off [at] about 6,000 ft. down runway 32R, climbed out in a wings-level attitude, and reached an altitude of about 300 ft. above the ground with its wings still level.
>
> Shortly thereafter, the aircraft began to turn and roll to the left, the nose pitched down, and the aircraft began to descend. As it descended, it continued to roll left until the wings were past the vertical position.
>
> Flight 191 crashed in an open field and trailer park about 4,680 ft. northwest of the departure end of runway 32R. The aircraft was demolished during the impact, explosion, and ground fire. Two hundred and seventy-one persons on board Flight 191 were killed, two persons on the ground were killed, and two persons on the ground sustained second- and third-degree burns.

The investigation into the accident revealed some truly chilling details. It is quite possible that the passengers of the plane watched their own deaths on TV. As do many planes, the doomed DC-10 had its own closed-circuit television system, which allowed the captain to provide the passengers with a live view of takeoffs and landings. The closed-circuit TV was operational for the DC-10's takeoff, and, after the engine fell off, it isn't known how long the camera continued to provide the view from the cockpit to the passenger cabin monitors. It is possible that the passengers may have been able to see the steep, drastic maneuvers the captain made in a desperate attempt to save the plane.

It was also learned that at approximately six thousand feet into the DC-10's "takeoff roll," pieces of the left engine's support pylon began to fall off the plane; the falling pieces could be seen by the air traffic controllers in the tower. At that point, the plane lifted off and one of the controllers, knowing something was seriously wrong, radioed Captain Walter Lux and asked him if he wanted to abort the takeoff and return and, if so, which runway he wanted to use.

There was silence from the DC-10 because Captain Lux and his crew were in a desperate battle to save their plane. The loss of the engine had also destroyed the captain's control panel, thereby rendering all cockpit controls useless. The plane went into a left turn in which the wings went completely vertical, and then tipped past the vertical as the nose of the plane pointed downward. The plane was only three hundred or so feet off the ground, so the severe swerve brought the wing down to the ground, and the plane crashed. The total destruction of the plane and the deaths of all on board were also due to the fact that the plane was fully loaded with fuel—the plane was headed for Los Angeles from Chicago on a nonstop flight. As we saw in September 2001, when two planes fully loaded with fuel were flown into the World Trade Center, even if the crash itself could be survivable, the inferno created by the burning fuel would not.

This was the worst air disaster in U.S. history, and the NTSB report blamed improper and deficient maintenance of the plane for the loss of the engine and concluded that the pylon that broke was not designed, or built, to handle "maintenance-induced damage." The blame was equally apportioned, however. The NTSB blamed the "vulnerability of the design of the pylon attachment" as well as "deficiencies in the Federal Aviation Administration surveillance and reporting systems that failed to detect and prevent the use of improper maintenance procedures." It also assigned culpability to the manufacturer (McDonnell-Douglas), and stated that lack of communication among all involved parties was a major contributing factor in the accident.

[1] There were 271 passengers and crewmembers on board; 2 people on the ground. Also, 2 people on the ground were seriously injured with second- and third-degree burns.

75

The 1988 Pan Am Lockerbie Bombing

LOCKERBIE, SCOTLAND

December 21, 1988

270 Dead

Quite clearly the detonation of high explosive material anywhere on board an aircraft is potentially catastrophic and the most effective means of protecting lives is to stop such material entering the aircraft in the first place.

—From the United Kingdom Air Accidents Investigation Branch 1990 report on Pan Am Flight 103

In these post–September 11 days, the world now knows that a bomb does not have to be placed on an airplane for it to be a terrorist target, and that the plane itself can be used as the bomb. (See chapter 46.) Earlier terrorist airplane bombings now take on a new resonance, one tinged dark from sad hindsight.

On December 21, 1988, a bomb on a Pan Am flight to New York exploded in the skies over Lockerbie, Scotland, killing all 259 passengers and crew on board, as well as 11 people on the ground in Lockerbie.

A bomb made from Semtex explosive was concealed in a Toshiba radio/cassette player, which was then wrapped in baby clothes and placed in a Samsonite suitcase in a luggage container positioned on the left side of Pan Am Flight 103's forward cargo hold. The deadly suitcase had been put on a Pan Am flight in Frankfurt, Germany, and then transferred to Flight 103 at London's Heathrow Airport, scheduled to depart for New York. The suitcase was removed from the Frankfurt plane and put on Flight 103 without being opened, X-rayed, or matched to a passenger.

In February 1990, the United Kingdom Air Accidents Investigation Branch released a report stating the following:

> It was established that the detonation of an IED [improvised explosive device] . . . directly caused the loss of the aircraft. The direct explosive forces produced a large hole in the fuselage structure and disrupted the main cabin floor. Major cracks continued to propagate from the large hole under the influence of the service pressure differential. The indirect explosive effects produced significant structural damage in areas remote from the site of the explosion. The combined effect of the direct and indirect explosive forces was to destroy the structural integrity of the forward fuselage, allow the nose and flight deck area to detach within a period of 2 to 3 seconds, and subsequently allow most of the remaining aircraft to disintegrate while it was descending nearly vertically from 19,000 to 9,000 feet.

The explosion at thirty-one thousand feet caused the front third of the plane to break off, after which passengers began pouring out the open end of the aircraft. Those that were not killed immediately by the explosion were dead by the time they hit the ground. In a scene of grisly horror, corpses began raining down on Lockerbie, some of whom were still strapped into their airplane seats. The dead landed on roofs, in the middle of the town's quiet streets, in the branches of trees, in people's backyards. One Flight 103 passenger landed on top of a sheep in a field, instantly killing the animal. In addition to dead people falling from the sky, pieces of the plane also crashed down on Lockerbie. The main fuel tank of the plane exploded and ignited upon impact when it crashed into a house, burning to death everyone inside.

Before December 1988, Lockerbie had been known for its dinosaur footprints. After this Christmas week bombing, the name of the town became forever associated with terrorism.

Who was responsible for the Pan Am Flight 103 bombing? And was the bombing a retaliatory act?

On July 3, 1988, during the Iraq-Iran War, the American warship USS *Vincennes* was escorting Iraqi oil tankers through the Strait of Hormuz. When a plane appeared on the *Vincennes* radar headed straight for the battleship, the

Vincennes radioed the plane demanding identification. When there was no response, the *Vincennes* shot the plane out of the sky. It was quickly learned that the reason the plane did not respond to the *Vincennes*'s hailings was that the U.S. ship, assuming the plane was an enemy aircraft, had broadcast its signal on a military frequency. The plane had actually been a civilian Iranian airbus, and the *Vincennes* missile had resulted in the deaths of all 290 onboard, including 66 children.

Five months later, a civilian plane headed for New York, loaded with Americans, was blown out of the sky. Accusations of retaliation began immediately.

In November 1991, arrest warrants were issued for two Libyan nationals—Abdelbaset Ali Mohmed Al-Megrahi and Al-Amin Fhima—both of whom were determined to be in Libya. The Libyan government refused to turn the suspects over to the police of any nation, and insisted on trying them in the Libyan courts. After years of high-level international negotiations, including rulings by both the United Nations Security Council and the World Court, it was agreed that the two Libyan nationals would be tried in a neutral country, the Netherlands, by a Scottish three-judge panel.

In January 2001, in a unanimous ruling by the three Scottish judges, Al-Megrahi was found guilty of murder; Fhima was found not guilty.

An appeal of Al-Megrahi's verdict is currently pending.

Whatever the resolution of the appeal, the ultimate reality for the families and survivors of both the Pan Am Flight 103 and the Lockerbie victims is that a terrorist act wiped out 270 lives. The determination of retaliation was not made during the trial, but Libya is one of Iran's two Arab allies (Syria is the other) and the notion of a Libyan bomb killing American civilian airplane passengers as payback for Americans killing Iranian civilian airplane passengers is not the least bit farfetched and still carries great credibility for many of those affected by the bombing, on both sides of the Atlantic.

76

The 1985 Stava Dam Failure

Stava, Italy

July 19, 1985

269 Dead

I saw the end of the world. I saw a white wall coming toward me. I couldn't tell if it was fire or what.

—A Stava survivor, talking to a reporter[1]

The sites of the hotels and houses had to be pointed out to me. It's as if they never existed.

—Giuseppe Zamberletti, Minister of Civil Protection, after a helicopter tour of Stava[2]

Grandinano Mary, piena della tolleranza che il signore è con voi . . .

Hail Mary, full of grace, the Lord is with thee . . .

The woman had lost count of how many rosaries she had said in the past twelve hours.

Benedetto è voi fra le donne e benedetta è la frutta del vostro womb, Jesus.

Blessed are thou amongst women and blessed is the fruit of thy womb, Jesus.

It was now past midnight, and the terrified Sardinian woman visiting Stava had been buried alive in the mud since shortly after noon of that day, when the thick liquid crashed into the hotel where she was staying and covered her like a filthy wet blanket that seemed to weigh as much as stone.

Mary santa, madre del dio, prega per noi i sinners . . .

Holy Mary, Mother of God, pray for us sinners . . .

The mud was as high as her chin, and she had to fight to keep her head up or her mouth would drop into the thick muck. Would she die here? Would anyone find her? She could hear people shouting and the clang of shovels and sounds of digging, but how would they know she was even in here? It had been so many hours, and so many rosaries, and no one had come. But she knew she must not lose her faith. If it was God's will that she die here, in the bowels of this flooded hotel, so be it. She would know when it was time to sink beneath the mud. But for now, she must still be strong and she must continue to pray and have faith.

Ora ed all'ora della nostra morte. Amen.

Now and at the hour of our death. Amen.

The woman took a short breath, being very careful not to inhale any mud, and began again.

Grandinano Mary, piena della tolleranza che il signore è con voi . . .

It was one in the morning.

The visitor from Sardinia was rescued the following morning just as the sun was coming up. Her prayers had been answered after she had spent eighteen hours in the mud.

Tailings are the dross that remains after ore has been processed, and tailings dams are barriers built to contain the slurry—tailings and water—that flows out of the mineral mines in pipes as part of the refining process.

There were two tailings dams above Stava, Italy, the first built in 1961, the second in 1970, to service a fluorite mine. Fluorite is a soft mineral—only coral, amber, gypsum, and talc are softer—used to make colored glass for windows, figurines, and glassware. The Stava mines were productive, and thus the tailings runoff was steady.

At 12:23 P.M. on July 19, 1985, both tailings dams above Stava collapsed.

Stava, long popular as a tourist destination, was especially crowded at this hour, since people who had wandered out of town on sightseeing trips, returned to town for the very important midday meal.

The flood of tailings slurry that rushed toward Stava at twenty-five miles per hour was enormous—it towered 100 feet high and was 150 feet wide. And because it was water laden with mineral runoff, it was much heavier than plain water and, as would be expected, it did far worse damage than if it had been plain water. Trees were plowed up as if a giant bulldozer had passed through. Cars were picked up and tossed about like toys. Buildings, some of which might have been able to withstand a flood of only water, were crushed and torn to pieces by the much more powerful tailings flood. People who were unfortunate enough to be in the path of the flood wave were turned into mush, some so badly that even their gender could not be determined.

Stava was obliterated, but the flood demon was not finished with this little corner of northern Italy. The surge picked up speed, close to forty miles per hour now, and headed for the small village of Tesoro, which was close by on the Stava River.

The wave arrived in less than five minutes, and Tesoro took an equally hard hit, with the massive loss of houses, bridges, trees, and many lives.

A thorough investigation of the dam failures revealed a pattern of neglect on the part of both owners (the mine was sold to new owners in 1982) and that none of the necessary improvements to prevent failure had been carried out. In fact, a technical paper published at a seminar in Gällivare, Switzerland, in September 2001 revealed that even the most routine of inspections of both dams had never been done by either owner.[3] The paper also noted, "It is evident that the Stava Dams reflect design and construction practices that would not be acceptable today." [4]

As in any major disaster caused by corporate negligence, or even just corporate bad luck, the Stava dam failures generated a great many lawsuits, extending back to the first owners as well as to the owners at the time of the collapse. These "residual liabilities"[5] prompted stricter Italian laws governing the design, construction, and maintenance of water-retaining dams. Tailings dams had for the most part been exempt from strict guidelines and regulations. All that changed after Stava.

1 Lee Davis, *Natural Disasters,* 161.

2 Ibid.

3 "Safe Tailings Dam Construction."

4 Ibid.

5 Ibid.

77

The Crash of Flight 800

East Moriches, Long Island, New York

July 17, 1996

230 Dead

The probable cause of the TWA Flight 800 accident was an explosion of the center wing fuel tank (CWT) . . . neither the energy release mechanism nor the location of the ignition inside the CWT could be determined from the available evidence.

—From the National Transportation Safety Board's official report on the crash

In summary, we carefully studied and considered all of the witness accounts. The witness reports and the streak of light are consistent with them having observed Flight 800 in crippled flight. They're not consistent with a missile. This concludes my presentation.

—National Transportation Safety Board spokesman David Mayer, at the final NTSB public hearing on the crash

More than 150 "credible" witnesses—including several scientists—have told the FBI and military experts they saw a missile destroy TWA Flight 800.

—*New York Post*[1]

July and August nights on the shores of Long Island are odd amalgams of heat and the smell and feel of salt air. The humidity of the day often fades by seven or eight, but it remains hot, and the water gives a tangy moisture to the air that is not at all unpleasant.

On the night of Wednesday, July 17, 1996, the man who would come to be known as Witness 649, left his Westhampton, Long Island, home, to take a walk, watching the night sky and listening to the waves of the Sound hit the shore as he strolled.

At precisely 8:31 P.M., while standing in a school parking lot, witness 649 saw a reddish streak rise from the ground, bear right, wiggle a little, and then head up into the sky. As his eyes followed the streak, he noticed a white light moving across the sky in a northeasterly direction. Witness 649 continued to watch, and within a few seconds, red streak met white light, and an explosion occurred at the spot in the sky where they collided. Flaming debris then fell into the water. Witness 649 had just watched the demise of TWA Flight 800 and all 230 people on board.

The July 1986 crash of TWA Flight 800 off the coast of Long Island killed all of the passengers and crew on board. Its fiery nighttime descent into the waters of Long Island Sound was witnessed by many people, both on shore and on the water.

Many of these witnesses reported seeing a projectile rise up and fly toward Flight 800. A few seconds later, there was an explosion in the sky, and the flaming wreckage of Flight 800 could then be seen descending into the water.

Was this projectile, this streak of red-pink light, a missile? And if it was, was it a terrorist attack, or could it have been an errant missile launching by one of the United States Navy's own ships engaging in nighttime military exercises? Could the witnesses be misinterpreting flaming debris from the plane itself as some kind of projectile? Was the *true* cause of the crash a bomb exploding on the plane?

Or, all of those questions notwithstanding, is the official National Transportation Safety Board report correct? Did an electrical short circuit (from faulty wiring) create an explosion in a fuel tank that instantly doomed the plane and its passengers? The NTSB concluded that the probable cause of the accident was an explosion of the center wing fuel tank, likely caused by an electrical short circuit outside of the center wing tank.

Yet hundreds of eyewitnesses—many of whom were considered credible enough to offer expert testimony in court (including military pilots and civilian helicopter pilots)—claim to have seen something that sounds remarkably like a surface-to-air missile head straight for Flight 800.

Whatever the cause of the explosion, the specific event that resulted in 230 bodies in the water and a plane at the bottom of Long Island Sound, has been determined with certainty: an explosion caused the nose of Flight 800 to separate from the body of the plane.

The CIA and NTSB state that the decapitated body of the plane (the part filled with the passengers) then rapidly ascended three thousand feet before peaking and then arcing forward and plunging into the water.

Recovery efforts commenced immediately and consisted of the recovery of the bodies of the passengers, and also whatever floating debris from the plane could be retrieved from the water's surface. More extensive recovery efforts continued over the next four months. Salvage and military divers made four thousand dives to the site of the wreck and were able to bring up 90 percent of the 17,500-ton (when empty) plane and reconstruct it in a warehouse on Long Island. The rebuilt 747 was carefully studied and used to reach the conclusions put forth in the official NTSB report.

Conspiracy theorists contend that the plane *was* shot down, that the wreckage bore unequivocal evidence of this fact, and that the FBI, CIA, NTSB, United States Navy, and the White House all conspired to cover up this evidence (even to the point of removing specific damning parts of the plane from the warehouse reconstruction site) and then create an "accident" scenario for the crash. The CIA created an animation of the explosion and the ascent of the main body of the plane to buttress its "official" story.

The circumstances surrounding the crash of TWA Flight 800 have spawned documentaries, books, multipart magazine and newspaper series, Web sites, petitions, and even full-page newspaper ads. One such full-page ad in the August 15, 2000, issue of *The Washington Times* shouted, "We Saw TWA Flight 800 Shot Down By Missiles and We Won't Be Silenced Anymore!" The ad stated that the NTSB and all of the other agencies involved in the Flight 800 investigation were lying and that "America must know the truth."

That truth may never be conclusively known about Flight 800. The NTSB and the others say one thing, a passionate and vocal group of investigators, witnesses, and family members say another.

Whatever the cause, 230 people who boarded Flight 800 for a trip to Paris ended up dead in the water a mere twelve minutes after taking off, in one of the worst air disasters in U.S. history.

[1] *New York Post*, September 22, 1996.

78

The Quintinshill Rail Crash

QUINTINSHILL JUNCTION, GRETNA, SCOTLAND

May 22, 1915

227 Dead

Concentrated on their great task few of the survivors were in a position to see another dreadful disaster rolling down upon them. Suddenly there came an appalling sequel. Through the fearful tangle of wreckage and injured and dead, and into the striving heroes of the stricken remnant of the two companies there ripped the northbound express, double-engined and running late. Never was there such a disaster nor such a scene on a British railway.

—*The Scotsman*

The wooden train car was on its side and dozens of dead and injured soldiers lay piled on top of each other inside, trapped in the wreckage. The car then caught fire from the gas that was used to light the train's interior and the flames quickly began to devour the bodies of the soldiers. If anyone had been able to get inside the train car, he would have been able to tell the dead from the living: the ones gravely injured were the ones screaming from being roasted alive. The soldiers on the bottom of the pile of bodies prayed for a quick end. Many of them could not even move their arms or legs. Some could do nothing but watch helplessly as the fire edged closer, the heat of the blaze burning the skin off their faces. Then a new horror brought unspeakable misery to the dying soldiers. The hundreds of bullets in the soldiers' ammunition belts, along with the boxes of additional ammo stored in the car, began to explode from the heat. Bullets detonated on the bodies of the dead and the living, resulting in some of the conscious soldiers feeling what it was like to be shot by dozens of bullets at the same time. Within minutes, everyone in the car was dead, but the bullets continued to explode and ravage the soldiers' bodies. Later, when rescuers finally managed to make their way into the car, hoping to rescue survivors, exploding bullets from the bodies of the dead killed many of them.

The horrible train accident in Gretna, Scotland, at Quintinshill Junction occurred ten months after the start of World War I, and the saddest, most regrettable aspect of the tragic event is that it was completely preventable. It is expected and unavoidable that soldiers will die in battle, but to lose hundreds of young, strong, healthy enlisted men because of carelessness, irresponsibility, and laziness is, perhaps, a greater tragedy than losing them in battle.

The Quintinshill railway crash was the worst in Great Britain's history. Two trains collided head-on, and then a third train plowed into the wreckage of the first two at high speed.

The troop train carried five hundred men of the Seventh Royal Scots Division, on their way to Gallipoli in Turkey. The troop train was 213 yards long and it was crushed down to an astonishing 67 yards by the force of the collision impact.

The responsibility for the accident was that of two signalmen, James Tinsley and George Meakin, who, in a series of blunders, recklessly allowed two trains to occupy the same line. After the troop train collided with a local passenger train, a third train, somehow allowed to be on the same line, crashed into the wreckage, compounding the damage and injuries, and multiplying the deaths.

The engineer of the troop train had fewer than ten seconds to react when he saw the passenger train directly in his path. It was, of course, not enough time for braking or even slowing, and the crash occurred at approximately 6:43 A.M. the morning of May 15. One minute later, the third doomed train, an express, arrived on the scene.

Tinsley and Meakin were guilty of multiple oversights and errors, not the least of which was not putting blocking "collars" over the signal controls so a line would not inadvertently be cleared for traffic when another train was using it.

The Seventh Royal Scots Division lost 215 men. The train's engineer and his fireman were also killed, as were 10 civilians. The total death count was 227. Additionally, 247 people were injured in the crash, some seriously.

Four months after the accident George Meakin and James Tinsley were tried for their crimes and both were found guilty of culpable homicide. Tinsley was sentenced to three years in prison; Meakin, to eighteen months. However, both men suffered complete nervous breakdowns while incarcerated and both were released for medical reasons after serving only one year of their sentences.

Today, a memorial to the 215 soldiers lost in the crash stands in the Rosebank Cemetery on Pilrig Street in Edinburgh, Scotland.

79

The 1966 Florence Art Flood

Florence, Italy

November 4–5, 1966

33–200 Dead[1]

$700 Million in Damages[2]

Inestimable Damage to Priceless Art

On average we have had a bad flood in Florence once every hundred years . . . but the one in 1966 was the worst of all. I think that the Florentines will have to get used to living with floods but people gradually tend to forget about such events. People end up by completely forgetting all about them. The young people of today have no idea about what happened in 1966, whereas it is important to make sure that people remember a fact like this. When Florence was flooded, it was a catastrophe because we were completely unprepared. We had forgotten.

—Professor Umberto Baldini, Head of Florence's Department of Restoration of the Board of Artistic Assets[3]

The Florence flood of November 1966 destroyed priceless, irreplaceable works of art and other extremely rare archival materials, and can justifiably be compared to the destruction of the library in Alexandria in 500 .

The Arno river passes through the center of Florence. At 4:15 on the morning of November 4, 1966, after a full day of ceaseless, heavy rain, the Arno overflowed its banks and rushed into the unprepared city at speeds of up to eighty miles per hour. The water carried cars, dead cows, furniture, and other detritus as it swooped through the streets.

The floodwaters roared through shops, homes, and any other buildings in its path. More than six thousand of the city's ten thousand stores were destroyed, including the majority of Florence's world-renowned goldsmith shops.

Thousands visit the tombs of Galileo, Michelangelo, and Machiavelli in the Sante Croce Basilica in Florence each year. Visitors stand in awe of the legacies of these Renaissance giants as they walk silently by their crypts. After the floods washed away thousands of homes, Sante Croce became a refuge for the homeless.

The basilica is home to frescoes by Renaissance masters and Giotto, as well as its most famous possession, Cimabue's *Crucifixion.* Cimabue's masterpiece, one of the few surviving works by the great father of Italian painting and teacher of Giotto, was ripped down by the 1966 floodwaters, and 70 percent of its paint was destroyed. Though it was eventually restored, many other art works were irretrievably lost or damaged beyond repair.

In 1966, Florence's museums, libraries, and galleries were home to such priceless artifacts as original handwritten musical scores by Alessandro Scarlatti, the personal writings of Amerigo Vespucci, hundreds of thousands of books, manuscripts, folios, first editions, newspapers, and other one-of-a-kind creations. It is estimated that close to two million individual volumes were submerged in the floodwaters. In addition to these rarities, the city abounded with paintings (including the enormous *Coronation of the Virgin* by Botticelli), drawings, sculptures, murals, statues, and frescoes, as well as unique works like Lorenzo Ghiberti's baptistery *Gates of Paradise* in the Duomo, which were torn off the building and dragged through the raging waters. The panels were recovered but were damaged beyond restoration.

Compounding the problem and adding to the damage done by the water was oil. When the floodwaters rushed into the basements of Florence's buildings, many oil tanks ruptured and pumped out all their fuel oil, which then combined with the water and dirt to create a thick, vile liquid that added to the damage the water alone would have done. Many books, paintings, and manuscripts were soaked in this grimy substance and much of it could not be removed.

The final damage toll on Florence and its surrounding areas was cataclysmic. There were over 3,000 miles of road torn up, 12,000 farms and farmhouses wiped out, 10,000 houses in the city leveled, 50,000 head of cattle killed, 16,000 pieces of farm equipment such as tractors and threshers destroyed, over 5,000 families ended up homeless, and 800 communities were crippled.

The plodding, incompetent city government of Florence took an unconscionable six days to begin moving cleanup equipment into the city. During that time, people used whatever they could, including their bare hands, to rummage through the oily sludge that filled their homes and businesses and recover what they could.

The world was aghast at the damage to the priceless art treasures, and volunteers from all over Europe and the United States flocked to Florence to aid in the cleanup and recovery of manuscripts, books, and artworks. One young American girl who had volunteered to help in the recovery effort said to a reporter, "My father should see us now. He thinks our generation has no values." Even with this Herculean effort, though, the loss of irreplaceable items was staggering.

The Florentine daily newspaper *La Nazione* called the flood "the most monstrous natural cataclysm in the history of Florence"; Italy's interior minister, Paolo Emilio Taviana, said, "There is no record of such a calamity in living memory."

Florence has added defenses against flooding and museums and libraries now deliberately keep priceless works of art on the higher levels of buildings. It is a shame, though, that it took a disaster like the 1966 flood to spur the caretakers of some of the world's greatest art to be prudent and careful with the precious treasures with which they have been entrusted.

[1] The wide range of reported deaths suggests a lack of accurate figures regarding deaths caused by the flood. The ten sources we consulted all stated a different figure for the number dead: 33, 35, 87, 112, 113, 117, 127, 150, 170, and 200.

[2] In 1966 dollars.

[3] 1996 interview in the *Florence Art News*.

80

The Oklahoma City Bombing

Murrah Federal Building, Oklahoma City, Oklahoma

April 19, 1995

168 Dead

A blizzard of papers blowing out of offices that have been heavily damaged by this bomb in the downtown area. I'm just about three hundred yards away from the front of this building that has been ripped off by this powerful blast . . . buildings all around me here have suffered extensive damage. Up on top of the roof of one of these buildings, a brick wall has been blown over . . . on this fourth floor of this parking garage, the elevator doors have been blown off the hinges. That was the force of this blast.

—Reporter Ross Simpson, live on the radio shortly after the bombing

Before the 2001 World Trade Center and Pentagon terrorist attacks (chapter 46), the Oklahoma City Bombing in 1995 was the single worst act of domestic terrorism in the history of the United States; although at the time, it was not known if the bombing was done by foreign terrorists, as was the 1993 World Trade Center attack, or by an American. It was quickly learned that the attack had been carried out by the latter.

Army Gulf War veteran Timothy McVeigh, who was twenty-seven at the time of the bombing and who was executed in June 2001 for the crime, claimed he carried out this bloody, wholesale act of mass destruction and mass murder in response to the federal government's April 1993 assault on David Koresh's Branch Davidian complex in Waco, Texas, a raid that resulted in the deaths of many of Koresh's followers. McVeigh saw the Waco tragedy as undeniable evidence of a government out of control and decided to exact his own form of vengeance against the perpetrators.

On April 19—two years to the day after the Waco debacle—McVeigh drove a yellow Ryder rental truck up to the front of the Alfred P. Murrah Federal Building in Oklahoma City, turned off the engine, and reportedly sat there a moment. He then climbed out and calmly walked away. He headed for his car, which had been parked some blocks away, and was still walking when the bomb went off. It was later learned that McVeigh had been wearing earplugs to protect his ears from the noise of the blast.

The back of McVeigh's Ryder truck was loaded with four thousand pounds of homemade explosives made from gasoline and fertilizer, a lethal cargo powerful enough to remove the entire front of the Murrah building, a bomb powerful enough to kill 168 people and injure over 500 more.

The truck bomb exploded at 9:02 A.M., just as federal workers were settling in at their desks; just as citizens were entering the building to conduct whatever business had been on their "to do" lists that day; just as the children in the building's day care center ("collateral damage" McVeigh would later heartlessly call them) were picking up toys to play with or books to read.

The Oklahoma City Bombing would have enormous societal consequences.

The Oklahoma City attack, which came two years after the first World Trade Center attack, inculcated a new sense of unease and anxiety in the American consciousness. Terrorism did not happen on American soil, we had previously believed. Terrorism happened in Palestine, and Beirut, and London, but not in America. The 1993 World Trade Center attack had been of foreign origin, so many Americans were willing to write it off as a fluke. But then Oklahoma City exploded onto the front pages and America's TV screens and suddenly there was a national realization that we were *not* safe, and also that it may not be a foreign terrorist attack that results in the deaths of many, many Americans.

The monstrous 2001 World Trade Center and Pentagon attacks were the ultimate wake-up call for Americans, and they conclusively convinced us that there were people all over the world who did not like us. Ironically, it was another *foreign* attack that ultimately validated the national paranoia that had begun in 1993, and which was amplified in 1995 by Timothy McVeigh. This trilogy of terrorism changed the face and heart of America for all time.

* * *

Timothy McVeigh was arrested on a minor traffic charge less than two hours after the Oklahoma City explosion. He was held on charges unrelated to the bombing and was minutes away from being freed when a connection was made between McVeigh and the truck that had been at the site of the bombing. He was charged with the bombing, convicted, and executed for his crimes.

Today, the Murrah Federal Building is gone. There was unanimous agreement among the victims' families and the American people that it should not be rebuilt and that nothing else should be constructed on the site. Instead, a memorial park was constructed with 168 chairs—bronze and stone chairs lined up in stark, simple lines, one for each of the victims. Nineteen of the chairs are small. They are for each of the children that were killed in the explosion.

81

The Ringling Bros. and Barnum & Bailey Circus Fire

HARTFORD, CONNECTICUT

July 6, 1944

168 Dead

I went back for more the last time when a man called to me and asked me to help him pull out his child. He called from the grandstand, and I reached up toward him. Then he fell back into the fire.

—Herman Wallenda, of The Flying Wallendas[1]

Every hearse, every livery car was in constant use; undertakers toiled night and day, some funeral parlors were holding services at fifteen-minute intervals. The quiet crowds gathered, dispersed, and gathered again in the cemeteries.

—*Time*[2]

The last thing a circus performer *ever* wants to hear during a show is "The Stars and Stripes Forever."

John Philip Sousa's stirring march has long been a staple at parades and patriotic events, but the song holds a much different meaning in the circus world. In a parade, the song stands for America, patriotism, and Old Glory. In the circus world, the song is a signal that there is something terribly wrong, and it is only played when disaster has struck or is imminent.

"The Stars and Stripes Forever" was played on the afternoon of July 6, 1944, in Hartford, Connecticut, when flames raced up the flammable canvas walls of the big top and began ferociously devouring the roof of the tent.

The Flying Wallendas were on bicycles on the high wire when the fire started on the side wall of the tent behind section A. The Wallendas quickly backed their bicycles to the platforms and climbed down their ladders as the fire rapidly began to spread. Bandleader Merle Evans quickly ordered the band to start the Sousa march (nicknamed the "disaster march" by circus folk), and circus workers throughout the tent and backstage immediately stopped what they were doing and raced for the exits. The fire spread so rapidly that, at first, the audience did not have time to react. This changed, however, when pieces of burning canvas from the flaming roof began falling on the crowd. Then everyone surged for the exits, which were quickly blocked by the masses of people. Children were trampled; adults were slammed into the metal animal chutes; and yet, as on the *Titanic*, the band played on.

In less than a minute, the entire roof of the tent had burned. Within fifteen minutes, the entire big top—which was 550 feet long, 250 feet wide, and 75 feet high—was gone. After the fire, investigators discovered that there was not a piece of intact, unburned canvas bigger than three square inches.

There were between 7,000 and 8,000 people in the tent for the matinee performance and the vast majority of them, including all the performers and circus workers, got out alive. However, 168 people died, and several hundred more were seriously injured in the fire. Two-thirds of the dead were children. Over 100 bodies were burned beyond recognition and piled in the center ring. Dental records were needed to identify them.

Some were lucky, though. Seven-year-old Elliot Smith survived only because the pile of people on top of him burned to death. One mother who made it out screamed frantically for her four children, all of whom she feared had been burned to death inside the tent. One by one, they ran up to her, until she had all four of her babies in her arms.

The circus midgets (and back then, it was *not* considered offensive to call them midgets) were the heroes of the day. Many of the little people repeatedly crawled under the flap of the tent to bring children out safely. Within a short time, the clothes they were wearing were smoking from the heat.

This July 1944 fire was the worst circus tragedy in United States history. It was learned that the tent had been waterproofed with paraffin cut with gasoline, which made it highly flammable. This kind of treatment, however, was routine for the time.

It was later revealed that the circus management had tried for years to buy a new flame retardant, developed by the military, but they were repeatedly denied it because of the war. Military people came to the circus after the fire, though, and gave them all they needed. From 1945 on, the canvas was treated with the new flame retardant. This was, of course, too late for the 168 who perished in the fire.

Five circus employees went to jail for involuntary manslaughter due to negligence. They did serve some time, but the state of Connecticut quickly pardoned them and released them shortly after their convictions.

The behavior and integrity of the Ringling Bros. organization following the fire is legendary. The company did not contest a single claim and took full responsibility for all the deaths and injuries. It ultimately paid out over $5 million in damages in an agreement by which all of the circus's net profits for ten years went to pay claims.

In 1950, the cause of the fire was finally discovered, although not by police investigatory work.

A Circleville, Ohio, man named Robert D. Segee confessed to starting the fire. He told police that an Indian riding a flaming horse had appeared to him and told him to start the fire. He also claimed that he blacked out after his vision, and when he came to, the fire had been set. Segee was tried and convicted in Ohio and sentenced to prison for two consecutive terms of twenty-two years—the maximum allowable by Ohio law—for setting the fire. It was finally learned that it was an arsonist who had set the fire and that all of the people killed did not have to die.

One of those who did not have to die has been known for decades as Little Miss 1565. She was a little girl whose body was never claimed at the morgue.

It is likely that whoever had brought her to the circus had perished in the fire and she had no other family to claim her—or to even know that she was missing.

It is so sad to reflect on how excited Little Miss 1565 must have been when she learned that she was going to the circus.

Today, her gravestone has no name.

[1] Jay Robert Nash, *Darkest Hours,* 471.
[2] "Six Minutes." *Time*, July 17, 1944, 19.

82

The Triangle Factory Fire

Greene Street and Washington Place, New York, New York

March 25, 1911

145 Dead

The occupants of floors over eighty feet from the ground cannot . . . be reached by the Fire Department's ladders, and must trust for escape to the stairways or exterior fire-escapes. In many of these buildings the occupants manufacture garments and other inflammable articles. The floors are littered with a quantity of cuttings, waste material and rubbish, and are often soaked with oil or grease. No regular effort is made to clear the floors. No fireproof receptacles are provided for the accumulated waste, which in some cases is not removed from the floors for many days. Many of the workmen, foremen and employers smoke during business hours and at meal times. Lighted gas jets are unprotected by globes or wire netting, and are placed near to the inflammable material . . . Fire drills are not held . . . exits are unmarked and the location of the stairways and exterior fire-escapes is often unknown. Access to the stairway and outside fire-escapes is obstructed by machinery, wooden partitions and piled-up merchandise, while in some cases the fire-escape balcony is at such a distance from the floor as to make it almost impossible for women employees to reach it without assistance . . . In some cases the window leading to fire-escapes are not large enough to permit the passage of grown persons readily. Automatic or manual fire-alarms are hardly ever provided . . .

—New York (State) Factory Investigating Commission, "Preliminary Report of the Factory Investigating Commission," 1912

The police had to use pay envelopes to identify the victims of this tragic factory fire, the worst in New York's history, and one of the worst industrial disasters of all time.

Many of the factory workers killed in this blaze were burned and mangled beyond recognition, but the fire broke out shortly before closing on a Saturday night and everyone had just been paid. A name on an envelope was the only way some victims could be identified.

Today, in our time of government regulations, workplace safety laws, OSHA, and union and media oversight, the working conditions in 1911 in the Triangle Shirtwaist Company's factory seem to come from some lurid novel about penurious overseers straight out of Dickens.

However, the truth is that, far from being some kind of reprehensible anomaly, the Triangle Shirtwaist's Factory was the norm for the time.

And only one miserable little fire escape.

—A sobbing New York City Coroner Holtzhauser, in *The New York Times*, March 26, 1911

The bosses would lock the doors to prevent workers from leaving and to keep them at their sewing machines.

The ten-story building had but one fire escape, and it was flimsy and inadequate.

The three floors of the factory were jammed with bolts of highly flammable material, without a fire extinguisher in sight.

Smoking was allowed everywhere.

The workforce of five hundred or so was made up mostly of female Jewish immigrants from Brooklyn, ranging in age from *thirteen* to twenty-three.

The word *unsanitary* does not even come close to adequately describing the working conditions in the shop. There is good reason these places were derogatorily called sweatshops.

Workers—including the thirteen- and fourteen-year-olds—regularly began work at six or seven in the morning and were often there until past eight at night, or later.

Considering the "time bomb"-type of conditions in garment factories in America in the early twentieth century, it is amazing that major tragedies such as the Triangle Factory Fire did not happen more often. Granted, the enormous brick building itself was essentially fireproof; but inside it was a death trap.

> *A thirteen-year-old girl hung for three minutes by her fingertips to the sill of a tenth floor window. A tongue of flame licked at her fingers, and she dropped to her death.*
>
> —*The New York Times*, March 26, 1911

Once the fire started on the eighth floor, the hundreds of young women made a panicked, mad rush for the stairs, the elevator, and the fire escape.

The fire quickly spread to the ninth and tenth floors and engulfed the stairs, however, making escape impossible. The elevator never made it back up to the top floors and some women burned to death waiting for the doors to open. Some women refused to wait and actually pried open the elevator doors. Thirty women jumped down the elevator shaft to escape the flames, and their dead bodies piled up at on top of the elevator car to be found later by firefighters. (The elevator operator told *The New York Times* that he felt the thud of the women's bodies hitting the elevator roof and that he remembered hearing the change from their pay envelopes jingle as it was scattered about.) On the higher floors, some women chose to leap out windows rather than burn to death. (This is precisely what happened at the World Trade Center in 2001 after the planes hit. For many people, death from an 80-story fall was preferable to burning alive.) (See chapters 46 and 71.)

The New York Fire Department arrived quickly, but they had difficulty getting close to the building because of the mass of corpses all over the sidewalk. Once they did clear the way and saw that the fire was on the eighth, ninth, and tenth floors, they realized that their ladders were useless: they reached only to the sixth floor. Firefighters spread out nylon nets to catch jumpers, but the women were so panicked that three or more would jump at one time into one net, which would rip from the strain, and the women would die from the fall.

The fire was quickly put out, but the long process of transporting the bodies to the morgue and identifying them had just begun.

In fifteen minutes, 145 employees had died, most of them in horrible, agonizing ways.

The owners and managers of the company escaped the fire. The two owners were later charged with manslaughter, but they were acquitted. It was learned that they had fled to the roof as soon as the fire broke out instead of opening the locked doors so the workers could escape. They eventually were ordered to pay $75 each to the families of the victims.

The Triangle Factory Fire resulted in the appointing of a factory investigatory commission, as well as new regulations for safety in the workplace.

Rose Cohen, the last survivor of the Triangle Factory Fire, died in 2001 at the age of 107.

83

The 1934 Fire on the *Morro Castle*

Off the Shore of Asbury Park, New Jersey

September 8, 1934

133 Dead[1]

I was alone with Mary Maloney and two friends having cocktails in the lounge. It was about 4 A.M. I don't know what happened. I first saw smoke, but didn't think it was much because the stewards said not to worry, it would be put out easy. So we went to see what was going on and suddenly the fire just jumped at us. I ran down and woke my roommate Helen Williams, and got a coat and a life preserver.

I was all for jumping overboard right away, but they told me to wait. Then I tried to go down a rope ladder, but my high heels caught in the second step and I fell in the water. I was in the water seven hours, I think.

—Twenty-one-year-old survivor Una Cullen, in *The New York Times,* September 9, 1934

The Forsaken Castle

Seen from the sky, the crippled *Morro Castle,* grounded a few hundred yards off the shore of Asbury Park, New Jersey, appeared surreal and incongruous in those shallow waters, like a four-foot-long toy battleship floating in a five-foot-long bathtub. A ship the size of the *Morro Castle* belonged on the open sea. After the September 1934 fire on the ship and the vessel's subsequent death in the Asbury Park waters, locals charged tourists to stand on the beach and stare at the ship as it floated in the shoal, burned out, blackened, and dead. The *Morro Castle* was in those waters for months, but the fascination never waned.

The death toll for this maritime disaster is relatively small in comparison with some of the other naval tragedies in this ranking (the *Toya Maru*, the *Dona Paz,* the *General Slocum,* and, of course, the *Titanic),* but the *Morro Castle* fire and subsequent grounding is one of the all-time worst passenger liner catastrophes in history, mainly because it did not have to happen. In fact, the incompetence, misjudgments, personal failures, and even crimes that led to its 133 deaths make the losses all the more tragic.

Anything that could have gone wrong during the doomed voyage of the *Morro Castle* apparently did, including the death (and suspected murder) of the ship's captain, a deadly fire on board, a terrible, unexpected hurricane, and a cowardly, hard-drinking, and nefarious crew that was involved with heroin and cocaine smuggling, rum smuggling, illegal gambling, illicit gunrunning, and a thriving clandestine stowaway business. Many members of the *Morro Castle* crew were hostile, lazy, and difficult, and they did not seem to manifest the professional sailor's creed that keeping the passenger safe is always the most important aspect of their vocation.

The passengers, however, seemed to be oblivious to all the internal problems on the ship, and the *Morro Castle*'s Cuba to New York cruise voyage was very popular and always fully booked.

The trouble for the ship's doomed voyage began the evening of Friday, September 7. The captain of the *Morro Castle,* Robert R. Willmott, was a gregarious type who was popular with the passengers and enjoyed dining with them and circulating among the tables in the dining room. That Friday night, however, Captain Willmott did not join the passengers during the dinner hour. Instead, he ordered steak and vegetables sent to his cabin. At seven P.M. he called the ship's physician, Dr. De Witt Van Zile and asked him to bring him an enema as soon as possible. The doctor left his cabin immediately to comply with the captain's request, and when he arrived at Willmott's quarters, he found the burly, white-haired seaman fully clothed, half in and half out of the cabin's small bathtub. The captain was dead, and within a short time, he began to exhibit the blue discoloration from rigor mortis setting in.

This was the beginning of a series of tragic circumstances that combined incompetence, terrible luck, and possible criminal acts resulting in many deaths of the passengers and the destruction of the ship.

After the captain's death, First Officer William F. Warms took command of the ship. Shortly thereafter, the *Morro Castle* was battered by a hurricane, which Warms was woefully unprepared to handle. However, more misfortune was yet to come.

Approximately seven hours after the captain's death, at 2:15 in the morning, a fire broke out in a cabinet in the passenger's writing room where 150 blankets that had been cleaned with a flammable liquid were stored next to the smokestack. (Initially, it was believed that a carelessly thrown cigarette had started the blaze.) Three crewmen tried to put out the fire themselves but were unsuccessful. The fire hoses were almost dry.

The fire started to spread throughout the ship, burning passengers alive in their cabins, but Warms did not send an SOS. He instead ordered that the ship speed ahead, believing he could make it to New York Harbor, which was forty miles away. The New Jersey coast was only eight miles away, but Warms insisted on heading for New York.

Radio operator George Rogers took it upon himself to send out distress signals, which brought several rescue ships, as well as the Coast Guard. Meantime, Warms finally ordered the anchor dropped, and passengers began jumping overboard. The lifeboats were filled with crewmen, who ignored the screams of their passengers and endeavored to save themselves.

Finally, the ship was empty, and all the survivors had been rescued.

Warms was indicted for negligence and sentenced to two years in prison. His sentence was overturned, however, and he never served a day in jail.

Rogers toured the country as the hero of the *Morro Castle,* but later it was suspected that he not only poisoned the captain, but also set the ship on fire. He was never charged with wrongdoing in the *Morro Castle* tragedy, but he was ultimately convicted of two counts of murder for killing two of his neighbors with a hammer.

A dead captain, a suspicious fire, a crew abandoning their passengers, a delayed distress signal, 133 dead.

Thus was the legacy of the elite *Morro Castle* passenger cruise ship.

[1] This is the most commonly cited number for the people killed in the *Morro Castle* disaster. However, as is frequently the case regarding death tolls, several sources report several figures, including 125, 133, 134, and 137 dead.

84

The Winecoff Hotel Fire

ATLANTA, GEORGIA

December 7, 1946

119 Dead

Her nightgown shone white against the flames behind her as she stood on the window ledge, high above the street. Then it, too, caught fire. She jumped. But she missed the net stretched by firemen. She landed astride overhead wires. There she hung in flames. Finally, her body broke loose and toppled to the ground.

—Newspaper account following the fire[1]

This is a great tragedy. The public is being defrauded when a hotel is advertised as "fireproof" but really isn't. Responsible agencies should prohibit the use of the word "fireproof" when a hotel is not really fireproof as the Winecoff obviously was not.

—Georgia Governor Ellis Arnall[2]

In one room, where five people lay dead, a canary sang amongst the corpses.

Thousands of people lined the streets around Atlanta's Winecoff Hotel, staring up in horror at the dozens of people standing on window ledges or hanging out of windows screaming for help.

The hotel was on fire and there was no escape.

Soon, people began jumping off the ledges, making the choice that situations such as these inevitably demand. Which is worse? Dying by being burned alive? Or dying from a fifteen-story fall? Many chose the fall, and, soon, the pavement was littered with the bodies of those who jumped rather than burn.

Firefighters quickly threw ladders against the building and began climbing to the windows where people were desperately screaming for rescue. Unfortunately, the fire department's ladders extended only to the tenth floor, and the building had fifteen stories. On the fifth floor, a firefighter raced to a woman hanging on a window ledge—just as she let go, he managed to swing her onto his back. As he began to back down the ladder, spectators gasped in shock as a panicked woman jumped off a ledge from several stories up, struck the firefighter and the rescued woman, and all three fell to the ground and died.

A woman on the eighth floor threw her four-year-old son out a window begging for someone to catch him. Someone did, and he survived, but his mother leaped to her death immediately thereafter.

Some guests decided to stay in their rooms with the door and windows closed. They reasoned that since there was no way to escape, they would be safest in their rooms because the firefighters would soon put out the fire and then they would come and rescue them. Almost of all these people died of asphyxiation. Their bodies were found in their rooms, rooms in which the telephone and doorknobs had melted from the one thousand five hundred-degree-Fahrenheit heat.

The builder of the hotel, W. Frank Winecoff, a permanent resident of the hotel, had a suite on the tenth floor. He perished in the fire.

One of the survivors, Major Jake Cahill, rescued his mother by putting a plank across the alley from the building next door to the hotel and leading her to safety. Later, as he walked away from the hotel, he found his coat on the sidewalk. Someone had stolen his traveler's checks and fountain pen as he was busy saving his mother's life.

After the fire, bodies were lined up in the street at the intersection of Peachtree and Carnegie Streets, directly across from the theater where the movie *Gone With the Wind* had made its world premiere. One of the most memorable sequences in that movie is, of course, of Atlanta burning.

The Winecoff Hotel has come to be known as "Atlanta's *Titanic.*" Just as the *Titanic* was touted as unsinkable and yet it sunk, so was the Winecoff declared fireproof and yet it burned. The Winecoff's newspaper ads before the catastrophe of 1946 boldly and proudly proclaimed that it was "Absolutely Fire Proof."

The term *fireproof* had a drastically different meaning in 1946 than it does today. The Winecoff did not have a sprinkler system, a fire alarm system, fire doors, or fire escapes. The hotel's fifteen stories were accessible only by one long, spiraling staircase and elevators to each floor. Apparently, the fact that the hotel was mainly built of twelve-inch-thick brick walls was enough for it to pass a safety inspection and be rated as a fireproof structure.

The fire started at 3:15 A.M. on the third floor of the hotel. A stray cigarette was long believed to have been the culprit, but in 1993, in their book *The Winecoff Fire: The Untold Story of America's Deadliest Hotel Fire,* Sam Heys and Allen B. Goodwin assert that the cause of the fire was actually arson and they name a suspect.

As soon as he was told that flames were racing through the hallways, the manager, Comer Rowan, called the fire department, and then began calling each room individually and shouting, "Fire!" when someone answered the phone. Rowan managed to call only a few rooms before the hotel switchboard died. The fire department arrived at 3:42 A.M. Everyone above the fifth floor was trapped by then, and it ultimately took six hours to put out the blaze.

In the end, everything inside the 194-room building burned, but the cement shell did not. Of the 280 guests registered at the hotel on December 7, 119 died, 90 others were seriously injured, and 71 escaped unscathed.

Within days after the tragedy, legislators across the United States began revising fire codes; nevertheless, the fire at the Winecoff Hotel still stands as the worst hotel fire in American history.

[1] Jay Robert Nash, *Darkest Hours,* 616.
[2] *The New York Times*, Sunday, December 8, 1946.

85

The 1981 Hyatt Regency Walkways Collapse

Kansas City, Missouri

July 17, 1981

114 Dead

Even if the now-notorious design shift in the hanger rod details had not been made, the entire design of all three walkways, including the one which did not collapse, was a significant violation of the Kansas City Building Code.

—From the U.S. Department of Commerce's National Bureau of Standards official report on the collapse

The radio that summer was playing Queen's "We Are the Champions," Blondie's "Heart of Glass," Elton John's "Little Jeannie," and, interminably, the Village People's "Y.M.C.A.," but not a note of those contemporary songs was heard at the Kansas City Hyatt Regency's weekly "Tea Dance." Swing music was the repertoire of choice at the tea dances, and the July 17, 1981, gathering drew the biggest crowd in the twelve months that the hotel had been open. More than fifteen hundred people bebopped to the musical stylings of the Steve Miller Orchestra in the four-story atrium in the hotel's spacious lobby, notable for its airy design and its three suspended walkways above the lobby floor.

People greatly enjoyed strolling the walkways and looking down on the action below, and that night, many found the swing music so intoxicating that there were also people dancing on the walkways.

At around 7:05 P.M. shortly after the Steve Miller Orchestra bandleader had counted off Duke Ellington's classic hit "Satin Doll" and people had started dancing to the song, there was a loud, sustained cracking/rumbling sound that could be heard above the music. Within seconds, and as everyone in the lobby watched in horror, two of the atrium's suspended walkways collapsed, one on top of the other, killing 114 people and injuring 200 others. The fourth-floor walkway collapsed onto the second-floor walkway. The third-floor walkway was offset opposite the other two walkways and it remained suspended and intact. Cement and steel rods and glass and bodies plunged to the floor, burying people under tons of wreckage and injuring others who were lucky enough not to have been standing beneath the walkways. The majority of the 314 people killed or injured were either standing on the atrium floor or were on the second-floor walkway.

Rescue workers and medical personnel rushed immediately to the Hyatt, but it was quickly determined that heavy equipment would be necessary to recover those who had been in the wrong place at the wrong time. Work went on through the night, but it wasn't until seven the following morning that the last body was retrieved from beneath the rubble.

Immediately, the questions began. How could walkways in a brand-new hotel collapse? If there had been something drastically wrong with the walkways, why had the problems not been uncovered by the Kansas City building inspectors before the hotel opened? Who was ultimately responsible for all the deaths and injuries?

After a lengthy investigation, including the participation of the National Bureau of Standards, two outside engineering companies, and a company specializing in structural failure analysis, it was determined that the reason for the collapse was due to a change in the design of the hanger rod connections for the walkways. The change—suggested by the steel manufacturer and approved by the engineering firm—had essentially transferred the bearing of the weight of the walkways from the building's ceiling onto two welds in the hanger box beam assemblies. The redesign from a single support rod that went all the way through all the hanger box assemblies, to individual rods connected to the hanger box by a threaded end and a bolt, was just plain bad structural engineering, and the change never should have been approved. The addition of a second rod increased significantly the weight load on both the nut and the box beam itself. The two halves of the box beam had been welded down its length, which seriously decreased its ability to carry the additional weight and, thus, hastened the splitting of the weld when the nut gave way and the box cracked.

Nonetheless, this design change had been approved; it was built that way, and it was then inspected and passed as safe.

At first, in classic "blame the victim" thinking, it was suspected that too many people had crowded onto the walkways and overloaded them. How could a walkway designed for a certain number of people be expected to support that number plus of people? This theory was soon proven to be untenable when it was learned that each of the hanging rods had been rated to support a 68,000-pound load. The total load weight on the walkways at the time of the collapse? Only 18,600 pounds, slightly over 25 percent of the load requirements.

The structural engineering firm blamed the subcontracted steel manufacturer; the steel company blamed the engineers.

In the end, blame was placed squarely on the structural engineering firm, with a legal ruling stating that the firm was guilty of "a number of mistakes, errors, omissions and inadequacies" and that it had failed "to conform to the accepted custom and practice of engineering for proper communication of the engineer's design intent." Also revealed at trial was that during the construction of the hotel, the atrium roof had collapsed and that the steel manufacturing firm had committed to checking all the steel joints and welds before signing off on the project. This seeming acceptance of responsibility by the steel manufacturer did not weigh heavily on the decision to assign the overwhelming burden of responsibility on the engineering firm that designed the atrium.

The two key engineers on the Hyatt project permanently lost their engineering licenses in Missouri, but both are now practicing structural engineers in other states.

The Kansas City Hyatt Regency closed for eleven weeks for repairs and sixty other Hyatt hotels with atriums performed detailed safety inspections on their own facilities. Over 150 lawsuits were filed following the disaster, almost all of which were settled out of court.

The Hyatt Regency walkways collapse remains one of the worst structural disasters in U. S. history.

86

The Great Nashville Train Wreck

NASHVILLE, TENNESSEE

July 9, 1918

101 Dead[1]

My father was horrified. He went down there and attempted to raise the car to relieve some of the victims who were under pressure. . . . The other thing I remember was a hand pinched under the car. The man was stuck there with two dead men on his lap. He was hollering, "Oh my God! Oh my God!" Nobody could do anything to help him.

—Frank Fletcher, who witnessed the devastation when he was fourteen[2]

The worst railway disaster in U.S. history occurred during World War I and it was given very little media attention when it happened. Many of the newspapers of the time didn't bother to cover it, and those that did gave it very little space.

A total of 101 people died in the head-on collision between two trains. To this day, there has never been a train accident with a higher death toll.

So why was the accident more or less ignored? Why wasn't there an outpouring of sympathy and support for the families of the victims, along with an investigation into the causes of this tragedy?

A couple of reasons have been suggested over the years, both of which have merit.

In July 1918, the United States had been at war for four long years. Along with Great Britain, France, Russia, Belgium, Italy, and Japan, the United States had been fighting Germany, Austria-Hungary, Turkey, and Bulgaria for four years and the American people were war-weary. There was so much nonstop news about war casualties, that civilian deaths, even in such a large number, did not seem to be of much interest to the populace, and the newspapers responded accordingly.

In November 1918, the armistice ending the war was signed, but in July of that year, the battles still raged.

The other reason the collision did not get much coverage was of a more insidious nature, and bespoke the prevalent racism permeating America at the beginning of the twentieth century.

Of the 101 killed, 87 were civilians, and 14 were crew. Of the 87 civilians, the majority were black. Some historians have estimated that upward of 80 percent of the dead civilians had been African Americans, but that ratio has been disputed in recent years as possibly being too high. Whatever the actual figure, the fact is that a vast number of the dead were black.

The newspapers did cover the story, however briefly, and one report said that almost fifty thousand people "visited" the site of the wreck; some to help, far more to gawk.

Unfortunately, there was a lot at which to gawk.

The two trains had rammed each other head-on at sixty miles per hour. The explosion had been heard two miles away and felt from almost as far. Some people nearby probably thought Tennessee was having an earthquake.

The scene was as grisly as it gets. Dismembered body parts were strewn everywhere; corpses filled the overturned cars, hung from the train windows, and littered the fields around the tracks. As soon as word of the accident had spread, the "dead wagons" began arriving. Body after body was piled into the wagons to be transported to the area funeral homes. There were so many dead that mortuaries piled up the coffins on top of each other. Embalmers had to be summoned from other towns to help prepare the bodies before they began to decay in the heat of Tennessee in July.

So how did this terrible collision happen? Better yet, why did it happen and couldn't it have been prevented?

The Nashville, Chattanooga, and St. Louis Railroad ran local trains, as well as express trains for longer runs. Train number 4, the local, with engineer David Kennedy, pulled out of Union Station at 7:07 A.M., the morning of July 9, seven minutes late. It was headed for Memphis, and it was loaded with workers headed for shifts at the area munitions plants, as well as soldiers, and ordinary travelers.

The procedure was for train number 4 to stop at the Shops station, where there was a double track loop, which allowed trains to switch tracks. Engineer Kennedy would wait until given the green light that the express, train number 1, had already passed through, thereby freeing the track that number 4 needed to use.

William Floyd, the engineer of train number 1, was also running late that morning—approximately thirty-five minutes late.

Kennedy waited at the Shops station, and at 7:15, he was given a signal by the tower operator that he was free to proceed. He set out immediately and headed for Harding at close to sixty miles per hour. (Some sources say that Kennedy ignored a red stop signal at the Shops station.)

At the same time, train number 1 was headed west to Shops, on the same track on which Kennedy's train number 4 was headed east.

The two trains collided a few miles outside of Shops, hitting each other at full speed.

At least 101 were killed, and 171 were injured.

The fault for the tragedy has long been placed on engineer Kennedy. Procedure mandated that he not move from Shops until the express had passed through. If he had been given the go signal from the station tower operator, perhaps some blame can be apportioned off Kennedy and on to the operator. Yet, Kennedy was supposed to visually confirm that the express had passed before proceeding. Since he was running late, it was understandable why he would accept the go signal from the tower: he may have thought that he missed seeing the express because of being off schedule. Nevertheless, Kennedy has been held culpable ever since.

At the time of the accident, U.S. railroads were under a U.S. government department. Survivors sued the Nashville, Chattanooga, and St. Louis Railroad, but the government defended the lawsuits. Reportedly, it offered the families $100 for each person lost.

The Great Nashville Train Wreck was a tragedy laden with a sad irony.

Many of the workers who were killed were on the train to report for their first day of work.

But the day of the accident was the *last* day of work for William Lloyd, the engineer of the express. If he had lived, July 10 would have been the first day of his retirement.

[1] Some historians claim that this number is too low, and that 115 or more actually died in the wreck.

[2] "The Great Nashville Wreck of 1918," www.ezl.com/~fireball/Disaster13.htm.

87

Hurricane Andrew

THE BAHAMAS, FLORIDA, LOUISIANA

August 24, 1992

76 Dead[1]

$30 Billion in Damages[2]

It sounded like two trains crashing. People were singing, crying, chanting, praying. Children were screaming every time was there was a sudden noise. It was awful.

—Survivor Marsha Repouchin, describing conditions in a shelter during the storm[3]

We saw complete destruction all around us. All the foliage was gone. You could see windows blown out, parts of roofs missing . . . We were like an island out of time, completely cut off. It was an extremely eerie feeling.

—Eighty-year-old survivor George Grim[4]

Hurricane Andrew was the most damaging hurricane in the history of the United States. It did $30 billion in damage and left more than a quarter of a million people homeless.

In August 1992, when people learned that a hurricane named Andrew was threatening southern Florida, it had been twenty-seven years since a major hurricane had visited the area. Hurricane Betsy, a category 3, struck the Miami area in 1965, killing 75 people and doing $1.4 billion in damage. However, 1965 was a long time ago to many Dade County residents (many of whom were not even born at the time of Betsy) and the common wisdom was that it was highly unlikely that Andrew would amount to all that much.

As we now know, the common wisdom was wrong about Andrew, which ended up being a category 4, and wreaked incredible devastation on southern Dade County and southeastern Louisiana.

Andrew packed winds of up to 175 miles per hour and it took down buildings as though they were made of paper. Southern Florida is a popular area for mobile homes and by the time Andrew left, there wasn't a single one standing.

Similar to many other Atlantic hurricanes, Andrew was born as a tropical depression in the Atlantic off Cape Verde in early August 1992, and it gained strength as it moved toward Puerto Rico a couple of days before striking Florida. On Friday, September 21, Andrew passed north of Puerto Rico and by then it had grown into a tropical storm. By Saturday, Andrew had achieved category 4 status. On Sunday, it set its sights on southern Florida, and in the early morning hours of Monday, September 24, Andrew hit Biscayne Bay in Miami in Dade County with fury and destruction.

Andrew wiped out 90 percent of the buildings in the area, and wind surges were clocked at as high as 190 miles per hour after making landfall.

The southern tip of the Florida peninsula is narrow and surrounded by water on three sides. Most hurricanes weaken when they leave the ocean and make their way across an energy-sapping land mass. This was not to happen with Andrew. The hurricane moved across southern Florida in only four hours and then eased into the Gulf of Mexico. The waters of the gulf allowed Andrew to maintain its strength and remain a category 4 storm. It traveled across the gulf, and next made landfall in Louisiana, just south of New Orleans. It then continued on a northerly path into Mississippi and Alabama, bringing heavy rain, before it died out as it neared Georgia.

Andrew began to weaken immediately after hitting Louisiana, and within ten hours, it was a tropical storm; twelve hours after that, it had been downgraded to a tropical depression. Even in its weakened state, though, the storm produced upward of ten inches of rain as it moved north through Mississippi and Alabama.

Andrew did the most damage to southern Florida. Homestead Air Force Base was demolished. Its F-16s and C-130 transport planes were evacuated to bases in South Carolina and Georgia, and they never returned to Florida. The Homestead military facility had contributed $400 million a year to the local economy and employed a workforce of eight thousand, many of whom were civilians from surrounding towns. The Dade County economy took a huge hit with the destruction of the base, and five years later, some rebuilding had taken place, but the Homestead workforce was only around one thousand people.

Andrew wiped out electrical power to a staggering 1.4 million homes and businesses in Florida. A curfew was imposed in Miami to stem looting. Sixty-three thousand homes were destroyed in the Sunshine State, while more than 100 oil platforms in the Gulf of Mexico were either damaged or destroyed when Andrew raged toward New Orleans.

In Florida, agricultural crops were wiped out; in Louisiana, almost a quarter of a million people lost electricity.

After the storm, there was concern about the garbage and debris, and the rats and mosquitoes they inevitably attracted. Disease became a worry, but local authorities, with help from the federal government, worked to reopen hospitals as soon as possible, and, thankfully, massive outbreaks of cholera, typhus, dysentery, and other disease that thrive in filthy, bacteria-rampant conditions did not occur.

Today, weather forecasting satellites and new technologies allow greater accuracy in predicting hurricane paths and allowing early warnings, while preventing incorrect warnings.

Jerry Jarrell of the National Weather Service's National Hurricane Center said of the new forecasting capabilities, "Advances in forecasting technology are vital. For every mile we don't have to 'overwarn' and evacuate, we save up to $1 million."

[1] Since 1992, there have been allegations from some Dade County residents as well as from people in the media that this figure is grossly understated. Also, as with other disasters of this magnitude, the "official" death toll varies widely depending on the source. As in the case of the Florence Art Flood (chapter 79), many different sources turned up many different figures: 14 *(World Almanac)*, 15 (National Hurricane Center), 23 (Patrick J. Fitzpatrick, *Natural Disasters: Hurricanes)*, 40 (National Hurricane Center), 50 (CNN), 58, (FEMA) 59 *(Nexus Magazine)*, 62 *(Monthly Weather Review)*, 65 (Hurricaneville.com), 69 (Lee Davis, *Natural Disasters)*, 76 *(Guinness Book of World Records)*.

[2] National Hurricane Center of the National Weather Service.

[3] Lee Davis, *Natural Disasters*, 256.

[4] Ibid., 256.

88

The 1989 San Francisco Earthquake

NORTHERN CALIFORNIA, FROM SANTA CRUZ TO SAN FRANCISCO

October 17, 1989

62 Dead

$6 Billion in Damages

($3 Billion in San Francisco)

We're having an earthquake!

—ABC broadcaster Al Michaels from Candlestick Park

"We'll get you out, Julio," the firefighter said to the sobbing six-year-old boy.

Julio Berumen's mother, Petro, had been driving on the lower deck of I-880 on the Nimitz Freeway in Oakland, California, when the earthquake of 1989 struck. The upper deck of the freeway came crashing down on Julio's car, killing his mother and his mother's friend in the front seat instantly, and leaving the little boy and his sister, Cathy, pinned beneath a slab of cement and their mother's dead body in the backseat.

The rescue workers had to crawl through a three-foot space to get to Julio's car. An immediate assessment revealed that Petro and her friend were dead, eight-year-old Cathy was badly hurt, and Julio apparently not seriously injured. Even though there was a grave risk that more of the upper deck of the freeway could collapse around them, rescue workers immediately began working to free Julio and Cathy. It took them an hour and half to extricate Cathy from the car. Doctors at the scene immediately determined that she had serious internal injuries and she was rushed to the hospital. Attention then turned to freeing Julio. The outlook for the six-year-old boy, who had been stroking his dead mother's hair and crying "Mama" throughout his ordeal, was grim. He was beneath a giant piece of freeway and yet he was alive and had to be removed from the car.

Four and a half hours after his sister was rescued, Julio was pulled from the wreckage. The process has been horrific, however. Firefighters had used a chainsaw to cut the body of Julio's mother's friend in half to make room, and a surgeon had to be called in to amputate Julio's right leg. Nevertheless, Julio survived and is now almost twenty years old.

The epicenter of the quake was south of San Jose in the triangle formed by Gilroy, Santa Cruz, and Watsonville. Eleven miles below the surface of the earth, the San Andreas Fault moved.

It was probably only the ninety-year-olds that experienced déjà vu when the earth started rocking on October 17, 1989, in San Francisco. That small group of native San Franciscans would have been six or seven when the 1906 magnitude 8.3 earthquake hit, and they likely had some vague memories of what it was like to survive such a devastating event.

The 1989 magnitude 7.1 quake did not claim anywhere near as many lives as did the 1906 disaster—62, as compared to over 3,000—but the dollar value of the damage—$500 million in 1906, $6 billion in 1989—was far more severe. Many buildings, bridges, and homes that were damaged or destroyed in the 1989 quake had been built after the 1906 quake, and there was $3 billion in damages in San Francisco alone.

The 1989 event also left 3,757 people injured, some seriously, and instantly created over 12,000 new homeless people.[1]

Many people who lost their homes were out of them when the earthquake hit. Little did they know when they locked their front doors behind them that morning that the next time they would return home would be with a Department of Public Works official who would allow them fifteen minutes to gather up what they could and then leave forever.

The quake hit at 5:04 P.M. and what many Americans recall most vividly was watching it on TV. The third game of that year's World Series was scheduled for play at Candlestick Park and the game was nationally televised. When the first tremors hit, the shaking was shown on TV, but only until the electricity went out.

(San Francisco ended up being without power for three days—full power was restored on October 20.)

Although the TV feed was cut almost immediately, many people who were in Candlestick later gave firsthand accounts. One especially vivid report came from army Staff Sergeant David Langdon, assigned to relief efforts following the quake:

> The spooky part of [the earthquake] was looking up in the stands, completely full. Imagine Candlestick Park completely coming apart and going back together. To see the slabs above the upper deck separate by feet and come back together, and watch the light stanchions sway left and right from the apex to the center, about fifteen feet either way, it was a sight to behold, if you've never seen it. Then to look out to the field and just see it roll as if it were an ocean, because it was moving like a wave, just like water; waves and waves and waves. Before panic could set in, it stopped, all within about ten to fifteen seconds. Fans reacted really great; they applauded at first thinking that this is San Francisco and it would be apropos to have an earthquake during the World Series. Until we found out the devastation it had done.[2]

As Staff Sergeant Langdon correctly noted, the initial quake lasted fifteen seconds, followed by a 5.2 magnitude aftershock thirty-seven minutes later. The quake also triggered a four-foot tsunami in Monterey Bay.

The San Francisco Fire Department reported thirty-four fires in the city from the time of the earthquake through midnight, October 19, 1989. Causes included natural gas explosions, faulty generators, knocked over candles, electrical wiring shorts, problems with coffeepots and stoves, and even people barbecuing indoors after the power went off.

There was sporadic looting and the San Francisco District Attorney issued a statement that anyone arrested for looting would be held without bail.

The earthquake also caused a section of the San Francisco–Oakland Bay Bridge to collapse, requiring the bridge to be closed for a month for repairs.

For the most part, San Franciscans took everything in stride. Five days after the quake, over twenty thousand people gathered in Golden Gate Park to hear Beethoven's Ninth Symphony performed by the San Francisco Symphony. That's the symphony that includes the soaring "Ode to Joy."

The fact that tens of thousands of people who had just gone through the worst earthquake in California history in almost nine decades could participate in an ode to the positive emotion of joy, powerfully illustrates the resilient nature of the human spirit.

[1] Museum of the City of San Francisco.

[2] From an oral history compiled by Eve Iversen at the University of California at Davis.

89

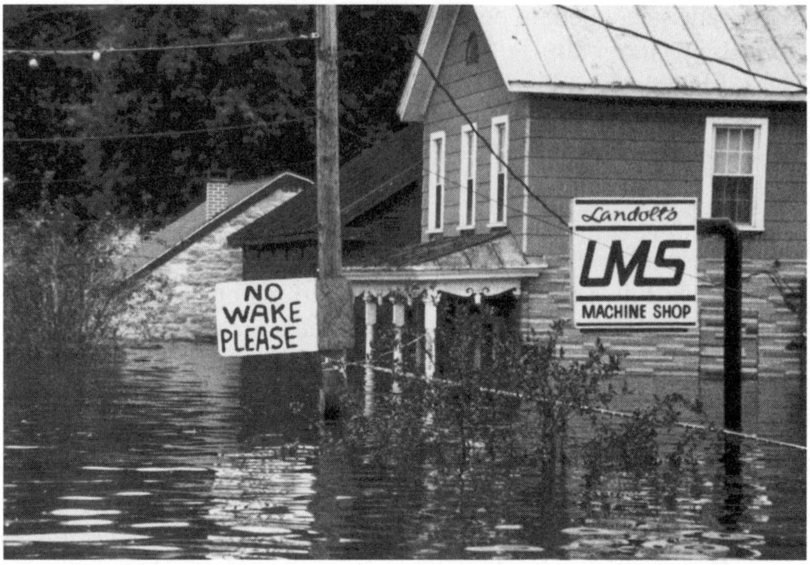

The 1993 U.S. Midwest Floods

Minnesota, North Dakota, South Dakota, Iowa, Illinois, Missouri, Nebraska, Wisconsin, Kansas

June, July, August 1993

52 Dead

$18–20 Billion in Damages

[The Mississippi] cannot be tamed, curbed or confined . . . . you cannot bar its path with an obstruction which it will not tear down, dance over and laugh at.

—Mark Twain

There was no warning whatever. The water started coming. It just kept coming.

—A Missouri farmer

Sometimes we live in a world of extremes. Feast or famine. Freeze or roast. Drought or flood.

When an area is suffering through a bone-dry, empty-sky, dust-everywhere drought, the people living in such a dust bowl cannot even begin to conceive of there one day being too much water. "I'll row to the general store if I have to," they might pray. "Just send as much rain as you can spare, dear Lord." During America's own dust bowl (chapter 95), the sand blew across the land like a pale brown snowstorm.

And then there is the other extreme, flood.

America has had problems with floods throughout her life, but she has never had to contend with floods such as the floods that inundated the Midwest during the summer of 1993. Lee W. Larson, chief of the Hydrologic Research Laboratory in the Office of Hydrology at NOAA, during a June 1996 lecture in Anaheim, California, said that the Midwest floods of 1993 "ranks as one of the greatest natural disasters ever to hit the United States," and noted, "it was certainly the largest and most significant flooding event ever to occur in the United States."[1]

There was a lot of rain and snow in the Midwest in 1992, and by the spring of 1993, the ground in the states bordering the Mississippi and Missouri Rivers was saturated. By June 1993, rivers were running high, and these factors combined to create a formula for disaster.

It started to rain on June 11, 1993, in southern Minnesota and before it stopped a foot had fallen, adding to already high rivers and streams. Close to another foot of rain fell a few days later, and the weather system that was drenching Minnesota and Iowa did not seem to want to leave the area.

June ended up being one of the wettest Junes in American history and the Mississippi rose so high that in early July all barge traffic was banned on its waters. Throughout the summer it rained and rained, causing the Mississippi to rise to record levels, and forcing evacuations in many low lying cities along its banks.

Davenport, Iowa, saw the Mississippi rise to more than six feet above flood stage; hundreds of people were evacuated; hundreds of bridges were closed to traffic.

Missouri was hit hard, with flash floods sweeping away cars and drowning the people in them, and turning acres of cropland into lakes. The Mississippi flooded the wells of West Alton, Missouri, and human waste mixed with the drinking water.

All along the Mississippi, the story was the same. Dams and levees were being washed away like someone washing mud off a driveway; none of them was built to withstand the massive amounts of water being pressed against them.

In Nebraska, thunderstorms hit with violent winds and torrential downpours.

Kansas City got seven inches of rain in five hours.

People in cities all up and down the banks of the Mississippi were evacuated by boat, and it was genuinely surreal to see rowboats in eight feet of water gliding down the main street of a town.

Doctors in hospitals had to use bottled water for scrubbing before surgery. In addition, after several days of flooding, people were revolted to see human waste floating throughout the floodwaters. Many people no doubt felt as if they were surrounded by the biggest, most disgusting toilet of all time. However, the repulsive aesthetics of the situation paled in comparison with the health risks. The *E. coli* bacteria as well as the tetanus bacteria *clostridium tetani* are abundant in feces and waters contaminated with feces. An open cut that comes in contact with such water could turn into a death sentence for the person exposed to the bacteria. Iowa and Missouri health officials issued urgent warnings for people to get tetanus shots, and to bathe after wading through the filthy water.

The Weather Channel's Weather.com Web site summed up the devastation of the U.S. Midwest Floods of 1993:

> By the end of summer, some locations had received over 30 inches of rain—nearly 200% of normal. Minnesota, Iowa, Illinois, and Missouri were hardest hit. At St. Louis, the river crested at 49.6 feet—over 19 feet above flood stage, and more than six feet above the old record set in 1973. The Mississippi remained over flood stage at St. Louis for over two months. Farther north, record flooding occurred on the Des Moines River, a tributary of the Mississippi. At one point flooding disabled a major water plant, and Des Moines, Iowa, a city of nearly 200,000 people, was without safe drinking water. Transportation and industry along the Mississippi was disrupted for months. Damages to surface and river transportation in the region were the worst ever incurred in the United States. Over 1,000 of the 1,300 levees designed to hold back flood waters failed, though major cities along the rivers, like St. Louis, were protected from flooding by massive flood walls. Over 70,000 people were displaced by the floods. Nearly 50,000 homes were damaged or destroyed and 52 people died. Over 12,000 square miles of productive farmland were rendered useless. Damage was estimated between $15–20 billion.

The floods of 1993 caused a major reevaluation of the United States's federal floodplain management policy, with special attention paid to the location and construction of levees and dams, and the management of wetlands.

Changes have been made, but there is still no guarantee that the Mississippi and Missouri floodplains would be able to withstand another onslaught like the rains of the summer of 1993.

Most home owner's insurance policies do not cover flood damages.

[1] Lee W. Larson, "Destructive Water."

90

Hurricane Hugo

Antigua, Barbuda, Dominica, Guadeloupe, Montserrat, Nevis, the British Virgin Islands, the U.S Virgin Islands, Puerto Rico, North Carolina, South Carolina

September 17–23, 1989

71 Dead

$8.5 Billion in Damages[1]

No jobs. No money. Checks and credit cards are of no value. The banks are closed. No electricity and no estimate of how many months until it is restored. No telephone service. The only communication with the rest of the country is by short-wave radio. No running water. No toilet facilities. No schools. No garbage disposal. No hospitals. Scarcely a leaf or flower on the island. Bees are biting everyone because of the loss of flora and fauna.

—St. Croix resident Michael DeLorenzo

There's a rule of thumb that for every additional 20 miles an hour, you double the damage . . . I've never seen anything like this.

—The Governor of Montserrat

We're all carpenters now, mon! —A survivor on Montserrat

Hurricane Hugo is the second costliest hurricane in U.S. history, eclipsed only by 1992's Hurricane Andrew. (See chapter 87.)

Hugo did a total of $8.5 billion in damage, of which approximately $1.4 was in Puerto Rico. The death toll for Hugo has been reported as ranging from 71 to 86, depending on the source, and depending on whether or not only the mainland United States is used for the calculation, or the total of all locales Hugo hit is factored into the sum. Most sources use the figure of 71.

Hugo's total journey was 350 miles long, and it hit the island of Montserrat first as a category 4 hurricane with sustained winds of 125 miles per hour. It left almost every one of Montserrat's 12,000 inhabitants homeless. Nine people died on Montserrat.

Next up was the island of Guadeloupe. There, Hugo killed 5 people and left 3,000 people homeless. It also destroyed almost a third of the island's roads.

Hugo then moved on to the tiny island of Nevis, causing 4 deaths, a storm surge twenty feet above normal, and destruction of a staggering 99 percent of the homes on the island.

The island of Antigua was next on Hugo's path, and 33,000 people there were made homeless. The hurricane, still maintaining winds of up to 115 miles per hour, then traveled to St. Croix and St. Thomas, bringing massive destruction with its high winds and flooding downpours.

On St. Croix, the storm's destruction was not the only problem.

After Hugo passed, the looting began immediately. Stores were robbed, and 220 prisoners fled the local prison after Hugo ripped it open. These criminals began stealing anything they could grab, and what was most horrifying for tourists was that the local police and the National Guardsmen joined in the looting, as did everyone from children to senior citizens. Tourists were also terrorized racially by the looters and many of the island's residents. There are confirmed reports that mobs of blacks—75 percent of St. Croix's population is black—began marching through the devastated streets terrorizing the white tourists and shouting "Whitey, go home!"

To restore order, then President George Bush had to send one thousand military policemen to the United States territory, enforcing martial law until things got back to some semblance of normal.

On St. Thomas, 80 percent of the island's buildings were destroyed. Next was Dominica, where no one died but the island's entire banana crop—its primary source of income—was wiped out.

After devastating the Caribbean Islands, Hugo moved on to Puerto Rico.

Still packing 120-mile-per-hour winds, the storm hit Puerto Rico's capital city, San Juan, especially hard. Vacationers in the luxury hotels were suddenly refugees in the dark without air-conditioning or electricity. Over 10,000 homes on Puerto Rico were destroyed by Hugo, 80 percent of its coffee crop was destroyed, and the airport was shut down by the damage.

After Hugo left Puerto Rico, it headed for the eastern coast of the United States, bypassing Florida and heading straight for the Carolinas.

Hugo hit Charleston, South Carolina, on Thursday, September 21, 1989, with 135-mile-per-hour winds, and immediately cut off all electricity to the city.

Half of Charleston's residents evacuated inland to shelters, but some stayed behind, finding themselves in a surreal, apocalyptic nightmare.

There was broken glass ankle deep in the streets; ships from the harbor were strewn along the city streets; windows in the destroyed homes regularly exploded from the fires; there were feet of mud inside buildings.

Hugo did over $1 million in damage to the Civil War site Fort Sumter; Charleston Air Force Base was essentially demolished; and Charleston's mayor was quoted as saying, "We have on our hands a degree of physical destruction that is unprecedented in everyone's living memory."[2]

One man returned to where his house was supposed to be in Charleston. All that stood on his lot was a water heater. The entire house had been picked up and hurled 120 feet north, into his neighbor's yard.

The next day Hugo moved inland two hundred miles to Charlotte, North Carolina, with seventy-mile-per-hour winds and gusts to ninety miles per hour.

After Hugo left the Carolinas, it started raining in the area in torrential downpours, which added greatly to the misery and delayed the cleanup.

Power was out for three-quarters of a million people in the Carolinas. The total population for North and South Carolina is approximately ten million people; thus, one in ten people had no electricity, thanks to Hurricane Hugo.

Over $100 million in damage was done to Carolina crops; $1 billion of damage was done to South Carolina's timber crop.

The final death toll attributed to Hugo was 71, with almost half of the deaths occurring in the United States.

The final numbers paint a grim picture of the destruction one storm can do to a region.

Destroyed were 3,785 homes and 5,185 mobile homes and 292,000 jobs were lost.

[1] Patrick J. Fitzpatrick, *Natural Disasters: Hurricanes,* 134.

[2] Lee Davis, *Natural Disasters,* 282.

91

The Explosion of the *Hindenburg*

LAKEHURST, NEW JERSEY

May 6, 1937

36 Dead

After watching [the dirigible crew's] methods, it is the firm conviction of this reporter that only a stroke of war or an unfathomable act of God will ever mar this German dirigible's passenger safety record.

—W. B. Courtney, *Collier's*, 1936

It's burning, bursting into flames and is falling on the mooring mast and all the folks, we—this is one of the worst catastrophes in the world! It's a terrific sight! Oh, the humanity and all the passengers!

—Herb Morrison, reporting live in Lakehurst, May 6, 1937

Adolf Hitler was especially proud of the German dirigible *Hindenburg*, and the swastika, adopted as the symbol of Nazi Germany in 1935, proudly adorned its tail fins. When told of the explosion of the *Hindenburg*, Hitler was reportedly "stunned," but refused formal comment. Later, although the official Nazi news agency announced that dirigible travel across the Atlantic would continue "unabated," the *Hindenburg* catastrophe effectively put an end to airship travel. (Ironically, the *San Francisco Chronicle* reported Hitler's shock at the accident on its May 7, 1937, front page, directly beneath the headline "Crowd Views Holocaust at Lakehurst.")

Years before the start of World War II, the United States didn't really trust Hitler and his National Socialist Party (Nazis), but we did business with them, and we allowed Germany-to-America airship flights. Passengers who could afford the flight—$400 each way—could get from Frankfurt to New Jersey in just over two days, and they could do it in luxury and with style. The vessel had staterooms with toilets, showers, and hot and cold running water, a dining room with long picture windows (that opened!) and service on fine china, and even a smoking room.

The *Hindenburg* was the largest airship of all time (one of two planned sister ships). She measured 803 feet in length, just 78 feet shorter than another doomed megaship, the nautical *Titanic*. (See chapter 50.) The *Hindenburg* was built by the Graf Zeppelin Company and was considered the ultimate way to travel by air. Four state-of-the-art, twelve-hundred-horsepower, Mercedes-Benz diesel engines powered it. Planes of the time were small, unsafe, and incapable of traveling any real distances.

The airship was originally conceived to be filled with lighter-than-air, nonflammable helium. When the Congress passed the Helium Control Act and refused to sell the Graf Zeppelin Company the helium it needed (fearing the Nazis might eventually use their airships for military purposes), the Graf Zeppelin Company decided to use the lightest of all gases, plentiful hydrogen, a gas that also happened to be highly flammable. However, the airship makers had no choice, and hydrogen was chosen as the replacement for helium, specifically, over seven million cubic feet of the extremely combustible gas.

In the 1930s, smoking was considered an ordinary and, in many cases, necessary part of life. Cigarettes, pipes, and cigars were lit up everywhere—even in hospital beds and, yes, on dirigibles—and the only concession to the potential dangers of smoking inside a giant bag filled with millions of cubic feet of flammable gas was to strictly control the means of passengers lighting their smoke of choice. An electric lighter was attached to a chain in the smoking room of the airship and this was the only means for lighting a cigarette. Passengers were searched for matches and lighters when they boarded, but after that, they could smoke at will on board in the sealed-off smoking room.

But it was not a passenger's carelessly tossed cigarette that caused the explosion of the *Hindenburg*.

As the *Hindenburg* approached the airfield in Lakehurst, New Jersey, members of the ground crew noticed a small fluttering of the airship's outer covering. Fifteen seconds later, flames shot from the area where the rippling had occurred, ignited the dirigible's cellulose skin (which had been impregnated with aluminum and a flammable dope resin), and sent a fountain of fire shooting up out of the rear section of the airship. Within thirty-two seconds, the *Hindenburg* was reduced to a burned-out shell, crumpled on the ground. All sixteen of the airship's hydrogen chambers were engulfed by the time the ship hit the ground.

The *Hindenburg* carried 61 crewmembers and 36 passengers. The fire and crash killed 13 passengers and 22 crewmen from on board and 1 civilian handler on the ground.

One fourteen-year-old boy was saved through a fluke of luck. As flames engulfed him, one of the *Hindenburg*'s ballast tanks burst and showered the boy with water, saving his life.

The arrival of the *Hindenburg* in New Jersey was of great public interest, so there were many newsreel cameramen filming its approach and mooring, as well as still photographers snapping pictures. Thus, the media recorded the fiery death of the *Hindenburg*, and newsreel footage of the dirigible on fire played for months in movie theaters in America and Europe.

No Garlic

What caused the *Hindenburg* to catch fire and explode?

Most experts agree that electricity in the atmosphere ignited the fire. For years, it was believed that the flammable hydrogen in the vessel's gas cells immediately ignited and caused the enormous conflagration.

New studies, however, have pointed to anomalies that have since resulted in a different conclusion.

Former NASA Hydrogen Fuel Program Manager, Richard G. Van Treuren, in an article titled "Blame Hydrogen?" in the May 1997 issue of *Air & Space Smithsonian* magazine, explains why he and many others no longer believe that ignited, burning hydrogen was to blame for the destruction of the *Hindenburg*.

The first discrepancy in the "burning hydrogen" theory is the captain's insistence that his control gauges did not show a hydrogen leak at the time of the fire, nor did anyone smell garlic. Garlic was added to the odorless hydrogen gas (much the way sulfur odor is added today to natural gas) to call attention to a leak. No garlic smell was reported by any of the survivors.

Another problem with the initial hypothesis about the fire is that newsreel footage of the crash of the airship shows that the front end of the dirigible bounced when it first struck the ground, indicating the presence of a significant quantity of buoyant hydrogen—which, theoretically, had already ignited and was burning.

Trueren's conclusion is that the *Hindenburg*'s mooring ropes acted to conduct electricity and that an electrical plasma event in the atmosphere produced thousands of degrees of electricity and ozone, and ozone is deadly to aluminum, which was the primary component of the *Hindenburg*'s outer shell. It was the aluminum-impregnated shell and the flammable dope it was coated with that burned, not the hydrogen.

* * *

The crash of the *Hindenburg*, with its resultant death toll, effectively put an end to airship travel. The safety record of this kind of transportation had previously been impeccable, but the *Hindenburg* negated all that in one brief, spectacular inferno, recorded and played to shocked audiences. Two years after the crash of the *Hindenburg*, the first transatlantic passenger airplane flight took place and the era of the lighter-than-air dirigible was over.

Postscript

The *Hindenburg* catastrophe effectively put an end to using dirigibles for transportation. However, the dirigible was given a new life in 2002 as a low-cost, high-efficiency alternative to communications satellites.

In 2002, the London firm Advanced Technology Group announced the launch of its StratSat airship, a helium-filled dirigible that is also powered by gas and solar power. The StratSat will hover twelve miles above earth, out of the air traffic routes, filled with over a ton of high-tech transmitting equipment. One StratSat will remain in position within a half-mile radius for three to five years, and will able to cover an area of approximately seventy-two square miles—about the size of a big city, or even a small country. Photran, a company sponsored by the Malaysian government was ATG's first customer.

92

The 1991 Oakland Hills Fires

The Hills Above Oakland and Berkeley, California

October 20–24, 1991

25 Dead

$2 Billion in Damages

The transfer of fires from trees to decks to roof gutters filled with dead pine needles caused one house after another to burn like one match in a matchbook lighting the next match . . . To be a witness to the sight of so many homes engulfed in flames and to have no fire-fighters in sight was terrifying.

—Witness Don Pearman of PCI & Associates

Sunday has long been a day of rest. Even during fire season.

But Sunday, October 20, 1991, turned into anything but a restful day in the

Oakland, California, hills when a firestorm consumed 1,600 acres, 2,500 homes and businesses, and 450 apartments and condominiums. No one knows how this fire—the worst urban fire in U.S. history and the worst fire in California's history—started, but it is believed that a "suspicious" blaze on Saturday, October 19, may have been the cause of this massive disaster.

The Saturday fire was quickly put out. The winds were only at five miles per hour, so it did not spread beyond its initial area.

The following morning, though, the enormous fire that would claim 25 lives erupted, and there is suspicion that smoldering duff (decaying leaves and branches on the forest floor) ignited and quickly grew into a conflagration, thanks to the high winds of the day.

The Oakland and Berkeley fire was an "interface fire." An interface fire is a fire that begins at the place were wildlife and urban construction meet and, in some places (backyards, decks, roofs) commingle.

All of the components of a major wildlife/urban interface fire were present on October 20, 1991, in Oakland: the area was experiencing extremely high air temperatures; there was an enormous amount of dry vegetation surrounding the houses; many of the houses were constructed with highly combustible materials; there had been a long dry spell (the area had been suffering through a five-year drought); and extremely high winds were racing through the hills. All of these elements, combined with a suspicious fire that may not have been completely put out, were a formula for disaster.

How quickly did the fire spread? Quickly enough to burn down 790 homes in its first hour. The intensity of the conflagration rapidly transformed the fire into a firestorm, a catastrophic meteorological event in which were formed fire tornadoes that suck up air at their base. This air feeds the flames at the top of the tornado, with the tornado essentially creating its own weather to keep itself alive.

Houses in the Oakland Hills area at the time cost at least $1 million to build, and they were in demand. Views from these homes were spectacular. The Golden Gate Bridge, the San Francisco Bay, and the city of San Francisco itself were laid out beneath the Oakland Hills.

Many of the houses were single-family dwellings, and the surrounding foliage camouflaged many of them. This proximity to flammable growth hanging all over many of the homes contributed greatly to the $2 billion in damages caused by the fire.

Fire services are often slow to reach outlying areas. When they do show up at a major wildlife fire, the primary goal of the firefighters is to contain the fire. Single dwellings are considered expendable. In cities, building fires are often put out quickly because of the proximity to fire-fighting services, equipment, and personnel, but it make take a half hour or longer for fire trucks to reach the isolated areas in the hills where the fires are raging. This was the situation with the Oakland fires.

And there were other things that were done wrong that made everything much worse.

Many of the Oakland Hills and Berkeley homes were built with flammable wooden shingle roofs, non-fire-resistant decks, and combustible construction materials. Also, many of the roofs were not steep enough. Some houses with wooden shingle roofs actually did not burn. Why? Because the roofs had such a steep pitch that the burning embers from the forest fire blown onto the house by the wind simply rolled off the steep roofs.

After the fire started to spread, the problems in fighting it and saving lives began with a vengeance.

Gas lines ruptured, and then ignited into fountains of flame. Electrical power was cut off and water reservoirs dried up. The winding, narrow roads in the area prevented firefighters from maneuvering into positions to fight the fire. Communications failed due to the heavy telephone and radio traffic by both fire personnel and civilians, and incident commanders could not coordinate firefighting efforts.

And the narrow roads were a death trap. The huge fire apparatus couldn't move through them, and the number of abandoned cars clogging the roads complicated this. During the Oakland fires, many people who started out in their cars in an attempt to flee to safety ended up abandoning their vehicles in the roads when they couldn't get out, then trying to run to safety. These abandoned vehicles became roadblocks for the fire trucks. Drivers were also trapped in the gridlocked roads, including a police car filled with evacuees and a police officer, all of whom died in the fire. Ironically, the isolation of the homes in the Oakland Hills might have qualified the area for "fire hazard area" status, which would have put in place certain preventative measures by the municipality before a fire started, but Oakland Hills did not qualify because of one factor: the homes in the area were accessible by paved roads.

Smoke gravely limited visibility and temperatures eventually reached two thousand degrees Fahrenheit—the temperature necessary to cremate a human body. The asphalt on the streets began bubbling from the intensity of the heat.

The winds died down to five miles per hour by Sunday night and the fire began moving back over already burned areas. This was a major improvement and firefighters had the fire contained by the third day and under control by the fourth. The total effort to put out the fire and to save lives was enormous, and involved 88 engine strike teams, 6 air tankers, 16 helitac units, 8 communications units, 2 management teams, 2 mechanics, more than 700 search and rescue personnel, 767 law-enforcement officers, the California Office of Emergency Services, Federal Emergency Management Agency, the Red Cross, and the Salvation Army. The police were unfortunately necessary, too: looters posing as volunteers burglarized the homes of people who had evacuated.

Thirty percent of the people who lost homes in the fire refused to return and rebuild, and the city lost a big part of its tax base.

Nevertheless, certain changes were made and today there is a policy in place that all reservoirs must be kept filled during fire season, and there are emergency generators in the area. Some of the dangerous building practices that contributed to the enormous losses have also been curtailed, and now fire prevention precautions are always part of new construction.

93

The Great London Fire of 1666

LONDON, ENGLAND

September 2–6, 1666

8 Dead

Thus lay in ashes the most venerable Churche, one of the antientest Pieces of early Piety in the Christian World.

—Diarist John Evelyn, writing on September 7, 1666, about the destruction by fire of St. Paul's Cathedral

Only eight people died in this massive conflagration, but the Great London Fire of 1666 still is noteworthy for having destroyed three-quarters of the capital city of the United Kingdom, essentially erasing what we now refer to as old London and occasioning the building of the London we know today.

The fire raged for five days, mainly because there was no way to fight a large fire in seventeenth-century London, especially once it spread out of control. (The Great Fire dramatically illustrated the public safety shortcomings in London and after the fire was out and the rebuilding had commenced, the world's first municipal fire department was formed. The fire also prompted the creation of the world's first fire insurance company. Better late than never.)

The fire started small, grew quickly, and spread extensively.

Thomas Farynor, one of King Charles's bakers, worked in his shop on Pudding Lane until ten P.M. on the evening of September 1, 1666. At that time, he extinguished his ovens (so he claimed later) and went upstairs to bed.

A few hours later, sometime between midnight and two in the morning (the historical records are somewhat contradictory), he and his family were awakened by smoke and flames from downstairs. Perhaps believing it was already too big to control, Farynor did not make any attempt to put out the fire, and he and his family fled their home by climbing out a window and scurrying across the neighboring roofs. Most of Farynor's household staff followed the master except for one maid, a young woman terrified of heights who chose to remain behind. She was burned to death by the flames and is considered the fire's first official victim.

As the fire raged, the lord mayor was summoned and he was rather displeased to have been awakened and rousted from his home. "Pssshh," he snapped angrily upon his arrival at Pudding Lane. "A woman could piss it out!" He went back to bed.

Shortly thereafter a wind blew flaming cinders across the lane from the bakery and set fire to hay stored for horses behind the Star Inn. The combination of London's tightly packed houses, wood-framed buildings, and a lively wind soon conspired to burn down the entire block on which once stood the Farynor Bakery.

The fire then spread throughout the entire city, fueled by exploding barrels of wine, lamp oil, resin, and brandy stored in warehouses that the fire consumed. Strong winds helped even more.

People began running toward the Thames, where watermen charged incredible sums to carry them to safety.

The fire burned until Thursday of that week before the winds died down and the fire-fighting efforts, such as they were, finally quenched the flames.

The English civil servant and diarist Samuel Pepys, wrote at length about the fire:

> [T]he Lieutenant of the Tower . . . tells me that it begun this morning in the King's bakers house in Pudding-lane, and that it hath burned down St. Magnes Church and most part of Fishstreete already . . . Poor people staying in their houses as long as till the very fire touched them, and then running into boats or clambering from one pair of stair by the water-side to another. And among other things, the poor pigeons I perceive were loath to leave their houses, but hovered about the windows and balconies till they were some of them burned, their wings, and fell down.

• • •

> [We] saw the fire grow; and as it grow darker, appeared more and more . . . upon steeples and between churches and houses, as far as we could see up the hill of the City, in a most horrid malicious bloody flame, nit like a fine flame of an ordinary fire . . . [We] saw the fire as only one entire arch of fire from this to the other side of the bridge, and in a bow up the hill, for an arch of above a mile long, and all on fire and flaming at once, and a horrid noise the flames made, and the cracking of houses at their ruine.[1]

There were many attempts to put out the fire. Firefighters tore down unburned houses that were in the path of the fire in order to stop the spread. (This did not go over well with the occupants of the untouched houses, many of whom were not even convinced that their homes were in danger.) Leather buckets of water wielded by human chains were poured endlessly on the flames. The British navy blew up houses with gunpowder to stop the fire's spread.

In the end, it was the dying of the wind that finally put an end to the inferno.

The toll was enormous. No fewer than 13,200 houses were burned, along with 85 of London's 109 churches. More than 100,000 people were left homeless, 400 streets were wiped out, totaling 396 acres of devastation. Hundreds of businesses went bankrupt.

After the smoke settled, London architects designed a beautiful new city, smartly laid out, with a balance of residences, businesses, parks, roads, and other amenities.

Impatience won out over aesthetics, however, and houses were built quickly, in many cases duplicating the crowded layout of Old London.

Now, however, the new London, as disorganized as the city planning might have been, today has a very efficient fire department.

[1] Samuel Pepys, *Diary,* in Eyewitness to History, 188.

94

The *Exxon Valdez* Oil Spill

Prince William Sound, Alaska

March 24, 1989

$3.03–$8.03 Billion[1] in Losses

Evidently we're losing some oil and we're going to be here a while.
—*Exxon Valdez* Captain Joseph Hazelwood

The *Exxon Valdez* oil spill changed the natural order of things in Prince William Sound, Alaska, and its full environmental impact has yet to be determined.

Due to the spill, a pod of killer whales living in the sound lost 13 of its 36 members in the two years following the catastrophe. Ten years later, this pod has not regained its former size and has added only 3 new members. And what is most shocking is that a mother whale and some of her offspring left their established pod to join a different pod—behavior never before seen in killer whales.

When the *Exxon Valdez* ran aground on Bligh Reef at 12:04 A.M. on March 24, 1989, it spilled 10.8 million gallons (257,000 barrels) of oil. This was equivalent to the amount of water in 125 Olympic-sized swimming pools, and was 20 percent of the *Valdez*'s 53,094,510-gallon cargo of oil.

The *Exxon Valdez* spill is the largest oil spill ever to occur in the United States, and it ranks as the thirty-fourth worst oil spill worldwide. It is, however, considered the worst spill of all time in terms of the damage it did to the environment. Approximately 1,300 miles of Alaska shoreline was polluted with oil, 200 miles of which were very heavily covered with oil. The spill ultimately stretched 460 miles, extending all the way down the Alaskan Peninsula to the village of Chignik.

Of the 10.8 million gallons of oil released from the ship, approximately 1.5 million gallons were recovered by cleaning crews; 1.4 million gallons sunk to the ocean floor; and 216,000 gallons remained on the beaches. The rest is believed to have either evaporated or degraded through the effect of natural forces such as winter storms, rain, and the effect of the tides.

(In what might be the most profound product endorsement in the history of commerce, the veterinarians, biologists, and volunteers who cleaned up the oil-drenched birds and sea otters of Prince William Sound following the *Exxon Valdez* oil spill, used Dawn diswashing detergent to clean the animals.)

The damage the oil did to the many species of wildlife in the area is still being felt more than ten years after the accident.

Tragically, the common loons, cormorants (pelagic, double-crested, and red-faced), harbor seals, harlequin ducks, killer whales, and pigeon guillemots in the area are not recovering at all from the damaging effects of the spill.

The black oystercatchers, common murres, marbled murrelets, mussels, Pacific herring, pink salmon, sea otters, sockeye salmon, and clams are in the process of recovering.

The bald eagles and river otters in the area have fully recovered.

How did the *Valdez* oil spill accident happen?

In simplest terms, the *Valdez*'s third mate and its helmsman both failed to make a right turn as they had been instructed to by Captain Joseph Hazelwood, who had retired to his cabin before the grounding. Captain Hazelwood was given a blood alcohol test several hours after the accident and was found to have alcohol in his blood. He has consistently denied being impaired and a jury found him not guilty of operating a seagoing vessel under the influence. He was, however, found guilty of negligent discharge of oil, and fined $50,000 and sentenced to one thousand hours of community service in Alaska.

The case against Exxon by the state of Alaska and the U.S. federal government was more complicated and took two years to resolve. On October 19, 1991, a three-part settlement package was approved by the U.S. District Court.

The final settlement consisted of a criminal plea agreement, a criminal restitution agreement, and a civil settlement.

In the criminal plea agreement, Exxon was fined $150 million, of which $125 million was forgiven in recognition of the company's efforts to clean up the spill and make private restitution.

In the criminal restitution agreement, Exxon paid $100 million to the state and federal governments for the damage the oil did to the land and wildlife.

In the civil settlement, Exxon agreed to pay $900 million over ten years into funds administered by the state and federal governments.

Even though the amount of oil spilled by the *Exxon Valdez* does not place it in the category of the largest spills, its impact has been enormous. The reason? The undeniable obscenity of spilling oil all over one of the most pristine and beautiful places in the world. An oil spill in the middle of the ocean, or in a highly trafficked, already polluted harbor does not bother people as much as one in an untouched wilderness. It can be compared to the difference between a car splashing mud on a man's dirty coveralls, and a woman's brand-new white dress. The damage to the dress is somehow profane, and it bothers us more. This is what happened with the *Valdez* oil spill. The world was aghast at the scenes of the magnificent vistas of Alaska and Prince William Sound sullied by thick, black oil, and the most heartwrenching photos of all were those of helpless animals covered completely in oil.

Oil is the lifeblood of every industrialized nation. It is the solvent that allows the machinery of commerce and industry to exist.

And yet, oil is hard to find, expensive to refine and transport, and dreadfully difficult to clean up.

Are spills like that of the *Exxon Valdez* the inevitable price we must pay for energy when we want it, and in the quantity in which we want it?

[1] $5.03 billion in awarded damages has been appealed and is still in the courts. June 14, 2002, Exxon Mobil filed a motion in federal court to reduce the awarded damages to less than $40 million.

95

The Dust Bowl

THE U. S. GREAT PLAINS: KANSAS, OKLAHOMA, ARKANSAS, TEXAS, NEW MEXICO, COLORADO, NEBRASKA, NORTH DAKOTA, SOUTH DAKOTA

1932–1937

$1 Billion[1] in Losses

"How many today, Hiram?" Sarah Pike had her hands in a drawer up to her wrists. She was kneading bread the only way she could to prevent the dust from getting into the dough.

Hiram Pike walked across the kitchen in his long johns, having removed his dust-covered overalls and boots out on the porch. At the sink, he ran his finger across the faucet, and left a line in the dust that covered the brass fixture. Hiram shook his head disgustedly and turned on the water.

"I just wiped that down not ten minutes ago," his wife, Sarah, said in response to his unspoken criticism. Everyone's nerves were on edge and Sarah knew that Hiram was always in a foul mood after a rabbit drive.

"I didn't say nuthin'," Hiram grunted.

Sarah knew better than to go on, so she kept kneading and tried to turn the topic away from the dust and back to the rabbits.

"How many today, Hiram?"

Hiram turned off the faucet, shook off his hands, and grabbed the faded dish towel from the hook next to the window. He automatically shook it out over the sink before he used it, and then turned to face his wife.

"Pret' near a thousand. I brought back four good-sized. Maybe you can make a stew." Jackrabbits were gamy and stringy but Sarah could usually make a decent meal out of one or two by adding spices and some of the root vegetables they had pickled and canned during better times.

Hiram loved animals and hated to see them suffer or die needlessly. He had no problem with slaughtering pigs or selling cattle for meat, but rabbit drives got to him. Every Sunday since the dust storms had started, dozens of local men would meet at an area where there had been lots of rabbits spotted. They would form a mile-wide circle that they would then tighten by marching toward the center, driving hundreds of jackrabbits ahead of them. The jackrabbit population had skyrocketed after the droughts started and they were notorious for eating anything that grew, including the meager crops the local farmers tried so desperately to keep alive. So on Sundays they would have a rabbit drive. Once the day's catch was trapped in the circle, the farmers and their sons would wade in and beat them all to death with clubs and pipes. Guns weren't allowed. Hiram participated, of course, but he hated it. And he was always testy when he got home.

"I'll see what I can do," Sarah said complacently.

"They're out on the porch."

"All right."

Hiram then headed toward the bedroom to remove his filthy long johns and put on clean ones. If there were clean ones, that is. Sometimes Sarah's laundry would be covered in mud if she happened to hang them on the line at the wrong time.

On his way to the bedroom, Hiram hoped his long johns would be clean. And he also hoped for rain.

Hiram knew the odds against either of his wishes coming true were slim. And he was right.

The Dust Bowl was a five-year period in American history when mismanagement of soil, terrible droughts, and the Great Depression combined to create a twenty-five-thousand-square-mile area of barren destitution in nine states. There was too much plowing, too much grazing, and not enough rain, and the result was a crippling of the land. Farmers lost their farms and their homes; land was abandoned. (John Steinbeck wrote the novel *The Grapes of Wrath* about this period.)

In 1934, the U.S. government's *Yearbook of Agriculture* spelled out the chilling statistics:

- 35 million acres of cultivated land had been destroyed by shortsighted crop growth.

- 100 million acres of tillable land had lost most of its topsoil; in some cases, the land had lost all of its topsoil.
- At the time the Yearbook was published, an additional 125 million acres were losing all or most of their topsoil.

People who spent too much time outside, futilely trying to prevent their soil from blowing away in the windstorms, would often end up choking and unable to breathe. Some would vomit mud. Doctors reported people dying because their lungs filled with sand.

In the World War I years (1914–1918), the midwestern farmers had been encouraged to grow as much wheat as possible in support of the war effort. This resulted in tens of thousands of acres of previously grass-covered land being used for widespread planting. The grass had always kept the soil anchored down, but when the grass was stripped away and crops were planted, the soil became vulnerable to high winds, blistering sun, lack of rain, and other environmental factors, and enormous areas were at risk if the rains didn't come. When the rains did *not* come, rich soil turned to dead dust; and when the winds followed, the dust blew like snow in a blizzard.

In April 1935, the *Dallas* (Texas) *Morning News* ran a humorous blurb that illustrated the reach of these midwestern dust storms:

> Texas housewives are refusing to clean house until Oklahoma, Kansas and Nebraska make up their minds to stay put.

Government efforts to help the impoverished farmers included grants, mortgage programs, and soil erosion prevention programs. Much of this was too little, too late, however, and many farmers abandoned their farms, packed up everything they owned, and headed to California to look for work. These farmers became migrant workers known as "Okies" from Steinbeck's *Grapes of Wrath.* It is estimated that over 300,000 farmers and their families lost everything during the Dust Bowl years.

The great drought ended when the rains came in 1938. It was too late for many who had given up, but wise soil management policies, combined with an improving overall economic climate and, of course, rain, transformed thousands of dry, dusty acres back into fields covered with "amber waves of grain."

Today, drought is still an issue for midwestern farmers, although there have been enormous steps taken to prevent a dust bowl of the 1930s from happening again.

There is, however, no guarantee that Mother Nature will cooperate.

[1] In 1930s dollars.

96

The 1979 Three Mile Island Nuclear Accident

Middletown, Pennsylvania

March 28, 1979

$1.1 Billion in Damages

We actually thought the plant was too well designed to have a serious accident. It was kind of like the Titanic.
—Former Nuclear Regulatory Commission official Harold Denton

In 1977, singer-songwriter Gil Scott-Heron wrote and recorded a song called "We Almost Lost Detroit," which was about the partial meltdown accident at the Enrico Fermi Nuclear Reactor I in Monroe, Michigan, in October 1966. The title of the song came from something an engineer at the plant actually said after the accident. The plant was shut down for four years following the accident but was restarted and put back into service in 1970. It was permanently shut down in 1972. The Fermi II reactor, at the same site, was completed in 1985 and will go out of service in 2025.

Two years after Scott-Heron's haunting song had gotten people thinking about—and fearing—a nuclear power plant meltdown, the Three Mile Island accident occurred in Unit 2 (TMI-2) of the facility's two reactors. The plant had been in service for three months when the accident happened and, before the accident, it had already been shut down in January 1979 for two weeks because of the failure of two safety valves.

The Three Mile Island accident released radiation into the atmosphere. Thankfully, the amount of radiation was very low and it did not cause any deaths, nor did it prompt the governor of Pennsylvania to call for a mass evacuation of the immediate area. (He did, however, ask people to stay in their homes with all the windows closed until officials could declare the situation stabilized.)

Even though the impact of the incident seems relatively benign (as compared to, say, the Chernobyl nuclear power plant accident—see chapter 36), the accident at Three Mile Island was the worst nuclear power plant accident in American history. Since the Three Mile Island accident in 1979, there has not been a single new nuclear power plant ordered for construction in the United States. This is a direct result of what happened at Three Mile Island. Even more indicative of the thinking about nuclear power in the past twenty years is the fact that fifty-nine nuclear reactors that had been planned, designed, and funded before Three Mile Island were canceled after the accident and never built. The only new nuclear power plants that have come online since Three Mile Island are those plants that were already completed or near completion at the time of the accident.

Questions about the safety of nuclear power cannot change some basic facts about its efficiency in generating electricity. According to the Nuclear Energy Institute, America's appetite for computers and its increasing reliance on a digital economy is expected to increase demand for electricity by up to 35 percent by 2010. Today, computers and peripherals account for 13 percent of all electricity use. This will rise to 25 percent by 2020.

The following chart illustrates why nuclear power is not going to go away—even with the threat and actual occurrence of accidents such as those at Three Mile Island, Enrico Fermi, and even Chernobyl.

1999 Electricity Production Costs[1]

Type of Energy	***Cost per Kilowatt-hour***
Natural gas	$.0352
Oil	$.0324
Coal	$.0207
Nuclear	$.0183

Nuclear power costs almost half what natural gas costs, and, in an energy-hungry world, this means a great deal. Thus are the increasing fears that accidents will continue, and, that someday, there will be one that will do apocalyptic damage.

What happened at the Three Mile Island nuclear power plant, and who or what is to blame?

The accident was a combination of mechanical failures and human error.

A valve that controlled the flow of cooling water in and out of the reactor did not close as it should have, and water began flowing out of the reactor. This caused the reactor core to become much too hot, over five thousand degrees Fahrenheit, which resulted in some of the fuel rods melting. This released radioactive gas and water into the area.

Alarms that should have gone off did not; gauges and dials that should have been visible were obscured by hanging inspection tags; gauges that *were* visible reported erroneous figures; temperature readings were distrusted by plant technicians . . . the list goes on. The end result is that half the core of the reactor ended up exposed and radioactivity levels in the system's primary water supplies reached 350 times normal levels before the situation was corrected, fifteen hours and fifty minutes after the accident began.

The possibility of a total reactor core meltdown at Three Mile Island was very real. If this had happened, an explosion would have devastated the building and spread radioactivity over hundreds of square miles in Middletown and other Pennsylvania cities and towns. (Three Mile Island is only a few miles from Harrisburg.) This is what tragically happened at Chernobyl and radioactive gas from that explosion spread all over Europe. If Three Mile Island had followed suit, it is not farfetched that radioactivity from the explosion could have drifted as far as Los Angeles.

It took eleven years to clean up the Three Mile Island accident and it cost $973 million. Its sister unit, TMI-1, was shut down for six years to make over one hundred modifications based on what went wrong with TMI-2, at a cost of $95 million. Although some experts claim that the amount of radiation released was so small that there should be only one extra death from cancer caused by the accident, it is clear that it is still too early to know the full impact on the environment and the population in the area surrounding the plant.

[1] Nuclear Energy Institute, 2001.

97

The 1929 U.S. Stock Market Crash

UNITED STATES

October 29, 1929

$30 Billion+ in losses

You had to stand in line to get a window to jump out of, and speculators were selling space for bodies in the East River.

—Humorist Will Rogers, commenting on the aftereffects of the 1929 stock market crash

The line stretched along the lobby, out the bank's double doors, all the way down the block, and around the corner. The dozens of people in line were on the verge of panic, and yet most tried to maintain whatever calm they could muster. By day's end, most of these people would have lost all the money they had in the bank. Almost none of them would manage to make it to the teller's window to withdraw what they had before their bank closed and, ultimately, failed, one of the four thousand or so banks that could not survive the run on their deposits triggered by the stock market crash of 1929.

* * *

Calvin Coolidge never saw it coming and Herbert Hoover made it worse.

Many historians contend that President Coolidge's reluctance to put governmental restrictions on stock market speculation led to the Stock Market Crash of 1929.

Herbert Hoover is blamed for making the Great Depression that followed the Crash worse by signing into law the Smoot-Hawley Tariff, which imposed staggeringly high taxes on imported goods. (A thousand economists pleaded with him to veto it, to no avail.) The intent of Smoot-Hawley was to discourage imports of goods that were also available in the United States, thereby protecting the small American manufacturers. It did not work out that way, however, and the actual result was an international trade war that deepened and lengthened the Great Depression.

There is debate over whether or not the Crash of 1929 was the actual (only) cause of the Great Depression. Since there were many causes for the Great Depression in the United States and the worldwide depression it triggered, it is somewhat misguided to try to look to a single precipitating event for something so catholic.

Yet, as a single event, the Crash of 1929 had a devastating effect on the United States and the world, and, thus, must be ranked as one of the worst domestic financial catastrophes in history.

On Thursday, October 24, 1929, America was given a preview of things to come. On that day, stock values plummeted drastically and the New York Stock Exchange was transformed into a madhouse of manic, frantic traders trying to dump whatever shares they could before they lost everything. There were over 1,100 traders on the floor that day to handle the sell orders. On a normal day, 750 would have been enough. The word had gotten out to New Yorkers that there was some kind of financial emergency in the offing and thousands gathered on Wall Street, trying desperately to learn what they could about what was going on inside.

"What have you heard?" "How much has the market dropped?" "What should we do?" All these questions buzzed through the anxious crowd as those who had been able to make it into the visitors' gallery came outside.

None other than Winston Churchill was in the gallery that day, and he probably watched with shock along with all the others as stocks went down, down, down.

At one o'clock, the downslide was halted when a group of the biggest bankers "chipped in" to invest $20 million in the most important stocks. This seemed to do the trick and about two-thirds of that day's losses were recovered by the end of the trading day.

However, the respite was temporary and after a few days of edgy ups and downs, the market crashed on October 29, "Black Tuesday," when $15 billion of wealth was lost in a single day. Before the economy turned around over a decade later, this figure would double, resulting in more than $30 billion of wealth erased from the United States economy.

The closest current analogy to what happened to individual shareholders on October 29, 1929, is what happened to Enron shareholders when the company filed for bankruptcy in early 2002. CNN interviewed many Enron employees who had invested their entire retirement fund in Enron stock and who lost everything when the stock value fell to pennies. One Enron employee's 401K account had been worth $1.2 million before the company had gone bankrupt. Afterward, his retirement account was worth $5,500. He told CNN he was planning to start over. The man was fifty-three at the time of the interview.

The Stock Market Crash did major damage to the United States economy. It was one of the factors that caused the Great Depression. Within three years from October 29, U.S. unemployment had skyrocketed from seven million people out of work to sixteen million.

What caused the Crash?

Some of the reasons suggested over the past six decades are severely overpriced stocks, fraud by brokers, excessive buying on margin, bad Federal Reserve policy, corporate bigwigs lying to the public about the safety of their investments and the health of the companies in which people were investing, President Hoover's incompetence, and other causes, some of which would put the most paranoid conspiracy theorists to shame.

Following the Crash, the government immediately cut interest rates, which increased the money supply, but then misguidedly raised interest rates in 1931, which lowered the availability of money and severely hindered economic growth.

It would take over a decade for the United States economy to bounce back, and during that period, we would live through the Dust Bowl (chapter 95), Hoovervilles, bread lines, bankruptcies, mortgage foreclosures, and a national depression of the psychological kind as well.

World War II, and its production and manpower demands—a forced growth, so to speak, was the economy's salvation.

One cannot help but wonder how long the Depression would have lasted if we had not gone to war in 1941.

98

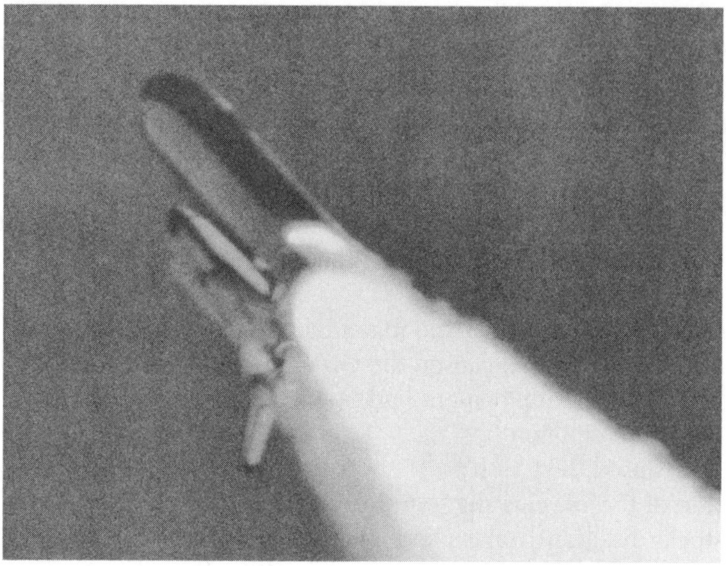

The Space Shuttle *Challenger* Explosion

9 Miles Above Earth, Headed to Orbit

January 28, 1986

7 Dead

Today, the frontier is space and the boundaries of human knowledge. Sometimes, when we reach for the stars, we fall short. But we must pick ourselves up again and press on despite the pain. Our nation is indeed fortunate that we can still draw on immense reservoirs of courage, character and fortitude—that we are still blessed with heroes like those of the space shuttle Challenger.

—President Ronald Reagan

Telemetered data indicate a wide variety of flight system actions that support the visual evidence of the photos as the Shuttle struggled futilely against the forces that were destroying it . . . The Orbiter, under severe aerodynamic loads, broke into several large sections which emerged from the fireball . . . The explosion 73 seconds after liftoff claimed crew and vehicle. Cause of explosion was determined to be an O-ring failure in right Solid Rocket Booster. Cold weather was a contributing factor.

—NASA

One of the most-asked questions about the space shuttle *Challenger* disaster is "Were the astronauts alive after the explosion?" Many want to know if the seven *Challenger* astronauts were conscious during their fiery plunge to the sea.

The answer is yes. At least for a few seconds, according to most experts, and possibly considerably longer. Exhaustive investigations following the accident revealed that three of the recovered astronauts' emergency-escape air packs had been turned on manually after the explosion. It was concluded that the force of the initial explosion would not have been enough to kill or render unconscious the astronauts and that their cause of death was hitting the water at 207 miles per hour. It is not known for how long the *Challenger* cabin retained air pressure or, for that matter, if it even did retain pressure after the explosion. So even if the astronauts were conscious after the explosion, it is likely that they were all unconscious within seconds and remained so as they hit the water.

The *Challenger* Seven were Michael Smith, Dick Scobee, Judith Resnik, Ronald McNair, Ellison Onizuka, Gregory Jarvis, and Christa McAuliffe.

The recovered, identifiable remains of the *Challenger* Seven were returned to their families on April 29, 1986. The unidentifiable remains were buried in Arlington National Cemetery on May 20, 1986.

One January 24, 1985, a year before the *Challenger* launch, NASA launched the space shuttle *Discovery.* The air temperature at the time of *Discovery*'s launch was fifty-three degrees Fahrenheit, and the engineers at Morton-Thiokol, the company that manufactured the solid rocket booster's O-rings, noted that there had been O-ring erosion at that temperature.

The expected temperature at launch time for the space shuttle *Challenger* was twenty-nine degrees Fahrenheit.

Morton-Thiokol's engineers, while admitting that they had no way to *prove* that there would be a problem with the O-rings at twenty-nine degrees (due to the absence of specific testing at lower temperatures), nonetheless cited *Discovery*'s erosion problems at fifty-three degrees and recommended to NASA that they postpone the launch of *Challenger*.

A NASA manager challenged the Morton-Thiokol engineers' conclusion and asked for a Morton-Thiokol management decision. The managers gave NASA a report citing their "engineering assessment" that the O-rings could handle the projected temperatures and that the launch should proceed as scheduled. Morton-Thiokol's project engineers refused to sign the report. Alan McDonald, Morton-Thiokol's director of the Solid Rocket Motors Project, was in Florida with

NASA and urged NASA to reject his company's managers' report and not launch. He was convinced that the cold weather created a situation that was enough of a risk to the O-rings to warrant postponing the launch. McDonald was overruled by NASA project managers and *Challenger* launched at 11:38 A.M. on January 28, 1986. There were icicles hanging off the launch pad and the shuttle at the time of launch.

The decision to launch *Challenger* was a bad one, and it resulted in the loss of 7 lives, the destruction of a multibillion-dollar spacecraft, and the two-year-shutdown of NASA's space shuttle program. It also marked the first time the United States had lost astronauts in a spacecraft failure during flight, and it caused Americans to lose faith in NASA. The *Challenger* disaster also led to the resignation of many key NASA people, and to the decision to use expendable rockets instead of the space shuttle to launch satellites into orbit.

A congressional committee assigned to investigate the disaster concluded that "meeting flight schedules and cutting cost were given a higher priority than flight safety."

The *Challenger* mission held enormous interest for the American public because of the presence on board of Concord, New Hampshire, high school teacher Christa McAuliffe—the first citizen in space—and the inauguration of NASA's "Teacher in Space" program. McAuliffe was scheduled to conduct lessons from space for her students, a groundbreaking and innovative program that generated tremendous enthusiasm among educators and students.

The *Challenger* mission also included the launching of a data relay satellite, and a series of experiments related to Halley's Comet.

The *Challenger* disaster is one of the one hundred worst *disasters* of all time in part because the conception, development, and launching of the space shuttle orbiters is one of the greatest human *achievements* of all time. The scale of the accomplishment is directly proportional to the scale of the disaster. The cause of the disaster was mechanical failure—the O-ring became so brittle in the cold, it could not prevent the igniting of the flammable gases it was meant to seal in. But the true culpability lies with the decision makers who dismissed the potential for mechanical failure and sent the *Challenger* hurtling to its doom.

99

The Apollo 1 Fire

CAPE KENNEDY, FLORIDA

January 27, 1967

3 Dead

There's always a possibility that you can have a catastrophic failure, of course. This can happen on any flight. It can happen on the last one as well as the first one. So you just plan as best as you can to take care of all these eventualities.

—Astronaut Virgil Grissom, in a television interview on CBS

This is our business, to find out of this thing will work for us. I don't see how you could help but be a little bit excited. I don't like to use the word "scary."

—Astronaut Roger Chaffee, in the same CBS interview

Line of Duty

The three astronauts had been strapped into their seats in the Apollo 1 command module (empty of fuel) for five and a half hours. The cabin had been sealed for over three hours and they had conducted a series of tests and simulations, most of which went well. Fifteen minutes before the liftoff simulation was to take place, the command module disconnected from its external power sources and went to internal power only—what is known as a "plugs out" test.

At 6:31, Astronaut Roger Chaffee said, "Fire. I smell fire." A serious electrical short had occurred in the wiring beneath Virgil Grissom's seat, and a fire, which would be fed by the pure oxygen in the cabin, started almost immediately.

Mission personnel watching on a closed-circuit camera could see flames through the porthole, but the astronauts could not unlatch the six bolts on the hatch door in time to escape. A few seconds later, the command module exploded, and the side of the cabin ripped open. Witnesses saw flames burst through the crack. By this time, it was too late for the three Apollo 1 astronauts. All three had died almost immediately of suffocation, and the 760-degree internal temperature in the command module had caused serious burns on their bodies, most of which were posthumous.

Five men had to work for almost six minutes to remove the module's three interconnected hatches. Inside the cabin, a horrible sight greeted the NASA team. The astronauts' bodies lay in a grisly mess of molten nylon and plastic, and their space suits had melted onto their bodies. Doctors arrived approximately eight minutes after the hatch was removed, but it took them seven hours to remove the three bodies.

Sailors are not supposed to die on land; firefighters are not supposed to die in the firehouse; cops are not supposed to die off duty; pilots are not supposed to die on the ground . . . and astronauts are not supposed to die on the launch pad in a fuelless spacecraft, before they are even out of Earth's atmosphere, let alone in space.

And yet, on Friday, January 27, 1967, three American astronauts—Virgil Grissom, Roger Chaffee, and Edward White—died when a fire broke out in their Apollo 1 capsule during a routine test on the launch pad and they were unable to free themselves.

In 1967, NASA was on a determined mission to fulfill President Kennedy's bold and visionary May 25, 1961, pledge to put a man on the moon before the end of the decade.[1] The United States was also in a space race with the Soviets, and thus NASA's build, train, and launch pace was frenetic.

A fourteen-volume report issued after the accident concluded that NASA had been seriously derelict in several areas, and a comprehensive investigation had uncovered evidence of "poor installation, design, and workmanship." The report also faulted NASA for woefully inadequate attention to safety issues, and the unspoken charge was that the space agency was moving too fast in order to beat the Russians and keep the politicians happy.

Congress decided that a complete top-to-bottom review of the space program was mandatory before launches continued.

NASA used this forced shutdown to reevaluate every facet of its spacecrafts and programs, to redesign extensively, and to replace parts and materials that were determined to be inferior, unsafe, or both.

The space agency spent eighteen months getting its house in order and ended up replacing all wiring with much higher-quality wiring, removing flammable materials from the spacecraft, developing fire-resistant materials for inside the modules and for the astronaut's space suits, and using only pure oxygen in the cabins under specific protocols designed for safety.

In a sense, the Apollo 1 accident allowed the United States to journey to the moon, land, and return home safely. It is extremely likely that if the Apollo 1 fire had not happened, and NASA had proceeded at the pace it was keeping for the Apollo program before the accident, the Moon mission would have failed. With the questionable reliability of the pre–Apollo 1 equipment and systems, we may have gotten to the Moon, but we may not have gotten back.

In retrospect, the only thing worse than having astronauts die in their command module on Earth would be for them to die in their spacecraft while stranded on the Moon.

After the Apollo 1 tragedy, NASA would not lose another astronaut in an accident for almost two decades. In 1986, the space shuttle *Challenger* exploded, killing all seven on board. (See chapter 98.)

[1] "First, I believe that this nation should commit itself to achieving the goal, before this decade is out, of landing a man on the moon and returning him safely to the earth. No single space project in this period will be more impressive to mankind, or more important for the long-range exploration of space; and none will be so difficult or expensive to accomplish. We propose to accelerate the development of the appropriate lunar spacecraft. We propose to develop alternate liquid and solid fuel boosters, much larger than any now being developed, until certain which is superior. We propose additional funds for other engine development and for unmanned explorations—explorations which are particularly important for one purpose which this nation will never overlook: the survival of the man who first makes this daring flight. But in a very real sense, it will not be one man going to the moon—if we make this judgment affirmatively, it will be an entire nation. For all of us must work to put him there." John F. Kennedy, "Special Message to the Congress on Urgent National Needs," May 25, 1961.

100

The 1851 Library of Congress Fire

THE CAPITOL BUILDING, WASHINGTON, D.C.

December 24, 1851

Priceless Loss of Irreplaceable Books and Documents

I agree with you that it is the duty of every good citizen to use all the opportunities, which occur to him, for preserving documents relating to the history of our country.

—Thomas Jefferson to Hugh P. Taylor, October 4, 1823

In his philosophy, freedom and enlightenment depended on each other; education, therefore, was a paramount responsibility of free government.

—Merrill D. Peterson, about Thomas Jefferson[1]

May 1815. Three pens lifted off the paper and dipped into three inkwells at the same time. The hand of Thomas Jefferson wielded one pen; the other two were attached to a complex arrangement of wooden rods, levers, and hinges, a machine known as a polygraph. These two pens followed Jefferson's hand and allowed him to make multiple copies of his writings without having to copy things over and over. Jefferson loved the polygraph, which had been invented in 1803 by English-born John Isaac Hawkins. In these days of instant digital reproduction of voluminous amounts of text, it is revelatory to reflect on how momentous it was in those days to be able to make one or two copies of a written work.

On the vellum sheet, Jefferson had written Memory, Reason, and Imagination at the top of three individual columns. Beneath Memory was "History"; beneath Reason was "Philosophy"; beneath Imagination was "Fine Arts." In each column, Jefferson had written many titles of books, organized by category, with the page count, size, and estimated age of the volume next to the title.

Jefferson was preparing an inventory of 6,487 books, which he was selling to the United States government for $23,950. These books would form the basis of the new Library of Congress.

On August 24, 1814, during the War of 1812, British troops burned the U.S. Capitol and the Library of Congress. Throughout the following autumn, Thomas Jefferson, now a retired former president and in dire need of funds (this was in the days before ex-presidents were compensated for life), offered to sell a large portion of his renowned personal library to the U.S. government to rebuild the Library of Congress. There was great debate in both houses over the offer; likely, the opposition Federalists would have preferred that the retired president donate his library for the good of the country. Jefferson, buried in debt, simply could not afford to give his books away, although today, with the perspective of history, we can be assured that if he could have, he would have.

On January 30, 1815, President James Madison signed a bill authorizing the purchase of Jefferson's books.

Jefferson continued to write, listing many of his books by memory, and as soon as Jefferson completed the inventory, his slaves would load several wagons with the precious cargo for its trip to Washington.

For thirty-six years, Jefferson's books would serve the members of Congress well, providing them with information on law, history, politics, economics, religion, and war, as well as offering them much of the great literature of the ages, from the ancient Greeks to Shakespeare.

In 1851, over 4,300 of Jefferson's priceless books would burn to ash, along with over 30,000 other volumes (of a total of 55,000) in a tragic fire at the Library of Congress in the Capitol building. Original portraits of the first five presidents would perish in the flames, as would priceless documents dating back to the days of Columbus, and the library's entire map collection. Some of Jefferson's books survived the inferno, as did one of his handwritten documents.

The original Declaration of Independence in Jefferson's own hand was rescued from the flames.

How can the loss of books and papers be considered a disaster? *The 100 Greatest Disasters of All Time* has looked at human tragedies with enormous death tolls and incalculable destruction. Yet, we close this volume with an incident in which was lost a treasure of objects that bespeak the essential manifestation of the human spirit.

This 1851 early-morning, Christmas Eve fire, which was caused by a faulty chimney flue in the Capitol building, caused extensive damage and a great loss of materials, but no lives were lost, so how can it truly be considered a disaster?

The answer to that question lies in the fact that a disaster with long-term repercussions can be as devastating to mankind as a great loss of life. The answer also lies in, improbably, something that happened in the third century, the destruction of the library in Alexandria, Egypt.

The library of Alexandria was founded in 290 B.C. by Ptolemy I and, over a period of five centuries, a succession of Ptolemy's descendants worked to accumulate hundreds of thousands of volumes of scientific writing, every work of Greek literature, and countless translated works from other cultures. The library essentially held almost every bit of knowledge that had been accumulated over the centuries.

The Library of Alexandria held between 450,000 and 530,000 manuscripts, which would probably equal between 100,000 to 150,000 books today. It was destroyed by Muslim invaders around 641; the manuscripts and documents were burned for fuel.

The caliph issued the following statement regarding the works housed in the library:

> *If these writings of the Greeks agree with the book of God, they are useless, and need not be preserved; if they disagree, they are pernicious, and ought to be destroyed.*[2]

This single event—the destruction of the library—did not alone usher in the Dark Ages, yet the loss of the knowledge and scholarship, and the inability of future students to learn from the writing of the great thinkers and scientists of the past, contributed enormously to the period of ignorance, superstition, and bigotry that followed.

Thus is the reason for the inclusion of the 1851 Library of Congress fire on this ranking. Some of the books and maps and documents lost would surely have been a valuable resource for future generations.

And such a loss, by any definition, is a disaster.

[1] Henry F. Goff, ed., *The Presidents,* 56.

[2] *The Catholic Encyclopedia.* www.newadvent.org.

THE TORNADO SCALE

Intensity	***Wind speed***
F0	40 mph
F1	74 mph
F2	112 mph
F3	156 mph
F4	208 mph
F5	262 mph

SOURCE: Developed by Dr. T. Fujita.

MEASURING AN EARTHQUAKE'S INTENSITY

The intensity of earthquakes is expressed in magnitude using the Richter scale—the numbers ranging from 1.5 to 10. These numbers indicate the severity of the quake and its subsequent damage.

The Richter scale, which was developed in 1935 by American seismologist Charles Richter, is logarithmic in nature, meaning that each successive whole number represents a tenfold increase in power and intensity.

Even though the Richter scale is not really used much by seismologists anymore (today's technology allows far more specific and accurate readings of seismic activity), earthquake magnitudes are still commonly expressed using the familiar Richter's scale.

Another system used to describe earthquake intensity is the Mercalli Earthquake Intensity scale, which was developed in 1902 by Italian seismologist Giuseppe Mercalli. Although now obsolete, the descriptions of the twelve levels of earthquake effects in populated areas as codified by Mercalli accurately portray the damage at varying levels of intensity and are included here for illustrative purposes. Anything from a level 9 up is extremely catastrophic.

The Mercalli Scale

Level I: (Richter 2) Generally not felt by people, but detectable by seismologists.

Level II: (Richter 2) Felt by a few people. Some objects, such as hanging baskets or lamps, may swing if suspended.

Level III: (Richter 3) Felt by a few people, but mostly indoors. This level has been described as feeling like the vibrations of a passing truck.

Level IV: (Richter 4) Felt by many people indoors, but very few people outdoors. Windows, dishes, and doors rattle.

Level V: (Richter 4) Felt by nearly everyone both indoors and outdoors. Sleepers awaken; small unstable objects may fall and break; doors move.

Level VI: (Richter 5) Felt by everyone. Some heavy furniture may move; people walk unsteadily; windows break; dishes fall and break; books fall off shelves; bushes and trees visibly shake.

Level VII: (Richter 5–6) It is difficult to stand and there is moderate to heavy damage to poorly constructed buildings. Plaster, tiles, loose bricks, and stones fall; there are small landslides along slopes; water becomes opaque as sediment is stirred up.

Level VIII: (Richter 6) It is difficult to steer cars and there is damage to chimneys, monuments, and towers. Elevated tanks fall, tree branches crack; steep slopes crack.

Level IX: (Richter 7) There is extensive damage to buildings; masonry is seriously damaged; foundations crack; there is serious damage to reservoirs; underground pipes break.

Level X: (Richter 7–8) Most masonry, frame structures, and foundations are destroyed. There are numerous large landslides; water is hurled onto the banks of rivers and lakes; railroad tracks bend in some places.

Level XI: (Richter 8+) Few masonry buildings are left standing; railroad tracks bend severely; many bridges are destroyed; underground pipelines are completely inoperative.

Level XII: (Richter 8+) Nearly total destruction. Large rock masses are displaced; objects are thrown violently into the air.

• • •

The Amount of Energy Released by an Earthquake

Magnitude	*Amount of TNT Energy*
4.0	6 tons
5.0	199 tons
6.0	6,270 tons
7.0	199,000 tons
8.0	6,270,000 tons
9.0	99,000,000 tons

SOURCE: G. Lennis, *Earthquakes and the Urban Environment, vol. 1.*

CHRONOLOGICAL LISTING OF THE 100 GREATEST DISASTERS OF ALL TIME

Note: Some of the disasters occurred over a period of time (the Black Death), or are currently ongoing (the Worldwide AIDS Epidemic). For purposes of this chronological listing, the beginning year of multiyear disasters is used for ranking.

79	The Eruption of Mount Vesuvius (34)
526	The Antioch, Syria, Earthquake (18)
542	The Plague of Justinian (17)
1333	The China Drought, Famine, and Epidemic (5)
1347	The Black Death (1)
1485	The English Sweating Sickness (10)
1520	The Mexico Smallpox Epidemic (9)
1556	The Great China Earthquake (14)
1666	The Great London Fire (93)
1755	The Lisbon, Portugal, Earthquake (26)
1780	The Great Hurricane (32)
1815	The Eruption of Tambora and the Year Without a Summer (22)
1846	The Irish Potato Famine (12)
1851	The Library of Congress Fire (100)
1856	The Rhodes Church Explosion (43)
1864	The Calcutta Cyclone (23)
1865	The Sinking of the *Sultana* (49)
1871	The Great Chicago Fire and Peshtigo Forest Fire (51)
1876	The China Famine (4)
1883	The Eruption of Mount Krakatoa (30)
1887	The Yellow River and Yangtze River Floods (11)
1888	The New York City Blizzard (56)
1889	The Johnstown Flood (47)
1891	The Russia Famine (16)
1896	The India Drought, Famine, and Disease Disaster (6)
1896	The Japanese Tsunami (33)

1979	The American Airlines DC-10 Crash (74)
1979	The Three Mile Island Nuclear Accident (96)
1979	The Worldwide AIDS Epidemic (3)
1981	The Hyatt Regency Walkways Collapse (85)
1981	The India Rail Accident (57)
1984	The Bhopal Chemical Leak (44)
1985	The Japan Air Lines Flight 123 Crash (65)
1985	The Stava Dam Failure (76)
1986	The Chernobyl Nuclear Accident (36)
1986	The Space Shuttle *Challenger* Explosion (98)
1987	The Collision of the *Dona Paz* and the *Vector* (42)
1988	The Armenia Earthquake (25)
1988	The Pan Am Lockerbie Bombing (75)
1989	The *Exxon Valdez* Oil Spill (94)
1989	Hurricane Hugo (90)
1989	The San Francisco Earthquake (88)
1990	The Iran Earthquake and Landslide (28)
1991	The Oakland Hills Fires (92)
1992	Hurricane Andrew (87)
1993	The U.S. Midwest Floods (89)
1995	The Kobe Earthquake (41)
1995	The Oklahoma City Bombing (80)
1996	The Crash of Flight 800 (77)
1996	The Saudi-Kazak Midair Collision (69)
1998	Hurricane Georges (60)
1998	Hurricane Mitch (35)
1999	The Izmit, Turkey, Earthquake (31)
2001	The September 11, 2001, Terrorist Attacks (46)
2002	The Egyptian Train Fire (67)

SELECT BIBLIOGRAPHY AND SUGGESTED READING

Alexander, John T. *Bubonic Plague in Early Modern Russia: Public Health & Urban Disaster.* Baltimore: John Hopkins University Press, 1980.

Allen, Everett. *A Wind to Shake the Earth: The Story of the 1938 Hurricane.* Boston: Little, Brown, 1976.

American Meteorological Society. *The 1938 Hurricane: An Historical and Pictorial Summary.* Boston: American Meteorological Society, 1988.

Axelrod, Alan. *The Complete Idiot's Guide to American History.* New York: Alpha Books, 1996.

Aylesworth, Thomas G. *Geological Disasters: Earthquakes and Volcanoes.* New York: Franklin Watts, 1979.

Berlin, G. Lennis. *Earthquakes and the Urban Environment.* Vol. 1. Boca Raton, FL: CRC Press, 1980.

Carey, John, ed. *Eyewitness to History.* New York: Avon Books, 1987.

Caufield, Catherine. *In the Rainforest.* Chicago: University of Chicago Press, 1991.

Chilton, David. *Power in the Blood.* Brentwood, TN: Wolgemuth & Hyatt, 1987.

Conquest, Robert. *The Harvest of Sorrow: Soviet Collectivization and the Terror-Famine.* New York: Oxford University Press, 1986.

Corliss, William R. *Handbook of Unusual Natural Phenomena: Eyewitness Accounts of Nature's Greatest Mysteries.* New York: Gramercy Books, 1995.

Cornell, James. *The Great International Disaster Book.* New York: Charles Scribner's Sons, 1976.

Cowan, John F. "West Virginia Coal Mines: Monongah Disaster." *West Virginia Dispatch,* December 8, 1907.

Davis, Lee. *Natural Disasters.* New York: Checkmark Books, 2002.

Drexler, Madeline. *Secret Agents: The Menace of Emerging Infections.* Washington, DC: Joseph Henry Press, 2002.

Edgar, W. "Russia's Conflict with Hunger." *American Review of Reviews,* 1892, 576

Erickson, Jon. *Quakes, Eruptions and Other Geologic Cataclysms.* New York: Facts on File, 1994.

"Famine in Soviet Ukraine and Its Main Reason." *Svoboda,* July 18, 1932.

Farrington, Karen. *Natural Disasters: The Terrifying Forces of Nature.* London, UK: PRC Publishing, 1999.

Fitzpatrick, Patrick J. *Natural Disasters: Hurricanes: A Reference Handbook.* Santa Barbara, CA: ABC-CLIO, 1999.

Flexner, Stuart, with Doris Flexner. *The Pessimist's Guide to History.* New York: Avon Books, 1992.

Francis, Arthur A. "Remembering the Great New England Hurricane of 1938." *Salem Evening News,* September 21, 1998.

Frey, Rebecca J. *Gale Encyclopedia of Medicine.* Farmington Hills, MI: Gale Group, 1999.

Garner, Joe. *We Interrupt This Broadcast: Relive the Events That Stopped Our Lives—from the Hindenburg to the Death of Princess Diana.* Naperville, IL: Sourcebooks, 1998.

Garraty, John A. *1,001 Things Everyone Should Know About American History.* Garden City, NY: Doubleday, 1989.

Gibbs, Philip. *The Pageant of the Years.* London: Heinemann, 1946.

Graff, Henry F., ed. *The Presidents: A Reference History.* New York: Charles Scribner's Sons, 1997.

Grafton, R. *A Chronicle at Large, and Meere History of the Affayres of Englande.* 1569.

Gregorovich, Andrew. "Black Famine in Ukraine 1932–33: A Struggle for Existence." *Forum Ukrainian Review,* No 24, 1974.

Hecker, J. F. C. *The Black Death.* London: Sydenham Society, 1832.

———. *The Dancing Mania.* 1832.

Hewitt, R. *From Earthquake Fire and Flood.* London, UK: George Allen & Unwin, Ltd., 1957.

Heys, Sam, and Allen B. Goodwin. *The Winecoff Fire: The Untold Story of America's Deadliest Hotel Fire.* Marietta, GA: Longstreet Press, 1993.

Howell, J. Z. "The Black Hole of Calcutta, 21 June 1756." *Annual Register,* 1758.

Iezzoni, Lynette. *Influenza 1918: The Worst Epidemic in American History.* New York: TV Books, 1999.

Jones, Michael Wynn. *Deadline Disaster: A Newspaper History.* Chicago: Henry Regnery Company, 1976.

Kennett, Frances. *The Greatest Disasters of the 20th Century.* London, UK: Cavendish Publications Ltd., 1975.

Ladurie, Emmanuel Le Roy. *Times of Feast, Times of Famine: A History of Climate Since the Year 1000.* New York: Farrar, Straus & Giroux, 1971.

Larson, Lee W. "Destructive Water: Water-Caused Natural Disasters—Their Abatement and Control." Lecture Presentation, IAHS Conference, Anaheim, California, June 24–28, 1996.

Lee, Min, ed. *Larousse Dictionary of North American History.* New York: Larousse, 1994.

Loewen, James W. *Lies My Teacher Told Me: Everything Your American History Textbook Got Wrong.* New York: The New Press, 1995.

McCullough, David. *The Johnstown Flood.* New York: Simon & Schuster, 1968.

McPherson, James M. *"To the Best of My Ability": The American Presidents.* New York: Dorling Kindersley, 2000.

MacPherson, Malcolm, ed. *The Black Box: All-New Cockpit Voice Recorder Accounts of In-Flight Accidents.* New York: Quill, 1998.

Marks, Geoffrey, and William K. Beatty. *Epidemics.* New York: Charles Scribner's Sons, 1976.

Morris, Charles. *Morris's Story of the Great Earthquake of 1908 and Other Historic Disasters.* Philadelphia: Universal Book and Bible House, 1909.

Nash, Bruce, and Allan Zullo. *The Misfortune 500.* New York: Pocket Books, 1988.

Nash, Jay Robert. *Darkest Hours: A Narrative Encyclopedia of Worldwide Disasters from Ancient Times to the Present.* New York: Wallaby, 1977.

Ochoa, George, and Melinda Corey. *The Timeline Book of Science.* New York: Stonesong Press, 1995.

Pararas-Carayannis, Dr. George. Correspondence with the author. January 18, 2002.

———. *The Big One: The Next Great California Earthquake.* Honolulu: Aston-Forbes, 2001.

Pepys, Samuel. *Diary.* Vol. 7. Edited by Robert Latham and William Matthews. London, UK: G. Bell & Sons, 1970–83.

Procopius. *Secret History.* Richard Atwater, trans. Ann Arbor, MI: University of Michigan Press, 1961.

Ritchie, David, and Alexander E. Gates. *Encyclopedia of Earthquakes and Volcanoes.* New York: Checkmark Books, 2001.

Robbins, Richard G. Jr. *Famine in Russia 1891–1892: The Imperial Government Responds to a Crisis.* New York: Columbia University Press, 1975.

Robins, Joyce. *The World's Greatest Disasters.* Secaucus, NJ: Chartwell Books, 1990.

"Safe Tailings Dam Construction." Technical paper. Seminar at Gällivare, Switzerland, September 20–21, 2001.

Schlager, Neil. *Breakdown: Deadly Technological Disasters.* Detroit: Visible Ink Press, 1995.

Sigerist, Henry E. *Civilization and Disease.* Chicago: University of Chicago Press, 1943.

Simpson, Howard. *Invisible Armies: The Impact of Disease on American History.* Indianapolis: Bobbs-Merrill, 1980.

"Six Minutes." *Time,* July 17, 1944.

Smith, Roger. *Catastrophes and Disasters.* Edinburgh, UK: W & R Chambers Ltd., 1992.

Spignesi, Stephen J. *The Complete Titanic: From the Ship's Earliest Blueprints to the Epic Film.* Secaucus, NJ: Citadel Press, 1998.

———. *The Italian 100: A Ranking of the Most Influential Cultural, Scientific, and Political Figures, Past and Present.* Secaucus, NJ: Citadel Press, 1998.

———. *The USA Book of Lists.* Franklin Lakes, NJ: New Page Books, 2001.

Stanton, Patrick. *Assessment of the Iranian Earthquake 20th of June 1990: A Field Report.* British Civil Defence paper presented at the International Conference: "Disaster and the Small Dwelling" at the Disaster Management Centre, Oxford Polytechnic, Headington, September 2–6, 1990.

Stein, Leon. *The Triangle Fire.* New York: Carroll & Graf/Quicksilver, 1962.

Thwaites, Guy, Mark Taviner, and Vanya Gant. "English Sweating Sickness, 1485–1551." *New England Journal of Medicine* 336, no. 8 (1997): 580–82.

Ui, Jun, ed. *Industrial Pollution in Japan.* Tokyo: United Nations University Press, 1992.

Vallee, David R., and Michael R. Dion. *Southern New England Tropical Storms and Hurricanes, A Ninety-Eight Year Summary 1909–1997.* Taunton, MA: National Weather Service, 1998.

Watson, Milton H. *Disasters at Sea.* Northamptonshire, UK: Patrick Stephens Ltd., 1987.

Weiss, Murray. "TWA Probers: Missile Witnesses 'Credible.' " *New York Post,* September 22, 1996.

Whittow, John. *Disasters: The Anatomy of Environmental Hazards.* Athens, GA: University of Georgia Press, 1979.

Wolcott, Martin Gilman. *The Evil 100.* New York: Citadel Press, 2002.

Yong, Chen. *The Great Tangshan Earthquake of 1976: An Anatomy of Disaster.* New York: Pergamon Press, 1988.

Newspapers, Journals, and Magazines

Air & Space Smithsonian
American Heritage
American Review of Reviews
Boston Evening Globe
Collier's
Discover
EPA Journal
Florence Art News
Guardian
The Hartford Courant
Honduras This Week
Life
Los Angeles Times
Montreal Daily Star
National Geographic
New England Journal of Medicine
New Haven Register
New York Herald
New York Post

The New York Times
Newsweek
Reader's Digest
Salem Evening News
San Francisco Chronicle
The Scotsman
Sketch
Svoboda
Telegraph (London)
Time
Times (London)
Ukrainian Weekly
USA Today
The Wall Street Journal
The Washington Post
Washington Times

Web Sites

www.airsafetyonline.com
www.aviationcrashes.com
www.britannica.com
www.cdc.gov (Centers for Disease Control)
www.cnn.com:
Wedeman, Ben, Rula Amin, Jerrold Kessel, the Associated Press. "Rescues bring flash of hope amid grim toll of Turkey quake." August 20, 1999.
Wedeman, Ben, Walter Rodgers, the Associated Press, Reuters. "Turkish leader admits mistakes in quake response." August 24, 1999.
www.crashdatabase.com
danger-ahead.railfan.net/accidents/samastipur/home.html (Bihar, India, Railway Crash)
www.disasterrelief.org
www.discovery.com
www.earthquake.com
www.epa.com (Environmental Protection Agency)
www.ezl.com/~fireball/Disaster13.htm (The Great Nashville Wreck of 1918)
www.gale.com (*Gale Encyclopedia of Medicine*; *Gale Encyclopedia of Alternative Medicine*)
www.geocities.com/DrGeorgePC
www.greatshipwrecks.com
www.honduras.com
www.hurricaneville.com
www.msha.gov (Mine Safety and Health Administration)
www.msnbc.com

www.nea.com (Nuclear Energy Agency)
www.newadvent.org *(Catholic Encyclopedia)*
www.ngdc.noaa.gov/cgi-bin/seg/m2h?seg/haz_ volume2.men+Earthquake+ Damage,+Armenian+SSR,12/1988_help (Earthquake Damage, the Armenian SSR, December 7, 1988) (National Oceanographic and Atmospheric Administration)
www.ngdc.noaa.gov/cgi-bin/seg/m2h?seg/haz_volume2.men+Eq+Damage,+ Northern+Iran,+6/21/1990_help (National Oceanographic and Atmospheric Administration)
www.nytimes.com
www.pbs.org
www.refdesk.com
www.rmsempressofireland.com
www.twa800.com/index.htm
www.washingtonpost.com
www.weather.com
www.yahoo.com

INDEX

ABOUT THE AUTHOR

Stephen J. Spignesi is a full-time writer who specializes in popular culture subjects, including historical biography, television, film, American and world history, and contemporary fiction.

Mr. Spignesi—christened "the world's leading authority on Stephen King" by *Entertainment Weekly* magazine—has written many authorized entertainment books and worked with Stephen King, Turner Entertainment, the Margaret Mitchell Estate, Andy Griffith, Viacom, and other entertainment industry personalities and entities on a wide range of projects. Mr. Spignesi has also contributed essays, chapters, articles, and introductions to a wide range of books.

Mr. Spignesi's more than thirty books have been translated into several languages and he has also written for *Harper's*, *Cinefantastique*, *Saturday Review*, *TV Guide*, *Mystery Scene*, *Gauntlet*, and *Midnight Graffiti* magazines, as well as *The New York Times*, the New York *Daily News*, the *New York Post*, the *New Haven Register*, the French literary journal *Tenébres*, and the Italian online literary journal, *Horror.It*. Mr. Spignesi has appeared on CNN, MSNBC, Fox News Channel, and other TV and radio outlets; he has also appeared in the 1998 E! documentary *The Kennedys: Power, Seduction, and Hollywood*, as a Kennedy family authority; and in the A&E biography of Stephen King that aired in January 2000. Mr. Spignesi's 1997 book *JFK Jr.* was a *New York Times* best-seller. His *Complete Stephen King Encyclopedia* was a 1991 Bram Stoker Award nominee.

In addition to writing, Mr. Spignesi lectures on a variety of popular culture and historical subjects and teaches writing in the Connecticut area. He is the founder and editor in chief of the small press publishing company The StephenJohn Press, which recently published the acclaimed feminist autobiography *Open Windows*.

Mr. Spignesi is a graduate of the University of New Haven and lives in New Haven, Connecticut, with his wife, Pam, and their cat, Carter, named for their favorite character on *ER*.

Books by Stephen J. Spignesi

Mayberry, My Hometown (1987, Popular Culture, Ink.)
The Complete Stephen King Encyclopedia (1990, Contemporary Books)
The Stephen King Quiz Book (1990, Signet)
The Second Stephen King Quiz Book (1992, Signet)
The Woody Allen Companion (1992, Andrews and McMeel)
The Official "Gone With the Wind" Companion (1993, Plume)
The V. C. Andrews Trivia and Quiz Book (1994, Signet)
The Odd Index: The Ultimate Compendium of Bizarre and Unusual Facts (1994, Plume)
What's Your Mad About You *IQ?* (1995, Citadel Press)
The Gore Galore Video Quiz Book (1995, Signet)
What's Your Friends *IQ?* (1996, Citadel Press)
The Celebrity Baby Name Book (1996, Plume)
The ER *Companion* (1996, Citadel Press)
J.F.K. Jr. (1997, Citadel Press; originally titled *The J.F.K. Jr. Scrapbook*)—*New York Times* best-seller
The Robin Williams Scrapbook (1997, Citadel Press)
The Italian 100: A Ranking of the Most Influential Cultural, Scientific, and Political Figures, Past and Present (1997, Citadel Press)
The Beatles Book of Lists (1998, Citadel Press)
Young Kennedys: The New Generation (1998, Avon; written as "Jay David Andrews")
The Lost Work of Stephen King: A Guide to Unpublished Manuscripts, Story Fragments, Alternative Versions, & Oddities (1998, Citadel Press).
The Complete Titanic: *From the Ship's Earliest Blueprints to the Epic Film* (1998, Citadel Press)
How to Be an Instant Expert (2000, Career Press)
She Came in Through the Kitchen Window: Recipes Inspired by the Beatles & Their Music (2000, Kensington Books)
The USA Book of Lists (2000, Career Press)
The UFO Book of Lists (2001, Kensington Books)
The Essential Stephen King: The Greatest Novels, Short Stories, Movies, and Other Creations of the World's Most Popular Writer (2001, New Page Books)
The Cat Book of Lists (2001, New Page Books)
The Hollywood Book of Lists (2001, Kensington Books)
The Essential Stephen King: The Complete & Uncut Edition (2001, GB Books)
Gems, Jewels, & Treasures: The Complete Jewelry Book (2002, QVC Publishing)
In the Crosshairs: The 75 Most Famous Assassinations and Assassination Attempts, from Julius Caesar to John Lennon (2002, New Page Books)